NEW STUDIES IN BIBLICAL THEOLOGY

D. A. Carson, Series Editor

NEW STUDIES IN BIBLICAL THEOLOGY

Possessed by God
DAVID PETERSON

Whoredom
RAYMOND C. ORTLUND, JR.

Whoredom

God's Unfaithful Wife
in Biblical Theology

Raymond C. Ortlund, Jr.

WILLIAM B. EERDMANS PUBLISHING COMPANY
GRAND RAPIDS, MICHIGAN

© 1996 Raymond C. Ortlund, Jr.

Published 1996 in the U.K. by
APOLLOS (an imprint of Inter-Varsity Press)
and in the United States of America by
Wm. B. Eerdmans Publishing Co.
255 Jefferson Ave. S.E., Grand Rapids, Michigan 49503

Printed in the United States of America

00 99 98 97 96   7 6 5 4 3 2 1

ISBN 0-8028-4285-2

Contents

Series preface

New Studies in Biblical Theology is a series of monographs that address key issues in the discipline of biblical theology. Contributions to the series focus on one or more of three areas: 1. the nature and status of biblical theology, including its relations with other disciplines (*e.g.* historical theology, exegesis, systematic theology, historical criticism, narrative theology); 2. the articulation and exposition of the structure of thought of a particular biblical writer or corpus; and 3. the delineation of a biblical theme across all or part of the biblical corpora.

Above all these monographs are creative attempts to help thinking Christians understand their Bibles better. The series aims simultaneously to instruct and to edify, to interact with the current literature, and to point the way ahead. In God's universe, mind and heart should not be divorced: in this series we will try not to separate what God has joined together. While the footnotes interact with the best of the scholarly literature, the text is uncluttered with untransliterated Greek and Hebrew, and tries to avoid too much technical jargon. The volumes are written within the framework of confessional evangelicalism, but there is always an attempt at thoughtful engagement with the sweep of the relevant literature.

This volume, the second in the series, traces out a biblical theme that has been largely overlooked in this century. My colleague Dr Ray Ortlund has combined scholarly and pastoral gifts to examine afresh what it means to confess that Yahweh is the Bridegroom of his covenant people Israel, and that Christ is the Bridegroom of the church. Not only does the development of this theme link large swathes of the canon together, but it simultaneously discloses the profoundly personal nature of God's covenanted love, exposes the odium of spiritual adultery ('whoredom'), and, conversely, enriches our view of marriage.

D. A. Carson
Trinity Evangelical Divinity School,
Deerfield, Illinois

Preface

The title of this book offends its author. Doubtless, it offends the reader as well. But in light of the biblical story to be surveyed in this volume the appropriateness of the title will become obvious. And so it stands, as offensive as is the sin to which it refers.

Formerly a more prominent theme in theological discourse and pastoral ministry than it is today, discussion of the vision of God as the husband of his people, with all that such a relationship entails for them, has recently been reopened by Nelly Stienstra in her 1993 monograph, *YHWH is the Husband of his People*. The following study was initially prompted by her excellent work but soon struck off in its own direction as an exposition of the biblical theme of harlotry toward God. What begins as Pentateuchal whispers rises later to prophetic cries and is eventually echoed in apostolic teaching. That message proclaims that, if Yahweh is the husband of his people, then their lapses from faithfulness to him may properly be regarded as the moral equivalent to whoredom. Such an analysis is not pleasant to the sensibilities. It may at first seem a strident exaggeration; but it is clearly declared in Scripture and offers a searching assessment of the nature of human sin which our own age has largely overlooked or even forgotten. Alternatively, the marital nature of the covenant intimates depths of communion with God for which the human soul yearns amid the barrenness of the modern world.

In order for unfaithfulness to God, branded as whoredom, to be meaningful, it is necessary to begin this study by setting forth the logic of human marriage as explained by Scripture. This understanding of the human marital bond provides the covenant community with the premise and ideal standard from which they may extrapolate in their thinking about their relationship with God. If a proper marriage makes visible nothing less than a 'one flesh' union, and if the covenant community's relationship with God is of a marital nature, then failure to live out complete union of the soul with God may be regarded as whoredom. Chapter 1, therefore, will expound Genesis 2:23–24, the foundational passage explaining the principial essence of human marriage.

Chapter 2 will open up a most striking fact. As the Pentateuch unfolds, it portrays Israel's relationship with God in terms which rely upon the desirability and moral authority of marital fidelity. The fact that God is the husband of his people is not yet fully disclosed; it is assumed. But the Pentateuch, flowing into the Deuteronomistic history, openly declares that, when the people of God share their devotion with any other than Yahweh, they commit whoredom.

What is suggested in the Pentateuch and historical books, then, is more fully and boldly developed by the prophets. Chapter 3 will expound the burden of Hosea 1 – 3 in this regard, and chapters 4 and 5 will survey other prophets.

Chapter 6 will demonstrate that this Old Testament concern was shared as well by Jesus and the writers of the New Testament, who bring to fulfilment the vision of a Saviour wedded to his people.

Chapter 7 will draw out hermeneutical, theological and pastoral conclusions from the study.

The major premise most fruitful for theological conversation within the Christian community must be the received Scriptures of the Old and New Testaments. Re-creating pre-canonical forms of the text is a valid, and ultimately necessary, exercise; but the further one moves back through these Scriptures into their earlier forms, the less common consent one may expect to encounter in our fragmented scholarly situation. This is not to say that such excavatory work could not succeed in a theological essay. But, given the aims and parameters limiting this project, the task of unravelling the canonical text and then stringing it out along antecedent lines would bog the study down in cumbersome and ever decreasingly convincing speculation.

Although an Appendix is included in this volume, responding to some recent feminist critique of the harlot metaphor, a brief comment may still be in order here. Some readers may initially be perplexed by the imagery to be encountered in the biblical texts studied in this volume. Barth was correct in noting that, within the whole of the biblical account, 'We have to reckon with the unfaithfulness of the wife, but never with the unfaithfulness of the Husband' (1958: 316). This biblical presentation does not, however, insinuate a negative judgment upon the moral character of women, as opposed to men, or seek to manipulate opinion against women, as opposed to men; it coheres with the larger biblical vision of ultimate reality in Christ and his church, the Bridegroom and the Bride. And all of his people, women and men alike, both betray him with their infidelities and yet by his grace will enter into the perfect consummation of the marriage, where together we all will inherit the only true human fulfilment that exists. If a reader comes to this book with special sensitivities to the metaphor of the unfaithful wife, then I commend the following as a fair-minded point of departure:

> Recent feminist theological writing has complained about the misogynistic nature of this biblical element. Without knowing the psychological make-up of the biblical writers it is not possible to evaluate the degree to which their writings may be characterized as misogynistic or otherwise. But given the metaphoric nature of the language used (masculine as much as feminine) caution is warranted before jumping to the wrong conclusions (Carroll 1986: 134).

If, after giving the biblical story a fair chance, a reader is able to agree that 'the Christian faith is the most exciting drama that ever staggered the imagination of man' (Sayers 1995: 3), then other, lesser interpretative questions are at least moderated in their urgency.

Because my own translational philosophy so often sympathizes with, and yet at times departs from, the tradition represented by the RSV and the NRSV, I will be interacting primarily with these two English translations, along with others, in my rendering of the biblical text into English.

I wish to express thanks to Prof. Donald A. Carson for inviting my participation in this important new series. His comments are invariably stimulating. I owe a debt of gratitude as well to the faculty and administration of Trinity Evangelical Divinity School, who provided the sabbatical leave during which this project could be completed.

I also wish to acknowledge with thanks the bibliographical research of my teaching assistant, Mr Bill Tooman.

As ever, my dear wife Jan defines the meaning of encouraging partnership.

May this book challenge the covenant community of today to think more clearly, to love more deeply and to reform more boldly, to the greater glory of God and to their own richer happiness.

Abbreviations

ABD	D. N. Freedman (ed.), *The Anchor Bible Dictionary*. New York, 1992.
ANET	J. B. Pritchard (ed.), *Ancient Near Eastern Texts Relating to the Old Testament*, 3rd edn. Princeton, 1969.
AV	The Authorized Version of the Bible, 1611.
BA	*Biblical Archaeologist.*
BAR	*Biblical Archaeology Review.*
BDB	F. Brown, S. R. Driver and C. A. Briggs, *A Hebrew and English Lexicon of the Old Testament*. Oxford, 1907.
BDF	F. Blass and A. Debrunner, *A Greek Grammar of the New Testament and Other Early Christian Literature*. Translated and revised by R. W. Funk. Chicago, 1961.
BHS	K. Elliger and W. Rudolph, *Biblica Hebraica Stuttgartensia*, 3rd edn. Stuttgart, 1987.
BJRL	*Bulletin of the John Rylands Library.*
EVV	English versions.
Gibson	J. C. L. Gibson, *Davidson's Introductory Hebrew Grammar: Syntax*, 4th edn. Edinburgh, 1994.
GKC	E. Kautzsch (ed.), *Gesenius' Hebrew Grammar*. Revised by A. E. Cowley. Oxford, 1910.
Joüon	P. Joüon, *A Grammar of Biblical Hebrew*. Translated and revised by T. Muraoka. Rome, 1991.
JSOT	*Journal for the Study of the Old Testament.*
KB	L. Koehler and W. Baumgartner, *The Hebrew and Aramaic Lexicon of the Old Testament*. Translated by M. E. J. Richardson. Volume I. Leiden, 1994.
LXX	The Septuagint (Greek version of the Old Testament).
MT	Masoretic Text.
NRSV	*The New Revised Standard Version*, Anglicized Edition, 1989, 1995.
OCD	N. G. L. Hammond and H. H. Scullard (eds.), *Oxford Classical Dictionary*, 2nd edn. Oxford, 1970.

OTS	*Oudtestamentische Studiën.*
REB	*The Revised English Bible,* 1989.
RSV	*The Revised Standard Version,* 1952, 1971, 1973.
SJT	*Scottish Journal of Theology.*
TDNT	G. Kittel and G. Friedrich, *Theological Dictionary of the New Testament.* Translated by G. W. Bromiley. 10 volumes. Grand Rapids, 1964–76.
TrinJ	*Trinity Journal.*
VT	*Vetus Testamentum.*
WO'C	B. K. Waltke and M. O'Connor, *An Introduction to Biblical Hebrew Syntax.* Winona Lake, 1990.

What am *I* to you, that you should command me to love you and,

if I do not,

you should be angry with me and threaten great miseries?

Augustine, *Confessions*, I, 5

Chapter One

In the beginning: human marriage as 'one flesh'

Like an untrained soldier thrown into the chaos of a battle already well advanced, the young nation of Israel was born into a world long violent with sin but unable to find the ways of peace. The late arriver urgently needed orientation. The teachings of the Pentateuch shaped Israel's distinctive sense of national identity and mission by setting forth the great issues engulfing the world in conflict and by calling Israel to a bold commitment to the purpose of God.[1] It placed the infant nation's present situation against a much larger backdrop, tracing the story all the way back to its remotest origins in the book of Genesis – the creation, the fall, the division of the nations into warring factions and then the call of Abraham to bring the blessing of God's rule to this troubled world. The covenant community could then see itself in a true light, rise above the vulgar preoccupations of common human existence and fulfill its holy calling.

Genesis 2:18–25, the account of the creation of the woman from the man, serves this larger purpose by opening up the profound inner meaning of the third line of Genesis 1:27:

> So God created man in his own image,
>   in the image of God he created him;
>   *male and female* he created them (RSV).

[1] The complex question of Pentateuchal formation continues to resist scholarly resolution. Whybray (1995: 12f.) assesses the current state of the question as follows: 'There is at the present moment no consensus whatever about when, why, how, and through whom the Pentateuch reached its present form, and opinions about the dates of composition of its various parts differ by more than five hundred years . . . The important question is not one of the sources available to the compiler but what the Pentateuch was intended to mean in its present form.' Until a consensus emerges, a cautious building of one's case upon the basis of the canonical Scriptures seems to be the course most capable, in principle, of gathering common ground.

One might have thought that this line merely prepares the way for verse 28, which assumes mankind's capacity for sexual reproduction: 'And God blessed them, and God said to them, "Be fruitful and multiply, and fill the earth . . ."' After all, the lower creation was addressed not dissimilarly in verse 22: 'And God blessed them, saying, "Be fruitful and multiply and fill the waters . . ."' But human sexuality has a far deeper meaning than mere animal instinct, even if that instinct and capacity were imparted to the animals also through divine blessing. Along with the rest of human nature, God uses human sexuality to serve his redemptive purpose in the world. And so the Torah places before Israel the deeper meaning of human sexuality through the account of the first man and woman in the garden of Eden in chapter 2.[2]

In verses 8–15 God prepares a place for the man. The garden is generously supplied not only with the necessities of life – food and water – which the original Israelite readers enduring the 'howling waste of the wilderness' (Dt. 32:10) must have envied, but also with rich luxuries to be wondered at under any circumstances.[3] Moreover, the tree of life within the garden functions as a sacramental device for sustaining the man indefinitely, presumably to be eaten daily to recharge the man's batteries, as it were.[4] Another, the tree of the knowledge of good and evil, serves as guardian symbol and standard of God's ultimate claim to rule in the garden. The man, for his part, is charged by God 'to till and keep'[5] the garden. Perhaps implied

---

[2] The literary interplay between chapters 1 and 2 of Genesis is developed fruitfully in Alter (1981: 140–147).

[3] Is. 51:3 and Ezk. 36:33–35, by assuming as ideal the experience associated with the garden of Eden, provide biblical commentary on the scene depicted so briefly but suggestively in Gn. 2.

[4] Hamilton (1990: 173) draws one's attention to 1 Tim. 6:16, which asserts that God alone possesses immortality.

[5] The sense may be, more particularly, 'to till and *guard*' the garden. One observes in Gn. 3:1ff. that evil is not unable to enter the scene, but the human couple are to bring it under their rule, as commanded in 1:28. When they fail in that responsibility, the cherubim, armed with a dreadful sword, guard (same verb as in 2:15, *viz.* √*šmr*) the way to the vast treasury of privilege represented by the garden. *Cf.* Delitzsch (1899: I:137): '. . . the meaning of ולשמרה is not restricted to keeping the garden from running wild or from injury by animals. He was also to keep it by withstanding the power of temptation, which was threatening to destroy him and Paradise with him.'

here is humanity's responsibility and opportunity to develop the garden until it would cover the entire earth, future generations living in one Edenic world, sustained by the divine means of grace and obedient to the Creator's authoritative definition of what is good and what is evil.[6]

In verses 16–17 God throws open to the man the freedom to enter into the joys of his new location of service.[7] The only restriction is the forbidden tree of the knowledge of good and evil, by which God places before the man the choice of life or death. The concept of evil and the threat of certain death may have perplexed the first man in his unfallen state, especially with the tree of life there always to fall back on; but the Israelite reader would not have missed the poignancy of it.

Then, in verse 18, amid abundant provision, meaningful responsibility, personal care from God and splendid promise for the future, God puts his finger on the one flaw in this otherwise ideal environment: 'It is not good that the man should be alone.' Total perfection requires one more creative act, narrated in verses 19–22. The scene of unspoiled surroundings, clearly defined moral parameters and a strong incentive to follow the divine command moves toward completion as God provides the man with a helper uniquely suited to collaborate with him as his partner in advancing the purpose of God.

We are now prepared to read verses 23–24 more closely:

> [23]Then the man said,
>   'This at last is bone of my bones
>   and flesh of my flesh;

[6] Kidner (1972: 61) observes, 'There is a hint of the cultural development intended for man when the narrative momentarily (10–14) breaks out of Eden to open up a vista into a world of diverse countries and resources. The digression, overstepping the bare details that locate the garden, discloses that there is more than primitive simplicity in store for the race: a complexity of unequally distributed skills and peoples, even if the reader knows the irony of it in the tragic connotations of the words "gold", "Assyria", "Euphrates".'

[7] One notes with interest that the entire verse – not only the prohibition of the one tree but also the generous provision of food from the other trees – falls under the main verb 'to command'. Moreover, the permission to eat is stated not grudgingly but strongly, with the infinitive absolute strengthening the verb 'to eat' and the whole garden ('eat of *every* tree'), with one exception, offered by God.

this one shall be called Woman,
for out of Man this one was taken.'
[24]Therefore a man shall leave his father and his
mother and cleave to his wife, and they shall become
one flesh.

In the course of his naming of the animals the man came to realize that there was no other creature in the garden which fully shared his own nature, for his naming of them entailed not mere labelling but analysis, so that each name would be appropriate to the nature of each creature.[8] This thoughtful exercise confronted him with one disappointment after another in relation to himself, so that he came to realize his own solitude within the vast complexity of the garden. He is now prepared for his final act of naming.

So 'God himself, like a father of the bride, leads the woman to the man' (von Rad 1972: 84). And the man, speaking either in praise to God or in unselfconscious wonder to himself, for these words are not directed to the woman but describe her in the third person – the man greets her with an intuitive sense of their congeniality. With the earliest recorded human words – and they are love poetry – the man expresses his exuberant joy at his first encounter with the woman. This one alone,[9] this one at last,[10] answers to the need of his heart, for she is bone of his bones and flesh of his flesh.[11] That is, he shares a close personal kinship with her as he does not with the animals, for he perceives that she has been built out of the stuff of his very body. A 'bone and flesh' mutuality, formally considered, may describe even a distant blood relation.[12] But here, in the man's glad recognition of the woman as his unique counterpart, sprung from himself, the sense is more personal and emotional. He

[8] Sifthei Chachamim comments: 'He grasped with his intellect the nature of every beast.' One observes the man's doing this in the case of the woman, in verse 23.

[9] Presumably, the conspicuous $z\bar{o}(')t$, 'this one', functions not dissimilarly to $w^e'\bar{o}t\hat{o}$, 'him', in Dt. 6:13: 'Him (only) shall you serve.' This creature only, unlike the animals, the man identifies with.

[10] Functioning adverbially, *happa'am* suggests the fulfilment of a desire hitherto frustrated. *Cf.* Gn. 29:34; 30:20.

[11] Rashi comments, 'Adam came to all the beasts and living creatures, but he found no satisfaction until he came to Eve.'

[12] *E.g.* Jdg. 9:2; 2 Sa. 19:13 [EVV 12].

rejoices in the woman as a creature truly fit for him. It is verse 24 which formalizes more clearly what this particular 'bone and flesh' relation entails.

Her name, '*iššâ(h)*, Woman,[13] relative to his own, '*îš*, Man,[14] declares publicly her status as his only true companion in the garden. Unlike the animals – indeed, unlike the man himself – she did not come up from the ground below but out from human flesh, putting her alone at the man's level. Verse 23b links this first meeting of man and woman with the larger task of the man's naming of the creatures and yet sets the woman apart as superior to the other creatures the man had already named.

One is struck by the fact that the man does not say that the woman was taken 'out of *me*' but 'out of *Man*'. He views both her and himself objectively. In 23a he speaks personally – 'bone of *my* bones and flesh of *my* flesh', which could be said literally of this first woman only. But in 23b the man speaks publicly and officially as the duly authorized Namer in the garden, setting a precedent for future generations of the race. He assumes his own identity as '*îš*, while formalizing the woman's identity as '*iššâ(h)*. The net effect makes clear her identity as fully human and yet different from himself.

Significantly, as will become evident in due course, this man with eyes undimmed by sin, in this moment of clear insight, nevertheless sees nothing before him but a woman in relationship to himself. The ultimate reality of a Saviour with his Bride, which the biblical story will eventually unveil as the mystery revealed through human marriage, does not fall within the range of the first man's perception. No adumbrations of that

[13] No proper etymology is intended but merely a euphonic similarity. The purpose is not technical but practical, which the feminine suffix adequately serves.

[14] Interestingly, the man is *hā'āḏām* in the passage until the last line of verse 23 and through verse 24, where he becomes '*îš*, while 25 resumes the use of *hā'āḏām*. Adding the feminine suffix to '*āḏām* would have produced the word for 'ground', which wordplay has its own function in relation to the whole human race. Moreover, '*āḏām* was already used in 1:27 for both sexes. *zākār* would have failed also, for *nᵉqēḇâ(h)* could not achieve the euphony, which itself suggests the close identification the man feels with the woman. Only '*îš* is capable of being exploited as a device for distinguishing the man and the woman while at the same time relating them closely.

mystery occur to him now. But what he does see and declare is enough for the curtain to rise meaningfully on the larger biblical drama.

Verse 24 breaks the continuity of the narrative – resumed in verse 25 – with the particle 'Therefore', intruding the narrator's own parenthetical comment.[15] The more general question concerns whether verse 24 should be read as an historical explanation of human custom[16] or as an authoritative injunction of human obligation.[17] If the verse is merely descriptive of a general pattern of human behaviour – the sexes tending to pair off in marriage – then one wonders why so obvious a point receives such formal attention in the solemn tones of verse 24. If this verse were excised altogether, it would still not be difficult to make a meaningful connection between the remaining narrative and later human customs in marriage. Our interpretative intuitions would supply the link readily. Moreover, one wonders why Scripture would encumber itself with an observation so heavily in need of qualification. The plain fact, witnessed to already in Genesis 4:19, is that the definition of marriage set forth here in 2:24 is by no means universally accepted. It was not in Israel, perhaps even in the case of Moses, the hero of the

---

[15] The compound particle *'al kēn* appears elsewhere when the author inserts his own explanatory remark into the narrative. *Cf.* Gn. 10:9; 11:9; 16:14; 19:22; 21:31; *etc.*

[16] This interpretation construes the *yqtl* verb (and, accordingly, the following waw-relative *qtl* forms) as bearing the force of a habitual imperfect, reflected in the present-tense verbs of the RSV: 'Therefore a man leaves his father and his mother and cleaves [NRSV clings] to his wife, and they become one flesh.' *Cf.* Skinner (1930: 70): 'An aetiological observation of the narrator'; Westermann (1984: 233): 'The etiological motif of v. 24 is then an addition, an explanation of "the basic drive of the sexes to each other".'

[17] This interpretation construes the *yqtl* verb form (and, accordingly, the following waw-relative *qtl* forms) as bearing the force of an instructive imperfect, reflected in the future-tense verbs of the AV: 'Therefore shall a man leave his father and his mother, and shall cleave unto his wife: and they shall be one flesh.' *Cf.* (Aalders 1981: 1:97): 'Although this translation [the present tense, as in the RSV] is linguistically possible, it makes the statement very dull . . . It is our conviction . . . that in these lines the sacred writer gives us the basic ordinance which establishes the close binding unity of man and woman in the marriage bond'; Keil & Delitzsch (1972: *ad loc.*): 'They are the words of Moses, written to bring out the truth embodied in the fact recorded as a divinely appointed result, to exhibit marriage as the deepest corporeal and spiritual unity of man and woman . . .'

Torah.[18] Finally, our Lord's use of this passage in Matthew 19:3–9 assumes the prescriptive force of verse 24. We shall read this verse, therefore, as the inspired author's pastoral application of verse 23 to his own historical situation.[19]

This being so, verse 24 thrusts into the midst of a pre-fall human scene a word directly addressing post-fall people. After all, Adam did not have a father and a mother to leave. By means of this conspicuous verse, then, the text insists that the reader see the larger point to be derived from verse 23. Verse 24 is intended to exercise guiding and correcting power in one's understanding of what marriage means and how one lives out that meaning in real life.

Three points are made in verse 24. First, a married man is to leave his father and his mother.[20] The expectation which the covenant community must accept as normative is that a new marriage will sever what is otherwise the strongest human bond, for it is the father and the mother whose very bodies give a man his life.[21] This requirement elevates the marital union above all other personal loyalties, under God. If, in marrying, a man withdraws his primary allegiance from his parents and redirects it to his wife so that they enter into a 'one flesh' existence, how much more does this distinguish marriage from all other relationships as well! Marriage is so profound a union that not only *may* one put one's wife ahead of all others, one *must* do so.

Secondly, a married man is to cleave to, or cling to, his wife. As the positive complement to the preceding clause, this requires

[18] Whether or not the Cushite woman whom Moses married (Nu. 12:1) was the same as his Midianite wife Zipporah (Ex. 2:21) is a debated question. *Cf.* Harrison (1990: 194f.).

[19] I take verse 24 as related, through *'al kēn*, to verse 23 in particular, rather than to the preceding narrative more generally, because of the 'flesh of my flesh'/'one flesh' connection it draws.

[20] The verb employed here, √ *zb*, is strong to the point of risking a misimpression, for it is used elsewhere of careless abandonment in which lawful obligations are disregarded, *e.g.* Jos. 22:3; Ps. 27:10; Is. 54:6.

[21] 1 Esdras 4:20–21, 25, viewed as a witness to an interpretative tradition in touch with the force of verse 24, corroborates this understanding. *Cf.* Jacob (1974: 21): 'Father and mother are the natural roots of the child; with its brothers and sisters it has grown on the same stem. Husband and wife are from different families. Yet man forsakes father and mother for his wife and thus dissolves the strongest ties of body and soul.'

and permits the man to devote his primary loyalty to his wife.[22] And what does this cleaving look like in life? The language suggests that, physically, the man takes his wife in his arms, so that in the course of normal life their marriage is frequently symbolized, celebrated and refreshed through sexual union. Emotionally, the man fixes upon her alone his deepest affections, under God, with a profound sense of attachment, contentment and fulfilment.[23] And formally or socially, the man lives with his wife in a covenant of strictly inviolable exclusivity, separating him from all others on the earth.[24]

Thirdly, the man and his wife are to become 'one flesh'. The new life created by a marriage fuses a man and wife together into one, fully shared human experience, prompting mutual care, tenderness and love. It is at this point that the logical connection with verse 23b becomes most clear. There, as also in verse 21, the

---

[22] The construction $\sqrt{dbq}$ with b^e is also used in Ru. 1:14 and 2 Sa. 20:2 for the fastening of oneself to another in devoted commitment.

[23] Paul Büchlein (Fagius), in *Critici Sacri* (1660 edn.), comments: 'Verbum דבק Hebraeis non simpliciter *adhaerere* significat, sed amanter et conjugali affectu; unde et R.D.K. in Radicibus per *associari* exponit. Quare et non raro, ubi veri et casti amoris mentio fit, idem verbi usurpat. Non ergo de carnis libidine in uxore explenda haec adhaesio intelligi debet, sed de amore potius conjugali, quo maritus uxorem, tanquam os et carnem suam, complecti, fovere, et nutrire debet, ut habet Epistola ad Ephes, cap. 5.' [The word דבק to the Hebrews means not simply *to cleave* but lovingly and with marital fondness; whence also Rabbi David Kimchi, in his *Book of Roots*, explains it by means of *to be united with*. For which reason, and not infrequently, where mention is made of true and pure love, the same makes use of the word. Therefore, this cleaving should not be understood of the lust of the flesh to be satisfied by a wife but rather of marital love, with which a husband should care for, cherish and nourish his wife as his own bone and flesh, as the epistle to the Ephesians, chapter 5, has it.]

[24] The covenantal nature of marriage in the OT has recently been expounded and defended by Gordon Paul Hugenberger (1994: 342). He defines a covenant as 'an elected, as opposed to natural, relationship of obligation established under divine sanction.' On p. 279, Hugenberger summarizes the covenantal meaning of sexual intercourse: 'Clearly, sexual union is the indispensable means for the consummation of marriage both in the Old Testament and elsewhere in the ancient Near East. While it is less certain, it seems probable that sexual union functioned in this manner precisely because it was viewed as an oath-sign . . . oath signs, such as eating together or giving one's hand in a hand shake, often function by offering a solemn depiction of the covenant commitment to unity being undertaken. With respect to sexual union, it is clear that this act is ideally suited to depict the "one flesh" reality which is definitional of marriage in Gn. 2:24.'

word 'flesh' is meant literally. Here in verse 24, however, a higher sense is intended. By metonymy, this use of 'flesh' accomplishes two things at once. On the one hand, it affirms the true, if not 'blood', kinship between the man and the woman.[25] On the other hand, it whispers the temporal limitation inherent in the marriage relationship.[26] What strikes the reader is both that this is a '*one* flesh' relationship, and also that it is a 'one *flesh*' relationship. A '*one* flesh' union is unparalleled in human relationships, which argues for the uniqueness of the marital bond – a point already established. But, additionally, any union defined in terms of *flesh* must be acknowledged to be less than ultimate in nature. It extends for the full length of this mortal life, but it cannot transcend this life. Marriage, therefore, is the deepest human relationship, but not even this relationship qualifies as a final experience. (Again, one bears in mind that verse 24 is an admonition to post-fall readers inserted into a record of pre-fall events.) There comes a day when every married man, stripped of everything he cherishes in this life, must let go even of his beloved wife's hand. Marriage is profound, but not ultimate.

To sum up, human marriage is premised in the making of the woman out of the very flesh of the man,[27] so that the bond of marriage reunites what was originally and literally one flesh. All other relational claims must yield to the primacy of marital union. It requires an exclusive, life-long bonding of one man with one woman in one life fully shared. It erects barriers around the man and woman, and it destroys all barriers between the man and the woman. God so joins them together that they belong fully to one another, and to one another only.

This is the vision of human marriage which provides the coherent network of meanings necessary for an understanding of the covenanted nation's relationship with Yahweh, as the story unfolds in the rest of Scripture.

[25] The word is used elsewhere as equivalent to 'relative(s); *cf.* Gn. 37:27; Lv. 18:6; Is. 58:7.

[26] The word can also connote that which is frail, transient, mortal; *cf.* Gn. 6:3; Dt. 5:26; 2 Ch. 32:8; Jb. 34:14–15; Ps. 56:5 [EVV 4]; 78:39; Is. 31:3; 40:6; Je. 17:5; 1 Cor. 15:50. *Cf.* Wolff 1974a: 26–31 – although Wolff places the use of 'flesh' in Gn. 2:24 into the referential category 'Body', paraphrasing the 'one flesh'-ness of marriage as 'a common body', which seems absurd.

[27] This point is emphasized in verse 23: '. . . for out of Man this one was taken.'

Chapter Two

Playing the harlot

For post-fall humanity, adulterated by sin, the Bible unfolds the drama of a loving God winning back to himself 'a pure bride for her one husband' (2 Cor. 11:2). Human marriage as original and ideal, defined in Genesis 2:23–24, provides the pre-understanding necessary for spiritual 'harlotry' to function as a meaningful moral category in the covenanted people's perception of themselves and of their 'marital' obligations to their Lord, until the biblical drama reaches its eventual dénouement.

As the Old Testament unfolds, one first encounters only intimations of Yahweh's marriage to his people. Such a relationship seems to have been assumed rather than declared, for Yahweh is explicitly identified as the 'husband' of Israel nowhere previous to the prophets.[1] Nevertheless, language suggestive of a marital bond is used of the covenant at the literary foundation of the Old Testament.[2]

My approach in tracking the linguistic markers of our theme is exegetical and not merely lexicographical, however. Out of

[1] The distinction between what Scripture asserts and what it assumes is not a fundamental one, for its assumptions are material to its teachings and a very telling aspect of them. Davidson (1904: 74) states it more boldly: '. . . it is not necessary to distinguish between what Scripture asserts and what it assumes, inasmuch as its assumptions may be considered its teaching even more than its direct affirmations.'

[2] Objections to early dating of Pentateuchal materials sometimes appeal to genuine anomalies in the text as evidences of some measure of post-authorial development, e.g. Gn. 12:6; 13:7; 14:14; Nu. 12:3; Dt. 34:5ff. In agreement with the larger impression of Old Testament formation as implied by its own canonical structure and internal witness, however, one observes a convincingly natural growth from episodic messages of Israel's harlotry in the Pentateuch and historical books to a more fully developed vision of Yahweh as the husband of his people in the prophets. If Israel's theology developed along historical lines radically different from those implied by the shape of the canon itself, then this pattern of development would be difficult to explain.

Israel's overall vision of God as King, Judge, Shepherd, Husband, and so on, an author would choose specific language for use in any given context as it was apt to evoke that particular aspect of God's ultimate meaning most congenial with the author's theological purpose in that passage. For this reason, I will not appeal to the usage of √*znh* (BDB 'commit fornication, be a harlot')[3] as my fundamental theological datum. Rather, through exegesis of the passages in which this language appears one is able to re-create the larger theological imagination which itself prompted the use of such language to begin with. The following proposals, therefore, grounded in exegesis, open up the nexus of meanings informed by the idea that the bond between Yahweh and Israel is marital in nature. In the Pentateuch and historical books, the indicators of this deeper theological substructure underlying the text are found in the references to Israel's whoredom in sharing her worship with other gods and in Yahweh's jealousy for her.[4] Our primary interest here lies in the former.

The donor conceptual field of marriage prescribes strict sexual faithfulness between husband and wife. Illegitimate sexual involvement, the dark reversal of the marital ideal, exposes the brokenness of a fallen race. The word group related to √*znh* is used literally of such unlawful sexual activity, *e.g.* Tamar's apparent prostitution in Genesis 38:24, as well as figuratively for betrayal[5] of one's union with God.

---

[3] The root is capable of being objectified with various English expressions. A major study is provided by Collins (1977).

[4] One might have proposed that √*ʿzb* and √*dbq* construed with *bᵉ* also be included, since they appear both in Gn. 2:24 and as covenantal language later in the Pentateuch, *e.g.* Dt. 11:22; 28:20; 29:24 [EVV 25]; 30:20. But drawing this connection would require a reversal of the marital roles, for in Gn. 2:24 it is the husband who leaves and cleaves but in the covenant it is Israel. Moreover, the leaving and cleaving in Gn. 2:24 entail a wholesome change of allegiance from parents to wife as two dimensions of one psychological adjustment; in the covenant, however, they are antithetical mentalities, the one opposed to Yahweh and the other devoted to him. The analogy is inapt.

[5] Radak, *Book of Roots*, *s.v.* זנה, makes the etymologically eccentric but conceptually suggestive proposal that 'one must join it [*i.e.*, √*znh*] with זנח, for the whore [*zônâ(h)*] is one who betrays; she abandons and forsakes [*taznîᵃḥ*]'.

Exodus 34:11–16

After the dreadful lapse of chapter 32, when through the making and worshipping of the golden calf the covenanted people compromised themselves with the paganism rampant in the surrounding cultures, their relationship with God was at risk. But Moses interceded, and God renewed the covenant with assurances of his on-going presence in their journey to the promised land. As a token of covenant renewal, God instructed Moses to make two new stone tablets, replacing the ones Moses broke in disgust when he saw the debauchery in the camp of Israel. Moses ascended Mount Sinai again with the new tablets, where the Lord revealed himself with a glorious declaration of his moral perfections and of his commitment to the covenant with fresh promises that he would demonstrate his power among his people.

Now, in verses 11–16, the Lord declares what he expects from them in return. His commands flow logically out of both his own nature and their recent flirtation with bull worship. They are intended to immunize Israel against the infection of nature religion, to which the people had exposed themselves. As the nation proceeds into the idolatrous surroundings of Canaanite civilization, their own recent behaviour does not encourage sanguine expectations. Without experience in agriculture, Israel will naturally turn to Canaanite practices for instruction. And if those practices, permeated with idolatry, seem to guarantee survival, the pressure on their faith to adapt to the local religion will be intense:[6]

---

[6] Habel (1964: 27) puts this tension in concrete terms: 'After the fervor of each of the holy wars [of the conquest] was spent, the very prosaic business of survival by settlement demanded agricultural techniques, Canaanite techniques. With cultivation, there came the lure of fertility rites, the unfortunate snare of the hungry peasant as well as the prosperous wine merchant. Time and again the writer of Judges recalls how the chosen people of Israel "served the Baals and Ashtaroth" and forsook Yahweh. The large number of Astarte plaques and figurines in Late Bronze Age deposits in Palestine indicates the frequency of Israelite contact with this way of life. Here, then, was a battle royal, for in the adoption of Canaanite culture the kingship of Yahweh was at stake. Wherever Israel established a compromising *modus vivendi* with the Canaanites this conflict was destined to continue.'

*11*Observe what I command you today. Behold, I will drive out before you the Amorites, the Canaanites, the Hittites, the Perizzites, the Hivites, and the Jebusites. *12*Take care, lest you make a covenant with the inhabitants of the land to which you are going, lest they become a snare among you.

Verse 11 begins with a call to universal obedience, and verse 12 with a call to particular watchfulness.[7] After falling so readily into idolatry with the golden calf, Israel[8] must never again be naïve about their bent toward moral and religious contamination from the surrounding peoples.[9] They must police themselves strictly. God, for his part, declares that he will drive out the pagan nations from the promised land, showing his opposition to the religious principles upon which their civilizations are based. How then can Israel, in covenant with a God of such commitments, make another covenant with the very nations he opposes?[10] The danger is that the paganism of these peoples – a real threat in view of the calf incident – would become a 'snare' among the people of God.[11] Verse 13 implies what that snare is and specifies how this danger is to be avoided:

*13*For you shall tear down their altars, and break their pillars, and cut down their Asherim *14*(for you shall worship no other god, for the LORD, whose name is Jealous, is a jealous God), *15*lest you make a covenant

[7] Verse 11 is introduced with a qal imperative of √šmr, and verse 12 with a niphal of the same verb. The former calls the nation to duty. *Cf.* Dt. 23:24; 29:8; 1 Ki. 2:43; 11:11. The latter calls the nation to caution. *Cf.* Ex. 19:12; Jdg. 13:4; 1 Sa. 19:2; Je. 9:3 [EVV 4].

[8] Although Israel is referred to in the third person in verse 10, they are doubtless in view here in 11, addressed in the second person.

[9] *Cf.* Childs (1976: 613): 'The whole emphasis of the admonition falls on Israel's complete separation from the inhabitants of the land.'

[10] Henry (*Exp: ad loc.*) comments, 'If God, in kindness to them, drove out the Canaanites, they ought, in duty to God, not to harbour them. What could be insisted on more reasonable than this? If God make war with the Canaanites, let not Israel make peace with them. If God take care that the Canaanites be not their lords, let them take care that they be not their snares.'

[11] The word *môqēš*, translated 'snare' by the RSV, is used for a lure employed in catching wildlife in Am. 3:5 and Jb. 40:24. Saul intended to use Michal as bait (*môqēš*) to catch David, according to 1 Sa. 18:21. Elsewhere it is used for various forms of personal entanglement which one would be safe to avoid.

with the inhabitants of the land, and when they play the harlot after their gods and sacrifice to their gods and one invites you, you eat of his sacrifice, [16]and you take wives from their daughters for your sons, and their daughters play the harlot after their gods and make your sons play the harlot after their gods.

According to verse 13, monuments of pagan worship deserve destruction. Ultimately, this is so because such forms of worship will distort Israel's vision of who God is. But Yahweh's purpose here is more proximate and immediately practical. These tangible emblems of pagan theology threaten to seduce Israel into compromise with pagan religious practice. The concern is that another golden calf or its equivalent could arise in Israel. That possibility will be precluded if Israel settles upon a determined policy of comprehensive destruction of such objects.[12]

Verse 14a claims exclusivity for Yahweh in the hearts and devotion of the people as the rationale for the policy of verse 13.[13] They are to worship no other God.[14] And, in turn, the incentive for singularity of devotion to Yahweh is, according to verse 14b, his own nature. He is a jealous God. Indeed, his very name is Jealous.[15] This is the language used in connection with the 'law of jealousy' in Numbers 5:11–31, instructing the

---

[12] *Cf.* Jacob (1992: 990): 'The verse employs a series of plural verbs, in contrast to the usual singular verbs; this is due to the multitude of the objects.'

[13] Verse 14, as the RSV and NRSV indicate, seems to be a parenthetical insertion into the text, providing the theological undergirding for the requirement of verse 13, before verses 15–16 provide the more practical concern lying behind verse 13.

[14] The phrase *'ēl 'aḥēr* is unique in the Old Testament. One observes *'ēl zār* ('strange god') in Pss. 44:21 [EVV 20] and 81:10 [EVV 9], the latter also showing *'ēl nēḵār* ('foreign god'), which appears as well in Dt. 32:12 and Mal. 2:11. Moreover, the plural *'ᵉlōhîm 'ᵃḥērîm* ('other gods') appears not infrequently in the Old Testament, *e.g.* in Ex. 20:3, which doubtless is the source of the commandment uttered here. But the singular 'other god' of our passage suggests a situation-specific rooting out of all forms of idolatry, one instance at a time, allowing no compromise at any point.

[15] The jealousy of Yahweh is his profoundly intense drive within to protect the interests of his own glory (Ex. 20:4–6; Ezk. 39:25), for he 'will admit no derogation from his majesty', to quote Eichrodt (1961: I:44). (Eichrodt calls the jealousy of God 'the basic element in the whole OT idea of God', *ibid.*, I:210.) The jealousy of Yahweh insists that his people observe his exclusive claims upon them (Dt. 6:13–15). Von Rad (1962: I:208) sets the biblical demand in a larger

community in what to do when a man is overwhelmed with a spirit of jealousy for his wife. *Mutatis mutandis,* Yahweh's jealousy for his wife Israel requires that she offer her devotion to no other lover, just as a man will share his wife with no other.[16] The covenant creates a sacred boundary not to be encroached upon. It warrants a lawful sense of entitlement within God, which, when violated, generates intense emotional upheaval:[17]

> They *stirred* him *to jealousy* with strange gods;
> with abominable practices they *provoked* him *to anger*
> (Dt. 32:16, RSV).

> They have *stirred* me *to jealousy* with what is no god;
> They have *provoked* me with their idols
> (Dt. 32:21, RSV).

> For they *provoked* him *to anger* with their high places;
> they *moved* him *to jealousy* with their graven images
> (Ps. 78:58, RSV).

And 'as his name is, so is he' (Cassuto 1967: 444).[18] When the

---

context: 'This intolerant claim to exclusive worship is something unique in the history of religion, for in antiquity the cults were on easy terms with one another and left devotees a free hand to ensure a blessing for themselves from other gods as well.'

[16] The sharpness of the description 'jealous' when applied to God suggests that there are two kinds of jealousy. In fallen man, jealousy can be selfish and irrational; in God, jealousy is pure love. The same divine fire which consumes idolatry, since it also yearns to show compassion, guarantees to keep Israel in his love (Joel 2:18; Zc. 1:12–16). God's morally perfect jealousy arises out of his joint longings both to vindicate his own glory and to enjoy true love with his people. Not infrequently, there is only partial overlap between the uses of a word when applied variously to both God and man. One must make all due allowance for the enlargement and purification of a word's meaning when it is applied to God, given the fullness of who he is. One must not impose upon God the imperfections and limitations which the same word may convey when applied to man. *Cf.* St Hilary of Poitiers, *De Trinitate,* IV.14: 'Our understanding of the [biblical] words is to be taken from the reasons why they were spoken, because the subject is not subordinated to the language but the language to the subject.'

[17] *Cf.* Pr. 6:34; 27:4; Song 8:6.

[18] On the name of God as the virtual equivalent to himself as revealed, see Gn. 12:8; Ex. 3:14–15; 23:21; Lv. 24:11; Dt. 28:58; 1 Ch. 29:13; Ps. 7:18 [EVV 17]; 18:50 [EVV 49]; Is. 56:6.

love of Jealous is offended, he burns.[19] His love is not morally indifferent, pouring out its benefits heedless of human response.[20] He expects and requires an ardent and faithful love in return.[21]

Verses 15–16 resume the thought begun in verse 12 and elaborate upon the snare awaiting Israel in the promised land if they are incautious in their relations with the indigenous peoples. The danger is that, by incremental degrees, the covenanted people could be absorbed into paganism. Interestingly, the utterance begun at verse 11 could conceivably have concluded at the end of verse 14, followed by the equivalent to verse 17.[22] The function of verses 15–16, then, is to amplify upon Yahweh's concern to warn and protect his people. These verses imply that, even if the land is completely cleared of the institutional manifestations of idolatry, *viz.* the altars, pillars and Asherim of verse 13, a danger still exists that the paganism they stand for could be renewed through friendly relations with the Canaanites who would retain a sense of affinity with and duty to their local gods.[23] Those deep psychological attachments would endure after the desecration of their sanctuaries, so that the danger of immorality from paganism would continue.

That danger unfolds by stages – first as a treaty of mutual advantage, then as an invitation to share in worship, then eating of a sacrifice made to a pagan god or goddess, and finally intermarriage with the Canaanites, with the result that all distinctions may in time be expected to dissolve. What begins as

---

[19] *Cf.* Dt. 4:11–12 with 24; Ps. 79:5. Jos. 24:19 suggests that his jealousy is contiguous with his holiness.

[20] *Cf.* Eichrodt (1961: I:217): '. . . human love possesses real value in his eyes.' *Cf.* Francis Vatable, in *Critici Sacri* (1660 edn), *ad loc.*: 'Non patitur ut alius deus secum colatur; solus pro Deo amari et coli vult.' [He does not permit that another god be worshipped with him; he wants to be loved and worshipped alone as God.]

[21] *Cf.* Calvin (*Inst.* 2:8:16): '. . . God is provoked to jealousy whenever we substitute our figments in place of him, as when a lewd woman, openly parading her adulterer before her husband's very eyes, infuriates his mind all the more.'

[22] Verse 17 reads,' 'You shall make for yourself no molten gods.' If the passage had been ordered in this theoretical way, verse 14 would not have been parenthetical.

[23] *Cf.* Jacob 1992: 991.

an agreement between friends eventuates in the extinction of Israel as a people uniquely covenanted to God.[24]

Strikingly, these verses describe pagan worship as whoredom – an attractive whoredom easily capable of spreading its enticements to others. English idiom might lead one to expect the verb √znh (RSV, 'play the harlot') to be construed with a form of the preposition 'with' rather than 'after'. But to 'play the harlot *after*' pagan gods is to cultivate a relationship with them, to render unto them one's obedience and devotion, to walk in their ways and pursue their ideals.[25] The net force of the idiom is not unlike 'to go/follow after' other gods,[26] except that, marked by √znh, the imagery is sexual rather than ambulatory because the larger controlling motif is marital.

The force of this language in verse 15 does not assume covenantal status for the Canaanite peoples, as if their 'playing the harlot after their gods' implied a legitimate but violated union with Yahweh, for the gods in view are '*their* gods'. Rather, verse 15 judges the moral character of their gods and the worship they require. The sense is very nearly – but not quite – literal, for pagan worship encouraged sexual immorality. But the expression remains figurative, for the language suggests that this whoredom is engaged in with the gods.

That the local customs for worship should be insultingly condemned as whoredom arises presumably from two factors. First, the theology of the Canaanite peoples evidences a preoccupation with fertility, lifting up before worshippers a vision of various gods and goddesses as sexually active.[27] Secondly, the ritual outworking of this theology reflected its vision of deity.[28] By contrast, classical Yahwistic theology nowhere presents him as a sexual being calling for sexual participation in

[24] The Chronicler sees morally culpable assimilation doing its destructive work in Israel's history in 1 Ch. 5:25. According to 2 Ch. 21:11ff., the covenanted people also became their own seducers.

[25] *Cf.* Lv. 17:7; 20:5–6; Nu. 15:39; Dt. 31:16; Jdg. 2:17; 8:27, 33. Note the parallelism in Ps. 73:27.

[26] *Cf.* Dt. 11:28; 28:14; Jdg. 2:19 (noting with interest verse 17); 1 Ki. 11:4–5, 10; 21:26.

[27] *E.g.* Gibson (1978: 72 [regarding Baal], 125 [regarding El]); Gordon (1962: 170): 'Fertility is the main concern of the Ugaritic myths.'

[28] *Cf.* Nu. 25:1–3; 2 Ki. 23:4–7. The apparently liturgical character of 'Shachar and Shalim and the Gracious Gods' in Gibson (1978: 123–127) may witness to the practical union of myth and ritual, although not all scholars would construe

worship. His creation of human sexuality finds its lawful outlet in the union of marriage, as defined by Genesis 2:23–24.

The Canaanite peoples 'playing the harlot after their gods', then, were plunging into a form of worship radically alien to Yahwism but highly congenial with the inner logic of their own theology. The real irony appears in verse 16, where this harlotry in relation to the local deities spreads through intermarriage into the covenant community of Israel. The expectation is that intermarriage will not convert and purify the Canaanites but the reverse; it will corrupt Israel. The marriages envisaged here, no doubt lawful as far as social convention is concerned, still entail whoredom, for human marriage is not ultimate. Israel has a prior commitment to a heavenly husband, who is jealous for the love of his people. It may be expected that intermarriage will import into Israel a blurring of the clear theological and moral distinctions which define the meaning of Yahwism. With the loss of a vivid sense of boundaries, such as make the very concept of marriage meaningful and special, harlotry with other gods is inevitable. This sharing of one's faith, devotion and obedience with any other than Yahweh is, in his reckoning of things, whoredom.

Exodus 34:11–16, therefore, lifts up before Israel a vision of Yahweh as one intensely jealous for the love of his people, with the corollary that their participation in foreign worship constitutes so repulsive a violation of the covenant that they reduce themselves thereby to the moral status of whores responding to the overtures of strangers.

Leviticus 17:7

Levitical law was given to set Israel apart as a people holy to Yahweh, like a gown adorning a bride for her husband. The whole of their lives was to be marked by the one dominant consideration of holiness to Yahweh, even including the butchering of animals and misuse of the blood, as in chapter 17.

---

that connection in the same sense or even accept its validity in principle. There is little question, however, regarding the low moral tone pervading Canaanite worship, so that the Old Testament's condemnation of the indigenous religion is hardly shocking.

So they shall no more slay their sacrifices for goat-
demons, after whom they play the harlot.

Verses 3–6 of this chapter decree that any man who slaughters
an ox, a lamb or a goat for personal consumption must first
present the animal to the duly authorized priest at the
tabernacle. It is to be, first and foremost, an offering to Yahweh.
The blood and fat are to be given up in sacrifice to Yahweh
before the man may take the rest for himself. The principle is
that 'All slaughter is sacrifice' (Snaith 1967: 118). Disregarding
this requirement brings bloodguilt upon a man,[29] the penalty for
which is that the guilty party will be 'cut off' from his people.[30]
Verse 5 implies that the purpose for this ruling is to bring stricter
official control to the people's slaughtering of animals, so that
everything is subsumed under the larger life purpose of
devotion to Yahweh. Up to this point, the people have been
sacrificing animals wherever they pleased in the open field. The
personal, *ad hoc* nature of this worship expression has permitted
abuses. That loophole is being closed by this law.

Verse 7 explains the conditions which require this ruling. The
people have a long-standing practice[31] of sacrificing animals out
in the countryside, far removed from priestly supervision, where
they have been offering their animals not to their rightful Lord
but to, of all things, goat-demons.[32] This practice must stop, for it

[29] The severity of the law may be explainable in the terms set forth by Poole
(*Comm*: I:234): 'The reason is, because he shed that blood which, though not
man's blood, yet was as precious, being sacred and appropriated to God, and
typically the price by which men's lives were ransomed.'

[30] Wenham (1979: 242) quotes H. H. Cohn concerning the force of this
penalty: 'The threat of being "cut off" by the hand of God, in His own time,
hovers over the offender constantly and inescapably; he is not unlike the
patient who is told by his doctors that his disease is incurable and that he might
die any day . . . The wrath of the omnipotent and omniscient God being
directed particularly at yourself of all people, and being certain to strike at you
with unforeseeable force and intensity any day of the year and any minute of
the hour, was a load too heavy for a believer to bear.'

[31] Ibn Ezra comments, 'The word *'ôḏ* is torah, for thus Israel was doing in
Egypt.' *Cf.* Jos. 24:14.

[32] A *śā'îr* is simply a goat, as in Lv. 4:23–24 and frequently elsewhere. The root
suggests the shaggy appearance of the animal. The *śe'îrim* in Lv. 17:7, however,
are more than mere animals. That is so, because the Israelites are sacrificing
animals *to* the *śe'îrim* as an act of spiritual harlotry, which denotes idolatry
elsewhere. These 'goats', then, are idols in goat form. *Cf.* 2 Ch. 11:15. Josephus,

involves the covenanted people in a whorish pursuit of false gods. Given that the people of God were sharing their worship with such loathsome idols, Yahweh's charge of whoredom seems almost mild. The holy bride of Yahweh was cavorting with weird, perverse gods, of such a nature as to be identified with lusty goats.

Leviticus 20:4–6

Leviticus 20 decrees the death penalty for various violations of holiness to Yahweh. In contrast to the moral chaos widely accepted in the nation which God is expelling from the promised land, Israel is to observe the distinctions entailed in God's moral order. To transgress his boundaries is to deny one's consecration to Yahweh, making one indistinguishable from those not covenanted to him, as if he had not bound Israel to himself at all. That would amount to a rejection of his beneficent rule and an attempt to destroy his name on the human scene. Hence, the severity of the penalties.

> [4]And if the people of the land do at all hide their eyes from that man, when he gives one of his children to Molech, and do not put him to death, [5]then I will set my face against that man and against his family, and will cut them off from among their people, him and all who follow after him in playing the harlot after Molech (RSV).

Against Apion, II, 7, charges that the Egyptians worshipped, among other things, he-goats; and Jos. 24:14 urges Israel to put away the gods their fathers worshipped in Egypt. The second interpretative step, bringing in the idea of demonic presence, comes from Dt. 32:17, which gives one to understand that, in some sense, demons inhabit and energize idol worship. *Cf.* Ps. 107:37–39. This connection is evident in the history of the interpretation of this word. After the LXX's paraphrastic 'vanities', *i.e.* false gods, the other ancient versions, *viz.* Targum Onkelos, the Syriac, the Vulgate and the Arabic, all concur in interpreting *śeʿîrîm* in Lv. 17:7 as 'demons'. Both Rashi and Ibn Ezra agree, although the latter validates his interpretation with a dubious etymology. The NRSV, therefore, is standing in this interpretative tradition with its rendering, 'goat-demons'. The RSV's 'satyrs' suggests goatish, Pan-like idols of a Greek nature. Pan's disposition would be apposite to the metaphor of sexual sin. *Cf.* *OCD*, *s.v.* 'Pan'. For a rather different view, see Snaith 1975: 115–118.

35

Verses 2–5 prescribe the death penalty for anyone, Israelite or resident outsider, who participates in the worship of Molech.[33] Verse 4 even requires that one not at all[34] disregard Molech worship in someone else, for Yahweh will deal as severely with an unconcerned observer as with an actual participant.[35] So no-one may touch Molech, and no-one may hesitate to confront another who does. Alternatively, verse 4 may insist that, if the people of the land[36] turn a blind eye to any Molech worship in their midst, God will himself execute the penalty and will extend it to the violator's family as well. Whatever the exact force of verse 4 may be, however, it gives the whole community a strong incentive to guard against the encroachment of Molech worship into a nation holy to Yahweh.

In verse 5 Yahweh repeats his threat of verse 3, declaring that the family of the Molech worshipper will also be cut off, doubtless because they would be the most likely to know of his idolatry and the least likely to expose it. But holiness to Yahweh takes priority over loyalty to family. Indeed, Yahweh declares that he will cut off 'all who follow after him in playing the harlot after Molech'.[37] The judgment, therefore, is not arbitrary. It covers

---

[33] *Cf.* Lv. 18:21; 1 Ki. 11:7; 2 Ki. 23:10; Ps. 106:37–39; Je. 32:35.

[34] The infinitive absolute *haʿlēm* has the effect of emphasizing the slightness of the action of the finite verb *yaʿlîmû* in fulfilling the condition to be answered by the penalty of verse 5. *Cf.* Gibson § 101: 'The intensification of meaning which results [from the complementary infinitive absolute, as here], however, is not of the kind associated with the Piel (e.g. שָׁבַר *break*, שִׁבֵּר *smash*); it does not simply apply to the finite verb but to the whole clause, the appropriate Eng. translation depending on what kind of clause it is.' *Cf.* GKC § 113 o: 'The infinitive absolute in this case [*i.e.* a conditional clause] emphasizes the importance of the condition on which some consequence depends.'

[35] *Cf.* Harrison (1980: 205): 'By overlooking the offence they imply a certain sympathy towards it, and such an attitude would demoralize the covenant community very quickly.'

[36] In this passage, 'the people of the land' would likely be the entire community of the Israelites, as opposed to their leaders only. The point would be that everyone, from top to bottom, shares in the responsibility for watchfulness, and not only the official leaders. For a survey of the considerable discussion on the meaning of 'the people of the land' here and elsewhere, see *ABD, s.v.* 'Am Ha'arez'.

[37] *I.e.* 'all who play the harlot following his example, by playing the harlot after Molech'. The first instance of √*znh* with *'aḥªrê* is not the idiom observed above in Ex. 34:15–16 and Lv. 17:7. It is an absolute use of √*znh* with the preposition simply indicating that the subjects in view are following another's lead. In the second instance of √*znh* with *'aḥªrê*, the idiom 'to play the harlot after . . . 'does

only those who play the harlot after Molech. But it is comprehensive. It covers *all* those who play the harlot after Molech. The observances of Molech worship are like an infection which must not be allowed to spread at all into the body of Israel, for they are lethal to holiness.

> ⁶If a person turns to mediums and spiritists, playing the harlot after them, I will set my face against that person and will cut him off from among his people.

The striking thing about verse 6 is that this harlotry does not involve the worship of false gods but the pursuit of false revelation through human agency. Consulting mediums and spiritists[38] also amounts to whoredom, because, like idolatry, resorting to their ministrations denies Yahweh's all-sufficiency. Just as the counsels of a perfectly wise husband should be satisfying to a fair-minded wife, so Yahweh's revelation in law, Urim and Thummim, prophetic word, and so on, should satisfy

---

appear. The repetition of the verbal idea in the infinitive *liznôt* is required here to 'reset' the variables necessary to the idiom √*znh* + preposition *'aḥªrê* + object of preposition, after the potentially confusing but contextually necessary *'aḥªrāyw* following *hazzōnîm*.

[38] The precise meaning of *hā'ōḇōt* and *hayyiddeʿōnîm* is difficult to determine, but the 'wizards' of the RSV and NRSV seem a bit too Arthurian. The LXX interprets these words as 'familiar spirits' and 'chanters', respectively, Targum Onkelos as 'conjurers' and 'familiar spirits', the Syriac as 'diviners' and 'soothsayers', the Vulgate as 'magicians' and 'soothsayers', the Arabic as 'magicians' and 'diviners' – although some of these versional proposals are themselves patient of fine interpretative nuances. Rashi, commenting on *'ōḇ* in Lv. 19:31, quotes Sanhedrin 7.7: ' "He that is a necromancer" (such is the python who speaks from his armpits).' Ibn Ezra, quoting Jb. 32:19, interprets the *'ōḇōt* in Lv. 19:31 as skin bottles, the primary devices used by the soothsayer. As for *yiddeʿōnî*, Rashi assumes an etymological connection with the name of a certain animal known as *ydwʿ* and comments, 'A *yiddeʿōnî* puts a bone of the animal, whose name is *ydwʿ*, into his mouth, and the bone "speaks",' describing the method of trickery used. Ibn Ezra draws a more convincing etymological connection with √*ydʿ*, 'to know', proposing that the *yiddeʿōnîm* are sought for knowledge of the future. Biblical usage leaves beyond doubt that these words refer somehow to spiritism. *Cf.* Lv. 19:31; 20:27; Dt. 18:11; 1 Sa. 28:3, 7–9; 2 Ki. 21:6 (2 Ch. 33:6); 23:24; 1 Ch. 10:13; Is. 8:19; 19:3; 29:4. The activities of the renegade Jezebel linked 'harlotries and sorceries', according to 2 Ki. 9:22. Molech's association with the cult of the dead may explain why verse 6, concerned with attempts to make contact with the dead, follows the paragraph prohibiting his worship. See *ABD*, *s.v.* 'Molech'.

the questions and perplexities of his people. To seek revelation beyond his provision insinuates failure in him, exposes a prying restlessness in the covenant people and subjects them to compromising guidance from degraded sources.

Numbers 15:38–40

After the mixed report of the spies, Israel's refusal to trust God for the conquest of the promised land and then their own desperate attempt to move forward without his empowering presence (Nu. 13 – 14), the narrative pauses in chapter 15 for God graciously to decree: 'Say to the people of Israel, When you come into the land you are to inhabit, which I give you . . .' (verse 2). Although the present generation of adults must die under the frown of God, his purpose has not been frustrated and Israel will take the land. The rulings declared in chapter 15 are to mark the lives of the younger generation of conquerors.

> [38]Speak to the people of Israel, and tell them to make tassels on the corners of their garments throughout their generations, and to put upon the tassel of each corner a cord of blue; [39]and it shall be to you a tassel to look upon and remember all the commandments of the LORD, to do them, not to follow after your own heart and your own eyes, after which you are playing the harlot, [40]so that you may remember and do all my commandments, and be holy to your God.

The adorning of Israelite garments with blue embellishments on their tassels[39] was, like other Mosaic laws, an encouragement

[39] The word ṣîṣit is interpreted in the LXX as 'hems', in Targum Onkelos, the Syriac and the Vulgate as 'fringes' and in the Arabic as 'forelocks (of hair)'. Rashi states that the tassel is so called 'because of the threads hanging on it, like "And he took me by a lock [ṣîṣit] of my head" (Ezk. 8:3). Another opinion is that ṣîṣit is so called because you see it, like "gazing [mēṣîṣ] from the lattice" (Song 2:9)'. Ibn Ezra writes, 'Two opinions are possible. The one is that they [i.e. the Israelites] will make ṣîṣit like "a lock of my head" (Ezk. 8:3). And they are the threads which extend, which are not braided . . . The second opinion is as our sages (of blessed memory) have transmitted. And because there are reliable evidences concerning the second interpretation, the first has ceased to be current. And they transmitted that this is the command regarding clothing

to perceive all of life, throughout one's daily routine, with careful attention to the law of God. The forgetful outlook, heedless of the many ways in which God's law filters down into the particularities of everyday life, does not remain neutral. It is led away according to the likes and dislikes, the merely personal sense of right and wrong, the prejudices and ignorance, of the wayward human heart,[40] involving one in harlotry. To prevent that outcome, this law required symbolic ornamentation upon Israelite clothing as a constant reminder of the relevance of God's law to all of life.[41] Such an outlook would dignify Israel as holy to God.[42]

Verse 39 does not specify idol worship as the harlotry in view. Nothing in the passage requires so narrow a referent.[43] This ambiguity has the positive exegetical function of broadening the field of reference to all the wayward desires of the heart and the lusts of the eyes. The language concerns Israel's 'playing the harlot' after their own hearts and eyes, implying without limitation the various temptations which may be imagined, perceived and caressed through the senses. But the law calls Israel both to deny what may seem right and expedient to oneself and to obey Yahweh even when the final outcome cannot be foreseen and assessed from a merely human perspective. Israel must trust Yahweh to be wiser than Israel in

---

which has four edges, and the *ṣîṣit* are *gᵉḏilîm* [*i.e.* the 'tassels' of Dt. 22:12]. I continue to interpret it this way.'

[40] Verse 39 uses the root √*twr* to describe the action of following after one's own heart and one's own eyes. This verb is also used in chapter 13 of Numbers of the spies' penetration into the land, exploring its possibilities. Pushing outward at the edges of God's law, rather than inward into the centre, is doubtless the impulse of the soul in view here.

[41] Ainsworth (*Ann*: II:40) explains 'the spiritual use of this ordinance' as the people of God clothing themselves with 'an heavenly affection to all the law and an holy conversation', which 'led them spiritually to put on the "wedding garment," Matt. 22:11, "the Lord Jesus Christ," Rom. 13:14, "the whole armour of God," Eph. 6:11, "and the new man, which after God is created in righteousness and holiness of truth," Eph. 4:24 . . .'

[42] The text does not say that the tassels will make the people holy, but that they will remind them to obey God's law, which obedience sets a people apart as holy. Milgrom (1983: 61–65) explains that the blue cord on the tassel signified the nobility of the covenanted people. *Cf.* Bertman 1961: 119–128.

[43] Budd (1984: 178) suggests that the author has in mind the reference to 'your harlotries' (*zᵉnûṯêḵem*) in Nu. 14:33, *i.e.* the acts of unfaithfulness to Yahweh committed by the first generation after the exodus.

all the decrees of his law. The net force of the declaration is that all the sinful preferences of the autonomous self, running contrary to the law of God, are a kind of whoredom, as if Yahweh's wisdom and ways were untrustworthy, with the result that his law would have to be supplemented out of one's own notions. Such an elevation of the sensate over the spiritual, of the whimsical over the authoritative, violates Israel's espousals to Yahweh.

Deuteronomy 31:16

In the course of the Deuteronomic covenant, chapters 31 – 34 set forth the succession arrangements, ensuring the perpetuity of Yahweh's rule over Israel after the death of Moses.[44] When Joshua is presented as Moses' successor, Yahweh calls Moses to make one last declaration to the people. He is to teach them the song recorded in chapter 32 as a blunt reminder to them of their guilt before God, when in subsequent generations they fall away from him. Yahweh introduces this final task by informing Moses of the nation's future prospects:

> And the LORD said to Moses, 'Behold, you are about to sleep with your fathers; then this people will rise and play the harlot after the foreign gods in their midst, the gods of the land into which they are going, and they will forsake me and break my covenant which I have made with them.'

After Moses' restraining influence is removed, Israel will seize the opportunity[45] to fulfill their desire for higher tolerance levels in their religious faith.[46] It is as if they are itching to try out the

---

[44] *Cf.* Kline 1975: 131–153.

[45] The clause *wᵉqām hā'ām hazzeh* does not indicate an action equal with the others in the statement but rather functions as an introductory indicator of initiative, followed by the series of verbs which comprise the actions of the statement. *Cf.* Dt. 9:12; 32:38; Jos. 6:26; Jdg. 7:9. Both the LXX and the Vulgate render *wᵉqām* with participial forms.

[46] *Cf.* Dt. 31:21: '. . . for I know the purposes which they are already forming, before I have brought them into the land that I swore to give'. Ibn Ezra comments, 'And the sense of *wᵉzānâ(h)* is to go out in one's thought from under God's authority.'

new gods in the land to which they are going,[47] for new surroundings offer new opportunities. But as they broaden the range of worship acceptable to themselves, Yahweh judges them to be harlots, abandoning their rightful husband and violating the sacred bond which unites them.

Judges 2:16–17

The author of Judges puts forward in summary form, in 2:6 – 3:6, the outstanding marks of Israel's history during this period – the cycle of apostasy, oppression, repentance and deliverance. Thus, the spiritual harlotry cited in 2:17 does not record merely a single episode but rather describes the character of the times.

> [16]Then the LORD raised up judges, who saved them out of the power of those who plundered them. [17]And they did not even listen to their judges, but they played

---

[47] Two matters require clarification. First, what is the sense of *'elōhê nēkar hā'āreṣ?* Rashi construes *nēkar* as a collective singular for the foreign nations of the land. This interpretation could be validated from 2 Sa. 22:45–46 (Ps. 18:45–46); Ne. 9:2; Ezk. 44:7; *etc.* Moreover, this would resolve the difficulty of the antecedent to the pronominal suffix in *b'qirbô.* Favouring an interpretation of the word as a qualitative abstraction, however, is the usage found in Gn. 35:2, 4; Jos. 24:20, 23; Jdg. 10:16; 1 Sa. 7:3; 2 Ch. 33:15; Je. 5:19 – which usage is surely more apposite to Dt. 31:16. The LXX is not entirely clear in its rendering, but the Vulgate's *post deos alienos in terra* is beyond question. Driver (1895: 340) suggests that *'elōhê nēkar* 'forms a compound idea, "gods of foreignness" = "foreign gods," which is then qualified by the gen. "of the land".' Secondly, how is one to interpret the syntax of *'ašer hû(') bā(') šammâ(h) b'qirbô?* Ibn Ezra acknowledges that the 3 m s suffix in *b'qirbô* could refer to *nēkar,* but he judges it more probable that it 'refers to "the land," for the masculine gender is attested, like "the land could not support [masc. sing.] them" (Gn. 13:16), and "The land is darkened [masc. sing.]" (Is. 9:18 [EVV 19])'. The resulting sense would be 'the land, into the midst of which you are proceeding'. The problem with this view is not only that one must posit the masculine gender for *hā'āreṣ* but also that the function of *šammâ(h)* becomes problematic. Driver, *ibid.,* argues that '"in its midst" can only mean "in the people's midst",' which the collective singular forms elsewhere in the verse would corroborate. He notes Jos. 24:23; 'Put away the foreign gods *which are in your midst'.* The net result is that the relative clause is to be perceived as concluding with *šammâ(h)* and *b'qirbô* as resuming (and concluding) the clause begun at *w'zānâ(h),* with *hā'ām hazzeh* as the antecedent to the pronominal suffix. The significance is that the foreign gods are already, even before the nation arrives in the land, being accepted into their midst, so ready are they to abandon Yahweh.

the harlot after other gods and bowed down to them;
they soon turned aside from the way in which their
fathers had walked, who had obeyed the commandments of the LORD, and they did not follow their
example.

The connection between verses 16 and 17 seems to be one of
astonishment. In the face of concrete evidences of Yahweh's
power to deliver his people through the judges, still Israel did
not remain in a listening frame of mind once the deliverance
was effected.[48] On the contrary,[49] their wont was to renew the
pursuit of their illegitimate, indeed discredited, lovers, who took
the forms of the popular gods of their defeated oppressors.
They entered into the pagan cultus, bowing down to the false
gods. They turned quickly[50] – implying a genuine affection for
the gods of Canaan and a correspondingly low estimate of
Yahweh's worth – away from the comparative faithfulness of
their forefathers (verse 7).

Judges 2:17 makes a similar point to Deuteronomy 31:16,
except that the latter projects its vision out into the future while
the former looks back through this era to highlight the
recurring cycle of events. The whoredom of the nation was
perceived clearly in advance, and the actual course of events
vindicated the prediction. The unfolding Old Testament story
presents, therefore, not an isolated incident of whoredom here
and there but a clearly evident pattern in Israel's behaviour,
revealing a persistent unfaithfulness within.

Judges 8:27, 33

After his extraordinary victory over the Midianites, Gideon

---

[48] I take the introductory marker $w^e gam$ as intensive in force. *Cf.* GKC § 153:
'It is to be observed that the force of these particles does not necessarily affect
the word which immediately follows . . . but very frequently extends to the
whole of the following sentence.' In this case, the intensive logic extends until
the *kî* clause.

[49] On the adversative *kî* after a negative clause, see GKC § 163 a.

[50] The two asyndetic clauses, the one beginning with *sārû* and the other with
lō(') 'āśû, have an explicative function in the logic of the sentence. The first
explains how quickly their turning aside to harlotry took place, and the other
emphasizes, in turn, how definite was their failure to sustain the faithfulness of
previous generations. *Cf.* Joüon § 177 a.

could have ruled the nation. And he did not even have to conspire for power. The people offered it to him. But he refused, asking for something else instead, something inspired not by political ambition but by misguided religious zeal. He asked for the golden earrings confiscated, among other things, as spoil from the defeated Midianites.

> [27]And Gideon made an ephod of it and put it in his city, in Ophrah; and all Israel played the harlot after it there, and it became a snare to Gideon and to his family (RSV).

The period of the judges was infamous for its widespread moral confusion. 'Every man did what was right in his own eyes' (21:25), and not even Gideon escaped the spirit of the times. Rather than respect the unique prerogatives of the Levites at the tabernacle in Shiloh, Gideon made his own personal ephod in Ophrah. As a device for enquiring of God,[51] an ephod may have offered Gideon not only constant access to personal guidance – something upon which he had relied more than once in the course of his leadership[52] – but also perhaps informal authority as a man made privy to the counsels of God. He may have even worn the ephod at times himself.[53] Whatever his motives may have been,[54] however, the consequence was plain. The ephod,

[51] *Cf. ABD, s.v.* 'Ephod', 2:550: 'Because the breastpiece containing the Urim and Thummim are attached to it, the ephod is an essential part of the divinatory apparatus of the Israelite cult.' *Cf.* 1 Sa. 23:6–12; 30:7–8.

[52] *Cf.* Jdg. 6:17–22, 36–40; 7:13–15.

[53] The verb √*yṣg*, however, creates the presumption that the ephod was somehow set up or put on display.

[54] Rashi comments, 'And he made it to be an ephod, as a memorial for the great deliverance.' Radak comments, 'He made it as a kind of loin covering, or garment, of gold. And he placed it in his city, so that it would be for a memorial of the great deliverance. And he himself made it to be a good thing, but after his death the sons of Israel played the harlot after it and made it a god.' Drusius, however, in *Critici Sacri, ad loc.*, qualifies Radak's view: 'Sunt tamen qui putant hoc factum fuisse demum post mortem Gedeonis, quod colligunt ex v. 33, qui sequitur, nescio quam solide. Nam ait ipse textus ibi quod tunc *Baales coluerint*, non quod scortati fuerint post Ephod.' [There are, however, those who think that this was not done until after the death of Gideon, which they gather from verse 33 which follows, I do not know how truly. For the text itself says there that then *they worshipped the Baals*, not that they played the harlot after the Ephod.]

outside its proper context and separated from the teaching ministry of the priests, seems to have attracted to itself the superstitions of the folk theology common among the people, so that they treated it with misplaced veneration, as if it were a pagan charm. They trusted in it rather than in Yahweh and neglected his formally established means of grace. And for Gideon himself and his household (who doubtless followed his example), it became a snare entangling them in yet further sins, unspecified in the text.

The arresting aspect of this episode is that a good man, presumably intending to do good, in grateful response to a divine victory, inadvertently leads the people of God into whoredom. And the object being lavished with affection is not a vulgar Asherah pole but a ritual object legitimate within the duly authorized Israelite cultus.[55] Not only is Israel capable of allowing Canaanite religion to steal its way into their hearts, they are also capable of reinterpreting the inner meaning of Yahwism so that the revealed religion is virtually Canaanized. Their accommodation can move both ways, but always to the detriment of faithfulness to Yahweh.

The linguistic formula for harlotry in this text – no different from, say, Exodus 34:16, where foreign gods are in view – encourages the presumption that, in the minds of the people, the ephod might as well have been an image of Baal, so unreasoning were they. Spiritual whoredom does not require that the object of devotion be foreign in nature. It may be Yahwistic. The whoredom consists in the psychology of the worshipper; it is not necessarily inherent in the outward object.

> [33]As soon as Gideon died, the people of Israel turned
> back and played the harlot after the Baals, and made
> Baal-berith their god.

With a readiness which revealed their true affections, Israel apostatized[56] upon their leader's death, whoring after the local fertility gods of Canaan. Evidently, they ascribed special status to a certain 'Lord of the covenant' (Baal-berith), whose temple was

---

[55] *Cf.* Ex. 28; 39.

[56] The verb $\sqrt{\check{s}w\underline{b}}$ is used absolutely of apostasy also in Jos. 23:12; Jdg. 2:19; 2 Ch. 7:19.

located at Shechem (Jdg. 9:4).[57] That this particular Baal had associations in some sense with the concept of covenant is doubtless significant. Israel affirmed and reaffirmed the covenant with Yahweh at Shechem.[58] Perhaps this is what attracted the Israelites to Baal-berith, for there may have seemed to be common ground between their ancestral faith and the indigenous religion. Whether that common ground was only apparent on the surface or manifested a true inner coherence was a question apparently lost upon the undiscerning Israelites. One wonders if they took comfort in the thought that here was a Baal truly congenial with their covenant faith. Yahweh must have felt flattered.

It is significant that the clearest marital images early in the story of the covenanted people are Israel's whoredom and Yahweh's jealousy in return. From the beginning, the marriage was strained. That tension will break out into open conflict in the prophetic literature.

[57] For a summary of the theories regarding the identity of Baal-berith and the connection between this deity and covenant theology in Israel, see *ABD*, *s.v.* 'Baal-berith', 1:550f.

[58] *Cf.* Jos. 8:30–35; 24:1–28.

Chapter Three

Committing great harlotry

The harlotry of Israel and the jealousy of Yahweh exploded in crisis in the eighth century BC. During the northern kingdom's autumn of prosperity and then their final spasms of self-destruction, the prophet Hosea was called to alert the people to the true reason for their national decline. It was not ultimately a failure of political manoeuvering, military power or financial resources. The explanation lay deep within the covenanted people themselves. Israel was an unfaithful wife, sharing her love with both Yahweh and the Baals, and her lawful husband could no longer support her affairs with other lovers through further manifestations of his mercies.

God called Hosea not only to speak to the nation but also to serve as a living symbol of the larger spiritual reality of Yahweh's love for promiscuous Israel. By this means the truth of their violations of the covenant was made visibly literal before them. Such a bold demonstration was necessary, because the people themselves could not see their departure from Yahweh:

> To me they cry,
> 'My God, we Israel know you!' (Ho. 8:2).

The pressing issue of the day in their eyes was not how to regain the favour of their offended Husband but how to stabilize the politically volatile situation to the east. Assyria was flexing its muscles. And it seemed that an alliance with Egypt to the west might shore up their weak position against the eastern aggressor. But the nation also sought to appease the Assyrians by buying them off with payments of tribute. So foreign policy vacillated between defiance and appeasement:

> Ephraim is like a dove,
> silly and without sense,

calling to Egypt, going to Assyria (Ho. 7:11, RSV).

Flitting about like a frightened bird, panicky Israel does not turn to the one true source of strength and security:

> The pride of Israel witnesses against him;
>> yet they do not return to the LORD their God,
>> nor seek him, for all this (Ho. 7:10, RSV).

The spiritual answers and resources offered in the covenant seemed unreal in the face of visible dangers. Deuteronomic faith seemed irrelevant, and the God of the exodus and Sinai remote. But it is not as though the people were irreligious:

> They love sacrifice;[1]
>> they sacrifice flesh and eat it;
>> but the LORD has no delight in them (Ho. 8:13a, RSV).

The people failed to make meaningful connections between their theology, history and worship, on the one hand, and their real-life problems, on the other hand. They put God, his covenant, his power, his wisdom, into a limiting category of thought – they could not bring themselves really to believe the assurance of Deuteronomy 28:1–14 – while 'the real world' was another category altogether with its own rules and its own resources. They acted as though faith in Yahweh alone were an impracticable policy for life. As a result, they dishonoured him even as they thought they continued to honour him.

Moreover, unalloyed, classical Yahwism was losing its compelling power among the people. It was being redefined with fewer sharp edges and more open doors as a broadly inclusive religion, increasingly tolerant of elements of paganism. What one observes in Hosea's historical situation is the admixture of contrary theologies made congenial not by logic or principle but by fashion and feeling. This syncretistic blending of Yahweh with the idols was answered through Hosea:

> O Ephraim, what have I to do with idols?

---

[1] I accept the emendation of the Hebrew text as suggested in the apparatus of *BHS* (8:13^{a–a}) and as reflected in the RSV.

> It is I who answer and look after you.
> I am like an evergreen cypress,
>> from me comes your fruit (Ho. 14:8 [Hebrew 9], RSV).

At issue was the all-sufficiency of Yahweh, with the question
perhaps put this way: Where does life, in all its richness and
fullness, come from? Does it come from Yahweh alone, or from
Yahweh plus others? If it comes from Yahweh alone, then one
will look obediently to him alone for that life. But if it comes
from Yahweh plus others, then one will spread one's allegiance
around, because Yahweh alone is not enough. The folk theology
permeating Israel at this time obscured the clarity of pure
Yahwism by mingling the alternatives together in one dimly
perceptible theological blur. Hosea sought to dispel the
confusion and restore clarity under the searching brilliance of
the classical theology of the Deuteronomic covenant.

The historical setting of Hosea's ministry, then, was marked by
a widespread lack of faith in Yahweh's all-sufficiency for Israel's
real-life needs and by a consequent failure to observe the
exclusive nature of their covenant with Yahweh. A 'spirit of
harlotry' (4:12; 5:4) pervaded the mentality of the times.

Hosea 1[2]

Hosea 1:1–9 charges Israel with flagrant whoredom and declares
Yahweh's withdrawing of his love by incremental degrees in the
face of their drift away from him.[3] It is not the purpose of this
section to expose the concrete forms of Israel's harlotry in their
national life but rather to confront them with a general, principial
condemnation and its dreadful consequences in the near future.

Verse 2 heads this opening section of the book:[4]

[2] Chapters 1 – 3 expound Hosea's insight into Israel's harlotry and provide
the framework within which the other references to her harlotry in chapters
4ff. function. *Cf.* Ho. 4:10, 12–15; 5:3–4; 9:1. Sometimes the literal and the
figurative references seem to merge. In Ho. 7:4 adultery serves as the figure,
and in 8:9 Israel's 'lovers' are drawn into view.

[3] *Cf.* Wolff (1974b: 23): 'The judgment announced here is accomplished only
step by step . . . In the same breath, Yahweh's active punishment (v 4) is
replaced by passivity (v 6), and even a complete withdrawal (v 9).'

[4] I take the first line of verse 2 not as the initial syntactical element of a longer
sentence comprising the verse, *pace* the RSV and NRSV, but as a heading for the
rest of the first chapter. The repetition of the divine name and the difference in

The beginning of the LORD's speaking through Hosea:

And the LORD said to Hosea, 'Go, take to yourself a wife of harlotry and children of harlotry, for the land commits great harlotry by forsaking the LORD.'

From its beginning, Hosea's prophetic ministry was shaped by the theme of Israel's whoredom as they pursued other gods and departed from strict faithfulness to Yahweh.[5] The northern kingdom, Yahweh charges, has become a brothel. It is not a matter of the isolated aberration here and there; nationwide,[6] the people have lapsed into egregious violations of their covenant with Yahweh, such that the generalization of verse 2b demands to be made.[7] This ugly, shocking accusation is to be made clearly evident to the people through Hosea's own heartache as a husband married to an adulterous woman.[8] He

---

the prepositions in relation to Hosea seem to favour this construction. In this case, *BHS* is correct to centre these words as a superscription, with the beginning of the prophecy as such after the athnach. The net result is that verse 1 serves as the superscription for the entire book, while verse 2a bears that function for 1:2b–9. The use of a finite verb in a construct chain, as in verse 2a, is attested also in Ex. 6:28; Lv. 25:48; 1 Sa. 25:15; Is. 29:1; Je. 6:15; *etc. Cf.* GKC § 130 d. Aquila's revision of the Greek tradition also suggests that an emendation is unnecessary: ἀρχὴ ἦν ἐλάλησε κύριος.

[5] The prepositional phrase *mēaḥᵃrê YHWH* may be compared with the idiom observed, *e.g.* in Ex. 34:15, 'to play the harlot after . . .' In Ho. 2:7 [EVV 5], Israel resolves to 'go after her lovers', which Hosea condemns as 'committing harlotry'. In 1:2, with the lawful husband as the object of the preposition, the compound with *min* is required, suggesting departure from following Yahweh. *Cf.* Nu. 14:43; 32:15 (with √*šwb*); Dt. 7:4 (with √*swr*). Bird (1989: 81) makes the interesting observation that the gods after whom Israel is playing the harlot are not mentioned here; only the aggrieved husband comes into view. Chapter 2 will mention her false lovers; here the emphasis falls fully upon the all-sufficient One who is being abandoned.

[6] 'The land' is metonymy for the entire nation. *Cf.* Ho. 4:1, 3.

[7] '*Egregious* violations of their covenant' is an attempt to tease out the force of the infinitive absolute in the phrase *zānō(h) tizneh*.

[8] Targum, Ibn Ezra, Radak, Calvin, the Geneva Bible, John Gill, *et al.*, evade the plain sense of the Lord's command in one way or another, since it seems to offend the dignity of the prophetic calling. *Cf.* Lv. 21:7, with regard to priests. But Israel's adultery, which Gomer's behaviour symbolized, was no less real for its being spiritual, and that relationship involved Yahweh. Rather than a violation of God's moral order, what we observe here is 'one of the most remarkable depictions of divine grace in the Old Testament', according to McComiskey (1992: I:17).

must deliberately choose for his wife someone who will be unfaithful to him and accept children who are not his own.[9]

Three declarations of judgment, in verses 3–9, flow out of and must be interpreted in connection with the charge in verse 2 that 'the land commits great harlotry', given the superscriptory function of that verse. The first word is sounded in verses 3–5:

> [3]So he went and took Gomer the daughter of Diblaim, and she conceived and bore him a son.
>
> [4]And the LORD said to him, 'Call his name Jezreel; for in a little while I will visit the bloodshed of Jezreel upon the house of Jehu, and I will put an end to the kingdom of the house of Israel. [5]And on that day, I will break the bow of Israel in the valley of Jezreel.'

Hosea and Gomer had a son[10] whose name hints at the doom coming upon the dynasty of Jehu and the whole northern kingdom. The place name 'Jezreel', notorious for violent bloodshed,[11] would conjure up such associations in the popular Israelite mind, much as 'Pearl Harbor' would for an American or 'Culloden Moor' for a Scot. Blood was crying out to God from that ground, and he now declares that he will soon resolve that

---

[9] The question of what precisely is implied about Gomer in the words *'ēšet zᵉnûnîm* is difficult. Wolff (1974b: 13) is probably correct to relate the *rûᵃḥ zᵉnûnîm* of 4:12 and 5:4 to the *'ēšet zᵉnûnîm* and the *yaldê zᵉnûnîm* of 1:2, so that *zᵉnûnîm* is construed as an abstraction. The exact force of the adjectival genitive in each case – in relation to the woman and to the children – is another question, and one that the text does not answer. The important thing is that the Hosean analogy should fit the larger reality of adulterous Israel in relation to Yahweh. That being so, a 'wife of whoredom' is one with a predisposition to whoredom. The phrase simply exposes in her a moral flaw analogous to the persistent bent toward harlotry staining Israel's character as the wife of Yahweh from her original espousals on. As for the children, they are begotten from adulterous affairs. *Cf.* 2:6–7 [EVV 4–5], where children are called *bᵉnê zᵉnûnîm*, 'for their *mother* has committed adultery'. For a survey of views on Hosea's marriage, see Rowley 1956–57: 200–223, supplemented with Davies 1993: 79–92.

[10] The prepositional phrase *lô* shows that this child, at least, was Hosea's own and not a 'child of harlotry'. *Cf.* Gn. 21:3. The lack of this phrase in verses 6 and 8 creates the presumption that the second and third children were not fathered by Hosea.

[11] It was at Jezreel that Naboth was betrayed and murdered (1 Ki. 21:1, 8–14) and that Joram and all who were loyal to his dynasty were killed (2 Ki. 9:14–26; 10:11).

moral tension. Bloodshed will come back to haunt Jehu's dynasty, destroying it with the same violence with which he destroyed the Omride dynasty.[12] Indeed, the entire nation as a political entity will cease to exist. God intends to break their capacity for military defence, leaving them helpless before the Assyrians.

Interestingly, the bloodshed of Jezreel constitutes spiritual whoredom. The first exposure of the land's 'great harlotry' is not religious but political. How does this explicate Israel's whoredom? The bloodshed of Jezreel as Machiavellian *Realpolitik* was whoredom toward God because it evidenced a 'whatever it takes' attitude of thrusting oneself forward at the expense of others. Spiritual adultery entails more than religious offences; whenever God is not trusted fully and obeyed exactly, including the realm of politics, his people deny the adequacy of his care and protection, so that they fend for themselves, on their own terms.

God's next message to his people is revealed through Gomer's second child, in verses 6–7:

> [6]She conceived again and bore a daughter. And the LORD said to him, 'Call her name Not Pitied, for I will no longer have pity on the house of Israel, but I will surely take them away. [7]But on the house of Judah I will have pity, and I will deliver them by the LORD their God; I will not deliver them by bow or by sword or by war or by horses or by horsemen.'

This utterance notifies Israel that God has changed his attitude and policy toward them to one of showing no mercy.[13]

---

[12] *Cf.* 2 Ki. 15:8–12. Both the RSV and NRSV interpret the construction of √*pqd* with *'al* in Hosea 1:4 as 'punish the house of Jehu for the blood of Jezreel' rather than 'visit the blood of Jezreel upon the house of Jehu'. McComiskey (1993: 93–101) demonstrates that this verse predicts an ironic visitation of bloodshed upon the house of Jehu. God will punish the house of Jehu for the blood of Jezreel *by* visiting upon them the blood of Jezreel. The punishment will take the form of their receiving what they themselves had dealt out. The moral warrant for this visitation of bloodshed is a separate question.

[13] The unusual collocation of two *yqtl* verb forms in *'ôsîp* . . . *'ăraḥēm* is the functional equivalent to the *yqtl* of √*yspp* + infinitive construct of √*rḥm*. *Cf.* Rashi; GKC § 120 c.

He has closed his heart. He will allow himself to feel nothing for them, even to the point of taking them away into destruction.[14] The southern kingdom of Judah, however, still has a place in his affections – the very mention of which would doubtless sharpen the edge of this judgment in the Israelite heart. Not far away, his protective mercies will deliver Judah from the same Assyrian invasion that will sweep Israel away.[15] But even for Judah, his means of defending them will show the futility of their own schemes and devices, so that he alone will be exalted as their Saviour. Yahweh insists upon his own direct intervention without the people's prayers and sacrifices to idols, without alliances with Egypt and payments to Assyria, as attempted in Israel's pursuit of false saviours. 'Not Pitied' bears witness to God's profound opposition to his people's whoredom, such that his jealous love restrains the merciful impulses prompted by that very love as he turns Israel away in the direction of certain destruction.

In the final oracle of confrontation, in verses 8–9, Yahweh uses the birth of Gomer's third child to put on public record his decisive break with Israel:

> [8]When she had weaned Not Pitied, she conceived and bore a son. [9]And the LORD said, 'Call his name Not My People, for you are not my people and I am Not I Am to you.'

The covenant of 'my people, your God' is cancelled. Hosea's Israel has drifted so far from any resemblance to a people authentic to God that they have become, in effect, a pagan

[14] The RSV and NRSV interpret *kî nāśō(') 'eśśā(') lāhem* as a reference to divine forgiveness. This understanding of the verb is possible. *Cf.* Gn. 18:24, 26. Linked, however, by *kî* with the preceding negative clause, this interpretation is not the most forthcoming. It seems more natural, in view of the logical structure of the larger unit (verses 6–7), that this clause matches the contrasting statement that God will deliver Judah. Calvin (*Hos: ad loc.*) comments: 'The prophet sets "to save" and "to take away" in opposition the one to the other.' The verb √*nś* is clearly used in this sense in 5:14. *Cf.* Ibn Janaḥ (*Book of Roots, s.v.* √*nś*: 'I will remove them and I will uproot them'), Ibn Ezra and Radak.

[15] The poignancy of this contrast is felt also in the reference to this salvation as coming 'by Yahweh *their* God', that is, Judah's God and not Israel's – which rejection he will announce with terrible directness in verses 8–9.

nation. They are not his, so he will not be theirs.[16] The great 'I
AM' of Exodus 3:14, who was there for them to bring them out of
Egyptian slavery, will not be there for them when the Assyrian
invader assaults their land.[17] Their adulterous violations of the
covenant have brought the nation so low that their warrants for
special consideration no longer exist in God's moral calculus.
They might as well be any other little nation being overrun by
the Assyrian hordes, as far as he is concerned. The announce-
ment of Not My People and Not I Am seems, therefore, the
equivalent to a divorce.

The next discrete unit in the prophecy – 1:10 – 2:1 in the
English text but 2:1–3 in the Hebrew – invests the three human
names of doom in 1:2–9 with new significance, reversing each
one into a promise of mercy and restoration. The divorce
announced in chapter 1 is truly in force, but only for the Israel
of Hosea's generation. Divine mercy is not defeated by human
sin, because God purposes to win a people for himself by
sovereign grace.

Hosea 2

The charge of 1:2 that 'the land commits great harlotry' now
appears in fuller form and with compelling proofs, in 2:2–13.[18]

---

[16] Burroughs (*Hos*: 25) comments, 'The people to whom Hosea prophesied
might have objected against him thus: What! Hosea, do you say that God will
not have any more mercy upon us? What! will not God have mercy upon his
own people? Is not God our God? Why do you threaten such things as these?
The prophet answers, It is true, God has been your God, and you have been his
people, but there is an end of those days; God now degrades you from those
glorious privileges that you formerly possessed, he will own you no more to be
his, and you shall have no further right to own him to be yours.'

[17] The RSV's and NRSV's 'I am not your God' is based upon a plausible, but
unnecessary, textual emendation. The traditional text, dependent for its
effectiveness upon an allusion to Ex. 3:14, states not what the reader expects
but what, upon reflection, includes by implication and exceeds in force the
meaning gained by the emendation. The joining of *lō(')* with *'ehyeh* by maqqeph
suggests the translation above, on the analogy of Not Pitied and Not My People,
although the latter two are not marked with maqqeph. The potential ambiguity
of this new divine name revealed in verse 9 – that ambiguity witnessed to by the
very emendation suggested to 'correct' it – requires the maqqeph.

[18] Radak comments, 'Now he returns to the words of rebuke which he uttered
at the beginning,' *i.e.* in 1:2.

The prophet 'undertakes the defence of God's cause', as Calvin puts it, so that the strong language of 1:2 can be seen to fit the facts:

> [2]Plead with your mother, plead –
>   for she is not my wife,
>   and I am not her husband –
> that she put away her harlotry from her face,
>   and her adultery from between her breasts;
> [3]lest I strip her naked
>   and make her as on the day she was born,
> and make her like a wilderness,
>   and turn her into a parched land,
>   and make her die of thirst.

Israel has made Yahweh a cuckold. And yet, even as he disowns her, he yearns for her repentance and restoration. He is prepared to carry out terrible threats, but he gives her an opportunity to evade that unwanted outcome.

He pleads with her.[19] His appeal is indirect, however, addressed not to Israel but to her children. The nation is the mother, and the individuals are the children.[20] Yahweh explains that he speaks not directly to Israel but rather to the 'children' about their 'mother', for she is no longer his wife and he is no longer her husband. They are not on good enough terms for a direct approach to be taken. She has left

---

[19] The verb √*ryb* seems not to be used in a technical sense here, since the literary form of the lawsuit is not assembled around the word, as it is in Ho. 4:1– 3, and since the second half of the verse sets forth a response, *viz.* national reformation, being called for. The RSV and NRSV are probably wise, therefore, to use the English 'plead' in this case.

[20] *Cf.* Targum, Rashi. Grotius, in *Critici Sacri* (1660 edn), *ad loc.*, writes, 'Jubentur singuli qui sibi bene esse cupiunt, accusare palam mala facta gentis totius, nempe 10 Tribuum, ut communes poenas evadant.' [The individuals who wish things to go well for them are commanded to reproach openly the bad deeds of the whole nation (the ten tribes, of course), that they may escape the general punishments.] Wolff (1974b: 33) comments, 'This bold distinction between mother and children opens up new paths enabling Hosea's audience within guilty Israel to take the side of Yahweh.' And Radak writes, 'The sense is that they are to plead, each one, with his neighbour, to bring them back to the good way.'

him. There is little likelihood that she will listen to her ex-husband. So his best chance of winning her back is through the pleas of the children. In real terms, the appeal is that the people would themselves rise up to protest official harlotry in the nation so that the leaders might initiate institutional reformation. The 'powers that be' are not listening to Yahweh's appeals through the prophet, but they might respond to a popular uprising.

Yahweh pleads with Israel to clean up her life.[21] She must remove her harlotry from her face and her adultery from between her breasts. She is like a woman adorning herself with 'meretricious finery'[22] to attract the attention of men other than her husband. She is a flirt – and a brazen, shameless one at that, 'strutting her stuff' openly before lascivious male eyes. But here the one who loves her still calls and invites her to remove all visible tokens of compromise from her way of life, to cease exposing herself to the degrading habit of seeking false lovers and, as the Targum paraphrases, to remove 'the worship of her idols from among her towns'. The high places and sanctuaries of Baal must go.

His plea is significant, because if she refuses to respond, the consequence will be disaster. Yahweh threatens to take her vulgar self-display all the way and strip her naked, as naked as she was the day she was born.[23] She will have nothing. She thought her openness to the Baals enlarged her chances of success, abundance and the enjoyment of life.[24] But the Baals provide nothing, and neither can they punish. The power of life and death lies with Yahweh alone, and he is able to blight her happiness and fertility and make the nation a virtual desert with

[21] The RSV and NRSV are probably correct in construing the second half of the verse as the purpose and content of the plea. *Cf.* Gibson § 87.

[22] So Calvin (*Hos*: *ad loc.*). He also comments that the nation 'had grown so callous as to wish to be known to be such as they were'.

[23] I doubt that Hosea's imagery here is intended to evoke a recollection of Israel's infancy with God as a nation, rather like Ezk. 16:4ff., because in this context he has already announced his separation from Israel. The covenant is no longer in force for this generation ('She is not my wife, and I am not her husband'). A threat of returning Israel to her pre-covenanted status, therefore, would not carry force at this point in the prophecy.

[24] Ibn Ezra connects this with the reference to idols in verse 7: 'The sense of "of thirst" is on account of the fact that she is saying, "[I will go after my lovers] who give my bread and my water and my drinks."'

no mitigation of the suffering entailed, even to the point of death.[25]

> [4]Upon her children also I will have no pity,
> because they are children of harlotry,
> [5]for their mother has played the harlot;
> she who conceived them has acted shamefully.
> For she said, 'I will go after my lovers,
> who give me my bread and my water,
> my wool and my flax, my oil and my drink.'

Verse 4 shows that Yahweh's judgment will not stop at the national and institutional level. It will reach down to touch individual Israelites as well.[26] There is no place for the lone individual to hide, no excuse that will secure anyone's safety, for '*she who conceived them* has acted shamefully'. Yahweh does not own them as 'my children' but brands them as the offspring of their immoral mother. They are Baal's brood, not Yahweh's family.[27] Their formal connection with Yahweh – and that itself now broken – is incidental to their true inner character. The 'spirit of harlotry' filling the nation has penetrated them as well, so that every individual playing a part in the larger national decline will also answer for it.

Israel's shameful act is that she has abandoned Yahweh – and she is condemned out of her own mouth, for Hosea quotes her[28] – by going after other lovers. She has consciously, deliberately

---

[25] The thirst in view may be intended as both literal and symbolic at the same time. The land would suffer drought, and the people would wither and die spiritually. *Cf.* Muggeridge (1972: 114f.): 'As I dimly realized, a people can be laid waste culturally as well as physically; not their lands but their inner life, as it were, sown with salt.'

[26] *Cf.* Keil & Delitzsch (1972: *ad loc.*): 'The fact that the children are specially mentioned after and along with the mother, when in reality mother and children are one, serves to give greater keenness to the threat, and guards against that carnal security, in which individuals imagine that, inasmuch as they are free from the sin and guilt of the nation as a whole, they will also be exempted from the threatened punishment.' That the prophet has the children pleading for their mother's repentance on Yahweh's behalf in verse 2, and now being included in judgment as culpable with her, is characteristic of the dynamic ambiguity of Hosea's style.

[27] *Cf.* McComiskey 1992: I:33.

[28] I presume that Hosea's quotation is his creative way of articulating the national mood, the *Zeitgeist.*

and persistently preferred them.[29] Unlike most whores, who allow themselves to be approached by their customers, Israel pursues hers. She courts their favour. Why? She is persuaded that they can give her what she wants out of life. Perhaps she is worried that they might not, unless she does pursue them. In any case, verse 13 leaves little doubt that Israel's 'lovers' are the idols. Deluded by prosperity, she credits them for her abundance.[30] The wealthy and powerful nations around her, whom she feared and envied, sought the favour of their gods by pagan devices and seemed to find compensation for doing so. McComiskey helps one to picture how this influence may have emerged in Israel's life:

> It began, perhaps, with something as innocuous as the placing of an image of Baal in a farmer's field. This is what their Canaanite neighbours did to increase production. It is what people did in this land, and it appeared to work. Gradually the invisible Yahweh lost ground to the baals whom the people could see and handle, whose religion was concerned with the necessities of life more than rigid moral demands. It was the baals, many Israelites came to believe, who fostered their crops and blessed them with children (1992: I:34).[31]

[29] The cohortative *'ēlᵉkâ(h)* notes the force of her resolve. *Cf.* Joüon § 114 c. Calvin (*Hos: ad loc.*) comments, 'But by introducing the word *said*, he amplifies the shamelessness of the people, who deliberately forsook their God who was to them as a legitimate husband. It indeed happens sometimes that a man is thoughtlessly drawn aside by a mistake or folly, but he soon repents; for we see many of the inexperienced deceived for a short time. But the prophet here shows that the Israelites premeditated their unfaithfulness, so that they wilfully departed from God. Hence, *she said.* And we know that this *said* means so much; and it is to be referred not to the outward word as pronounced but to the inward purpose. *She* therefore *said*, that is, she made this resolution; as though he said, "Let no one make this frivolous excuse, that they were deceived, that they did it in their simplicity; ye are, he says, avowedly perfidious, ye have with a premeditated purpose sought this divorce." '

[30] *Cf.* Drusius, in *Critici Sacri, ad loc.*: '*Post amatores meos*] Post vitulos qui in Dan et Bethel, quibus attribuebat omnem suam felicitatem.' [*After my lovers*: After the calves which were in Dan and Bethel, to which she was ascribing all her happiness.]

[31] *Cf.* Wells 1994: 88–117.

Israel's whoredom in turning to false lovers was also, and not
surprisingly, base in motivation, for what her lovers had to offer
was merely earthly. There was no sublimity in their provision –
which, of course, was not really theirs to begin with. But the
mundane was all they could even claim to offer; and, tellingly, it
was all Israel sought. The nation was arriving at wrong
conclusions, partly because they were asking the wrong
questions and cherishing the wrong desires. Longing for bodily
things only, a lifestyle of 'licking the earth', rather than seeking
higher things found in Yahweh alone – this was itself a fatal
step.[32] The sensate came to govern the ethos of the covenanted
people. That they would go to bed with the Baals to gratify these
desires is hardly surprising.

> [6]Therefore I will hedge up her[33] way with thorns;
>   and I will build a wall against her,
>   so that she cannot find her paths.
> [7]She shall pursue her lovers,
>   but not overtake them;
> and she shall seek them,
>   but shall not find them.
> Then she shall say, 'I will go
>   and return to my first husband,
>   for it was better with me then than now.'
> [8]She did not know
>   that it was I who gave her
>   the grain, the wine, and the oil,
> and who lavished upon her silver
>   and gold which they used for Baal.
> [9]Therefore I will take back
>   my grain in its time,
>   and my wine in its season;
> and I will take away my wool and my flax,
>   which were to cover her nakedness (RSV).

[32] Cf. Drusius, in *Critici Sacri, ad loc.*: '*Qui dant panem meum*, etc.] Pane et aqua
vivimus; lana et lino vestimur; oleo utimur ad venustatem, item ad robur
conciliandum corpori.' [*Who give my bread, etc.*: By bread and water we live; by
wool and flax we are clothed; oil we use for elegance, also for gaining strength
for the body.]

[33] I accept the emendation of the Heb. text as suggested in the apparatus of
BHS (2:8[b]) and as reflected in the RSV and NRSV.

Israel's guilt in verse 5 demands Yahweh's action in verse 6. She is running after her lovers with boundless determination. 'Nothing hath, and she resolves nothing shall, hinder her' (Poole *Comm*: II:854). So her husband intervenes by confining her. The course the nation has chosen to take – a path supposedly leading through idolatry to prosperity – is being closed off by sovereignly imposed affliction. When she approaches the familiar ways of soliciting the idols, she finds no help, no pleasure, no pay-off, but only pain and frustration.[34] It is not working any more. Yahweh brings his people into tightened economic conditions, depriving them of the rewards they thought they received for their devotion to Baal.

But still, Israel does not give up, so enamoured is she of her lovers. Verse 7a shows that she is not readily responsive to divine discipline. Even within the restrictions imposed by her husband, she persists in her idolatrous affections. She is earnest. She is sincere, a true believer. There must be some other explanation for her straightened conditions. Perhaps she has not been trying hard enough. The sacrifices, the incense, the ceremonies, the prophetic assurances, the priestly mumbo-jumbo – they are all renewed with frantic urgency.[35] But her efforts fail. There is no voice; no-one answers, no-one heeds her cries. Her lovers, to whom she has given so much, abandon her. That is how it appears to her, anyway. But the truth is the opposite. Yahweh, himself foretelling this outcome, loves his wife too much to allow her whoredom for ever to succeed.

In order to win Israel back to himself, Yahweh intends to discredit the Baals, who promise prosperity to their worshippers, by withholding that very prosperity. Then Israel will see who really bestows life. Her deprivation will be so severe as to prove illuminating. As in verse 5, Israel will make another deliberate choice.[36] Realizing that she would be better off with her original

---

[34] The reference to a hedge of thorns, rendering the course Israel intends impassable, suggests the image not of an adulteress but of an animal. This mixing of metaphors, however, is no problem for Hosea's fertile imagination. It blends the thoughts of Israel's promiscuity and brutish character into one.

[35] One notes with interest the piel form of $\sqrt{rdp}$, which more commonly occurs in the qal.

[36] The repetition of *'ām^{e}râ(h) 'ēl^{e}ḵâ(h)* in verses 5 and 7 must be more than an impressive coincidence, especially since the respective resolves expressed are directly contrary to one another. *Cf.* Poole (*Comm*: II:854): '*For then it was better*

husband, the prodigal wife will resolve to go back to him – not primarily out of love for him but out of disappointment with others, not as a result of prophetic warning or even the children's appeal (verse 2), but out of painful experience. But even with that motivation, she will seek reconciliation with her husband. The memories of his goodness, nourishment and faithfulness during her earlier national history[37] will rekindle a hope that perhaps that which has been lost between them might be restored.

What has kept Yahweh's wife away from him and pursuing other lovers is revealed in verse 8. She did not know where the fullness of life really comes from.[38] With 'an inexcusable stupidity', as Calvin puts it, she misinterpreted her experience as the outpouring of life from the Baals, requiring of her favours in return.[39] She, of all people,[40] familiar with her true husband throughout the centuries of her history, taught about his creative abundance in the Torah – *she* did not perceive her daily life as his generous provision, and his alone.[41] Instead, she

---

with me than now: How much the tune is changed! In ver. 5, all her gallantry, her feasts, her rich apparel, these are gifts of her lovers; not a word of her Husband's greatest kindnesses. But now she sees and confesseth the least of her Husband's kindnesses was better than the greatest kindness of these her paramours, and at worst with her Husband she was better than at best with adulterers.'

[37] Drusius, in *Critici Sacri, ad loc.*, unpacks the word 'then': *Tunc*] Cum ei soli servirem. [*Then*: When I served him alone.]

[38] Rashi wisely suggests that her ignorance was a failure to 'lay to heart' what she indeed knew theoretically. Her ignorance was not absolute. If quizzed, she could perhaps have given a 'correct' answer. But she failed to internalize the practical entailments of her monotheism. She shared her worship between Yahweh and the Baals; or perhaps she 'Baalized' Yahweh to such a degree that the distinctions were blurred beyond recognition. But God was not acceptably glorified, for he was not exclusively and purely glorified. Burroughs (*Hos*: 98f.) comments, 'In God's account, men know no more than they lay to heart and make good use of . . . Affected ignorance coming through distemper of heart is no excuse, but rather an aggravation.'

[39] Ibn Ezra aptly refers here to Je. 44:18.

[40] The 3 f s pronoun at the beginning of the verse is emphatic, as is also the 1 c s pronoun in the object clause.

[41] *Cf.* Ringgren (1987: 425): 'In other words, the real sacred marriage which produces fertility is that between Yahweh and his people, not the one celebrated in the fertility cult. We have before us a transformation of the fertility religion. *The love that pervades nature is Yahweh's love*, and it should be met by the people's love for their God.' (Italics added.)

took the very riches lavished upon her by Yahweh and by a perverse anti-conversion of their true meaning employed them in the cult of Baal.

Israel's fraudulent use of Yahweh's loving gifts compels him, according to verse 9, to take them back.[42] This verse states the literal reality portrayed by the figurative language of verse 6, both being introduced with 'Therefore'. Yahweh will deprive his wife of the things she loves at the moment when she most eagerly expects them. At the very time of harvest, the grain and wine will fail. Yahweh reasserts his title to his property.[43] They are his resources to dispose of as he sees fit.[44] He, and not the Baals, controls the harvest. He alone is Israel's life. According to verse 5, Israel asserted an independent possession of her blessings: '*my* bread and *my* water . . .' Now Yahweh answers her by claiming '*my* grain and *my* wine . . .' The true moral order of things is being brought back into focus. Neither will she be able any longer to conceal the shame of her whoredom from view.[45] Her blighted economy will make clear that her lawful husband has directly confronted and exposed her love affairs with the gods of fertility.

> [10]And now, I will uncover her lewdness
>   in the sight of her lovers,
>   and none shall rescue her out of my hand.
> [11]And I will put an end to all her mirth,
>   her festivals, her new moons, her sabbaths,

[42] Literally, the text says, 'I will return and I will take.' But the RSV's paraphrase is a valid interpretation of the force of the idiom. *Cf.* GKC § 120 d–e; Gibson § 97 (b).

[43] The Geneva Bible (1560) paraphrases, '. . . [I] wil recover my woll and my flaxe *lent*, to cover her shame.' (Italics theirs.)

[44] Andersen & Freedman (1980: 246) comment on the nuance of *wᵉhiṣṣaltî*: 'This vigorous action makes it clear that stolen property is being recovered. Just as *hirbêtî*, "I lavished," is more emphatic than *nātattî*, "I gave," in Hos. 2:10 [EVV 8], so here *hiṣṣaltî* is more forceful than the preceding *lāqaḥtî*, "I will take back." '

[45] The term *'erwâ(h)* connotes the shame associated with the exposure of one's nakedness. *Cf.* Lv. 20:17; 1 Sa. 20:30; Is. 20:4; 47:3; Ezk. 16:36. Moreover, in this context it hints at Israel's sexual escapades with her lovers. God is saying that the dirty secrets of her whoredom will be made plain for all to see, as he withdraws from her the prosperity which seems to cover the shame of her idolatry and render it respectable.

and all her appointed feasts.
¹²And I will lay waste her vines and her fig trees,
of which she said,
'These are my pay,
which my lovers have given me.'
I will make them a forest,
and the wild animals shall devour them.
¹³And I will visit upon her the feast days of the Baals,
when she burned incense to them
and decked herself with her ring and jewellery,
and went after her lovers;
but me she forgot, says the LORD.

Yahweh resolves to demonstrate his reality to Israel, upon whose Yahwism a pall of unreality has settled.[46] His promises seem ineffectual, his threats idle. In verse 10, therefore, he determines to demonstrate that he alone holds sway over the fortunes of his people. In particular, Yahweh declares that he will expose his wife's 'lewdness'[47] – presumably referring to her whole pattern of behaviour rehearsed already in the passage. The nation's outward prosperity conceals the truth of their inner moral rot. They do not have to face it or think deeply about it, much less repent over it. They may even congratulate themselves that they can live as they please, compromising the covenant, and Yahweh will not do a thing about it. This attitude

---

[46] One notes with interest that, from verse 2 on, Yahweh and Israel are the only significant actors. Only they are the subjects of the verbs – with the exception of verse 5, where Israel *says* that her lovers provide for her. From Hosea's perspective, they do nothing. Only Yahweh and Israel actually participate in reality, and his participation overrules hers. She is now to be restored to this theocentric perspective.

[47] The NRSV translates *nablût* as 'shame'. I prefer the RSV's 'lewdness' because of the sexual flavour of the passage. The word is a hapax, however, and patient of various nuances. The root II √*nbl* (in BDB's registration) suggests foolishness or stupidity. Indeed, the Vulgate translates *et nunc revelabo stultitiam eius*. Ibn Ezra writes that this word is 'from the root of *nᵉbālâ(h)*, according to the [morphological] paradigm of "for childhood [*yaldût*] and youth [*šaḥᵃrût*] are vanity" (Ec. 11:10), for nakedness revealed is *nᵉbālâ(h)*'. That is, *nablût* is cognate with *nᵉbālâ(h)* but takes the abstract form. The latter word is used in connection with various forms of disgusting sexual behaviour, *e.g.* Gn. 34:7; Dt. 22:21; Jdg. 19:23–24; 20:6, 10; 2 Sa. 13:12; Je. 29:23.

Yahweh will shatter by blighting the land, revealing the truth of Israel's violations of the covenant as threatened in the curses of Deuteronomy 28. And as these catastrophes roll over Israel, the people may plead to their lovers, the Baals, to deliver them. They may plead for the fruitful rains upon which their survival and happiness depend. And Israel's lovers will be standing there, as it were, watching all of this happen, but they will be powerless to act. The Baals will be seen to be utterly ineffectual. As Yahweh exposes his adulterous wife, he also taunts the Baals. She is abandoned, but she may not entertain hopes that her lovers will take her in and provide for her. If she refuses the mercies of Yahweh, her lawful husband, she may have no-one else's – and that, by *Yahweh's* decision.

Verses 11–12 explain more literally what the misery of verse 10 will look like. First, according to verse 11, Yahweh will cancel Israel's religious festivities.[48] Although arguable as formally lawful, they have become so Baalized as to cease being Yahweh's celebrations and thus have been reduced to '*her* festivals, *her* new moons, *her* sabbaths'.[49] Yahweh disowns these occasions, condemning them as too corrupted to continue. So the national calendar will be erased of Israel's normal course of religious celebrations, for they have become more carnivals than holy days. The national routine will no longer be punctuated with occasions of rest and refreshment; all days will blend together into a spirit-crushing monotony.[50]

Secondly, according to verse 12, Yahweh will strike the land with barrenness. Israel perceives her vines and fig trees,[51] which

---

[48] The verb *wᵉhišbattî* is answered in tragic irony with the object *wᵉšabbattāh*. Yahweh deprives Israel of the rest entailed in faith. The first object of the verb, *kol mᵉśôśāh*, is metonymy for the various celebrations, immediately enumerated in apposition, as occasions for joy. *kol mᵉśôśāh* is matched at the end of the verse with *wᵉkōl môʿᵃḏāh*, summing up all her festivities. Not one celebration will be allowed to continue.

[49] Burroughs (*Hos*: 105) comments, 'It appears that Israel, though an apostatizing people, designed to dreadful judgments, yet were a merry, jocund people; they went on still in their mirth and joviality.'

[50] Grotius, in *Critici Sacri, ad loc.*, comments, 'Nullum illis otium dabitur a laboribus.' [No rest will be given them from their labours.] Always winter, never Christmas.

[51] 'Vine and fig tree' constitute synechdoche for all forms of pleasant provision consistent with affluence. *Cf.* 1 Ki. 5:5 [EVV 4:25]; 2 Ki. 18:31 [Is. 36:16]; Je. 5:17; Joel 2:22; Mi. 4:4; Zc. 3:10.

add flavour to her life, as the pay-off[52] she receives for submitting to the rites of Baal worship. But Yahweh intends to subvert her faith.[53] Indeed, her carefully cultivated vineyards and orchards will suffer more than a dry season now and then. Yahweh will reduce them to wilderness, barren and unfruitful, where roaming animals feed at will.

The celebrations held in honour of the Baals will come back to haunt Israel, according to verse 13, which concludes the exposé of Israel's adultery begun in 2:2.[54] If she thought she was getting away with anything, she was wrong. Yahweh will confront her, and all those days of easy pleasure with her lovers must be repaid.[55] The festivals of verse 11, dismissed there as Israel's rather than Yahweh's, are here exposed even more searchingly. But we are to think not only of Canaanite observances imported into Israel; we are also to envision the ancient celebrations of the Mosaic law by now so permeated with pagan assumptions and aims that they are truer to the Baals than to Yahweh. Hence, 'the days of the Baals', when Israel goes after her lovers and forgets her proper husband. The last line of the verse ('but me she forgot') would lack point, unless the festivals in view were truly Yahwistic institutions which had been perverted to serve Baalistic ends. Israel's worship has degenerated to the level of Canaanite religion.[56] Hosea 4:12–14 helps one to picture the scene more vividly:

> [12]My people enquire of a thing of wood,
>   and their staff gives them oracles.
> For a spirit of harlotry has led them astray,

---

[52] The hapax *'eṭnâ(h)* need not be emended to *'eṭnan*, although the semantic value is doubtless the same. It refers to the pay a whore receives from her customer. *Cf.* Dt. 23:19; Is. 23:17–18; Ezk. 16:31, 34, 41; Ho. 9:1. Burroughs (*Hos.* 124) observes that Israel's harlotry 'makes her so impudent, that she uses that very word'. The unique form attested here is likely a wordplay on *tᵉ'ēnâ(h)*, 'fig tree'.

[53] Radak comments, 'Because she has said that from the hand of her lovers come the grain and the wine and the oil and all good things, I will make them a devastation. And she will know whether these good things of hers are from me or from them.'

[54] On the force of $\sqrt{pqd}$ construed with *'al*, see the discussion at 1:4.

[55] A striking feature of this passage is its sharp insistence upon requital without specifying either the time or the means or agency of punishment.

[56] *Cf.* 2 Ki. 17:7–18.

and they have left their God to play the harlot.
*13*They sacrifice on the tops of the mountains,
and make offerings upon the hills,
under oak, poplar, and terebinth,
because their shade is good.
Therefore your daughters play the harlot,
and your brides commit adultery.
*14*I will not punish your daughters when they play the harlot,
nor your brides when they commit adultery;
for the men themselves go aside with harlots,
and sacrifice with cult prostitutes,
and a people without understanding shall come to ruin (RSV).

Verse 13 of chapter 2 is significant because it makes explicit the connection between Israel's religious worship (burning incense to the Baals) and her spiritual adultery (going after lovers). It identifies Israel's lovers as the Baals, and portrays her as a woman adorning herself to attract them.[57] In other words, Israel spares no expense or effort to win the favour of the Baals. But the net force of the verse as a whole is to insist that her festive worship of the Baals will not translate into joy and prosperity but will instead discover unintended misery. In chasing after the Baals, Israel will be shocked to encounter not her gallant lovers but her heartbroken, angry husband. With tragic irony, Yahweh contrasts Israel's eagerness for the Baals, described in some detail,[58] with the brief 'But me she forgot'.[59]

---

[57] The verb √ *'dh* is used of a woman adorning herself to attract the interest of adulterers in Je. 4:30 and Ezk. 23:40. (Elsewhere, it is used of a woman's proper adorning of herself.) The ring could ornament either the nose (Ezk. 16:12) or the ear (Ex. 32:2). The hapax *helyâ(h)* is no doubt contiguous semantically with *ḥᵃlî*, mentioned in Pr. 25:12 (in connection with a *nezem*) and Song 7:2 [EVV 7:1]. A morphological analogy would be *šibyâ(h)* relative to *šᵉbî*, both meaning 'captivity, captives'. *Cf.* Ibn Ezra: 'He compares [Israel] with a whore who puts a ring upon her nose and an ornament [*ḥᵃlî*] on her neck to beautify herself, in order to find favour in the eyes of an adulterer.'

[58] Interestingly, the *yqtl* verb *taqṭîr* is followed by *wyqtl* forms. *Cf.* Joüon § 118 n. This would be tolerated within Hosea's unusual style presumably because *taqṭîr* is a frequentative imperfect referring to ongoing activity in the past.

[59] The direct object pronoun is the more conspicuous for having been front-loaded in the clause, while the verb's position as the last word of the oracle renders it the more forceful. Each word bears emphasis. Wolff (1974b: 40) sensitively observes, 'Hosea's God is personally offended by Israel's apostasy.'

Israel cherished glad expectations of the Baals, but felt little interest in Yahweh. She courted their favour, but neglected him. She adorned herself for them, but slighted him. He swears that her betrayal of his love will not succeed.[60]

Avenging his wife's adulteries is not God's ultimate aim, however. He intends to win her love back to himself. Verses 14–23 set forth this intention.[61]

> [14]Therefore, behold, I will allure her,
>   and bring her into the wilderness,
>   and speak tenderly to her.
> [15]And from there I will give her her vineyards,
>   and make the Valley of Achor a door of hope.
> And there she shall answer as in the days of her youth,
>   as at the time when she came out of the land of Egypt (RSV).

Israel has forgotten Yahweh, but he is determined to make himself loved once again. Amazingly, his response to her indifference is not further judgment but, in this case, the artful strategy of an ardent lover.[62] He intends to allure her,[63] rekindling the romance they enjoyed in their early years together. He sees that he cannot reason with her. That accomplishes nothing. She does not listen to her husband any more. So he will entice her. He will draw her back into a reunion with himself that, had she anticipated it, she would not have been willing to accept. And so God will more than match the

---

[60] The prophetic seal of authenticity, n^e'um YHWH, concludes the section with solemn finality and formalizes his commitment to follow through on everything he has declared in this section.

[61] The resolution to the tensions of 2:2–13 is suggested in 2:14–23. The wilderness where Israel is to die of thirst (3) becomes the scene of her restoration to love (14), the wild animals which are to devour Israel's harvest (12) are covenanted in peace (18), the grain and wine which Yahweh will repossess (9) he will provide (22). Cf. Andersen & Freedman 1980: 264.

[62] In verses 6 and 9 one observes the particle lākēn signalling a move from exposure of sin to divine punishment. Verse 14, however, clashes with the reader's expectations. Cf. Burroughs (Hos: 129): '. . . the grace of God knows how to make another manner of inference than we could have imagined.'

[63] The prophet takes a risk in employing the verb √pth, for it is also used of sexual seduction in Ex. 22:15 [EVV 16]. The LXX interprets with διὰ τοῦτο ἰδοὺ ἐγὼ πλανῶ αὐτήν and the Vulgate with propter hoc ecce ego lactabo eam. The pronoun 'ānōkî is emphatic, standing in contrast with 'but me she forgot' in verse 13.

seductions of the Baals with his own prevenient grace, proving himself an irresistible lover.

Yahweh will reinvigorate Israel's first love by leading them back into the wilderness. Rather than a prediction of exile into the provinces of Assyria, the second line of verse 14 alludes to Israel's nomadic life in the Sinai long ago, when, by comparison with Hosea's day, she was closer to her husband. The point is that the opulence of Samaria will never provide the surroundings in which her heart can be won back. But separated from her lovers, deprived of her pleasures through adversity, she will fall in love with Yahweh again. He will manifest his love in winning ways,[64] and she will be his.

Verse 15 declares that the Baal rites will no longer be needed, for he will provide for Israel in her wilderness. From there, by Yahwistic miracle rather than Baalistic magic, he will bestow upon her the good things of life.[65] The very experience of deep trouble with Yahweh ('the Valley of Achor') will itself open up a fresh tomorrow for the nation.[66] The covenant will be renewed and Israel will receive Yahweh's love with responsive hearts, as in their honeymoon period when she came out of Egypt. He will speak tenderly, and she will respond.[67] Israel's harlotry has not damaged the relationship beyond redemption.

And, when her heart within has been won over, Israel will manifest outward signs of true repentance and restoration to her husband:

[64] To 'speak to the heart' (RSV 'speak tenderly') is to speak so as to touch the affections. Cf. Gn. 34:3; 50:21; Jdg. 19:3; Is. 40:2.

[65] Calvin (Hos: ad loc.) comments, 'The prophet said in the last verse, "I will speak to her heart"; now he adds, "I will bring a sure and clear evidence of my favour, that they may feel assured that I am reconciled to them."' 'Her vineyards' is synecdoche for all the joys of life; but (to quote Calvin again), '. . . he has chosen vines, because in vines the bounty of God especially appears. For bread is necessary to support life; wine abounds, and to it is ascribed the property of exhilarating the heart.'

[66] Alluding to Jos. 7, the prophet implies that Israel will rediscover what it means to move forward into new divine mercies through sin-bred trouble. Hosea has already shown that God is able to reverse the judgments of Jezreel, Not Pitied and Not My People into assurances of restoration.

[67] Cf. Wolff (1974b: 43): 'That וענתה implies both an answer and a "following after" is indicated by the next word "there" (שמה) which syntactically presupposes a constructio praegnans (as in 1:2b; 2:20b, and 3:5b), i.e. a verb of motion is implied: "she answers and follows after" = "she follows willingly".'

[16]And on that day, says the LORD, you will call me, 'My husband,' and no longer will you call me, 'My Baal.' [17]For I will remove the names of the Baals from her mouth, and they shall be mentioned by name no more.

Israel's renewed love for Yahweh will show itself in worship cleansed of all compromise, so that she clearly affirms him for what he truly is, *viz.* her lawful husband. At the present time, Hosea implies, she tolerates a culpable ambiguity in her invoking of Yahweh.[68] She appeals to her *ba'al* – not that that is inherently wrong, for Yahweh is indeed her lord. But in a historical situation seductively confusing at that very point, such ambiguity leads to adultery. 'My Baal' – patient of two interpretations, one faithful and the other promiscuous – will be rejected by a renewed Israel eager to know and serve her divine husband with clarity of vision. Given Israel's covenant theology, 'My husband' allows for no uncertainty, and she will seize upon this endearing expression as the only form of address consistent with her deepest intentions. Purified Yahwism inspired by singleness of heart will mark Yahweh's wife when, in that day of wilderness-like affliction, the emptiness of Baalism becomes vividly clear and Yahweh alone is left, subduing her to a loving and tender responsiveness. The old Baals – the Baal of Peor, Baal Berith, and others with their various names – will no longer even be mentioned, except perhaps in abhorrence. In the course of time, it will be Baal, not Yahweh, who is forgotten.[69]

Verse 18 promises that, in that day when Yahweh entices Israel into the wilderness, he will so order life for his people that both animal and human savagery will be restrained, securing the

---

[68] Ibn Ezra comments, 'Rabbi Marinus [*i.e.* Ibn Janaḥ] said, "Even a name which is ambiguous, like 'Baal', which is the name of an idol, or like 'For a young man will marry [*yiḇ'al*] a virgin' (Is. 62:5) you will no longer remember." '

[69] Drusius, in *Critici Sacri, ad loc.*, renders salient the force of verse 17: 'Non solum cultum eorum obliterabo, sed etiam memoriam nominum quibus appellantur.' [I will blot out not only the worship of them but also the memory of the names by which they are called upon.]

nation's external peace even as she enjoys renewed peace with God. All outward circumstances will favour her.

Verses 19–20 resume the marriage metaphor:[70]

> [19]And I will betroth you to me for ever; I will betroth you to me in righteousness and in justice, in steadfast love, and in mercy. [20]I will betroth you to me in faithfulness; and you shall know the LORD (RSV).

The mystery of grace revealed here is a promise of covenant renewal – although even the word renewal is weak, for this oracle promises not merely the reinvigoration of the old marriage but the creation of a new one. A fresh betrothal, as if Israel were starting out again as a pure virgin, is set before the corrupted nation as their future hope. The declaration 'I will betroth you to me' appears three times with emphatic force.[71] This verb describes the formalizing of an arrangement which gives a man warrant for expecting to take a certain woman as his wife.[72] It is striking that a premarital term is exploited by the prophet to portray Israel's future. The positive exegetical function of this is not to suggest that God intends to stop short of a full marriage with Israel but rather to suggest the unspoiled newness of their union on that day. The ugly past will be forgotten and they will start over again, as if nothing had ever gone wrong.

And unlike the first marriage, which was such a disaster that it could not be salvaged, this new marriage will last for ever, strengthened by the moral qualities of righteousness and justice, steadfast love and mercy – all of which translate into a marriage

[70] One notes the 3 f s suffix in 17 ('her mouth'), the 3 m p pronoun in 18 ('for them' – unnecessarily emended in both the RSV and NRSV to 'for you') and the 2 f s suffixes in 19–20 ('you' [feminine singular]).

[71] The three appearances of w^e' $\bar{e}ra\acute{s}t\underline{i}\underline{k}$ do not point to consecutive actions but to one, enunciated three times in order to convey the certainty with which God declares his intentions and, at the same time, to provide syntactical launching points for his heaping of terms upon terms to describe the glorious inner character of the new marriage, viz. righteousness and justice, etc.

[72] Cf. 2 Sa. 3:14 – although the Hosean text does not use √'rś with b^e in the sense of 'betroth at the price of X'. Cf. footnote 74 below. Dt. 20:7 and 28:30 assume that 'betrothal' leads to and is fulfilled in sexual union and cohabitation. Dt. 22:23–24 indicate that betrothal entails such an obligation between a man and a woman that the woman may already be termed his 'wife'.

secured by faithfulness.[73] This relationship will be inviolable, for Yahweh will impart to Israel new moral character.[74] Whatever communicable virtues are necessary and meaningful on Israel's side of the relationship Yahweh will include in his provision of the relationship itself.

The burden of verses 19–20, then, is twofold. It reveals, first, God's gracious determination to renew his marriage with Israel[75] and, secondly, the certainty that this time the ground rules of a loving marriage will indeed be fulfilled. Israel will not again betray her divine husband. Instead, she will 'know the LORD' in personal communion.

Verses 21–23, which do not take advantage of the marriage metaphor, bring the assurances begun in verse 14 to their eschatological *ne plus ultra* in language to challenge the imagination.[76]

---

[73] One might quibble with the RSV's English equivalents to some of these words, but Hosea's emphasis doubtless lies on the net impact of the whole. These atomically weighted terms are meant to have the cumulative effect of assuring Israel that *all* the ideals of the covenant will be fulfilled in their new love affair with God.

[74] Rashi glosses 'in righteousness and in justice' with the comment, 'with which you will conduct yourselves'. But, while that is doubtless true, it explains only one side of this outcome, and the less profound one at that. Calvin's explanation is more satisfying: 'Except God then re-creates us a new people to himself, there is no more stability in the covenant he makes now with us than in the old which he made formerly with the fathers under the law; for when we compare ourselves with the Israelites, we find that we are nothing better. It is, therefore, necessary that God should work inwardly and efficaciously on our hearts, that his covenant may stand firm.' This must be the case, for the perfect betrothal promised here stands in contrast to the failed marriage before. Moreover, while covenant faithfulness will indeed distinguish the new bride, the terms used here are meant to describe not Israel *per se* but the betrothal, that is, the quality of the new marriage, and it is the betrothal which God initiates and provides. Therefore, one may reasonably posit God as the ultimate explanation for and ongoing source of this national moral renewal. *Cf.* Rom. 8:3–4. For Rashi's comment to stand as the final word, one would have to assert that the prepositional phrases 'in righteousness' *etc.* are to be construed with the direct object of the verb, *viz.* 'you'. But that is improbable, for the whole sequence begins with 'I will betroth you to me for ever [*l^e'ôlām*]', and that prepositional phrase cannot reasonably be so construed. Rather, it seems that the prepositional phrases modify the entire statement 'I will betroth you to me', for that is the factor fully repeated in each case.

[75] *Cf.* Gill (*ExpOT*: 4:583): 'Let it be observed, here are no conditions throughout; it is only *I will,* and *thou shalt.*'

[76] McComiskey (1992: 1:47) describes the text as 'a highly metaphorical account that is almost surreal'.

That day of Israel's restoration will bring final resolution to all the moral tensions brought to light in chapters 1 – 2. Israel's obduracy will dissolve, Yahweh will show himself abundant in blessing and grace, and even the natural surroundings will sprout forth with new life. Safe to say, this grand prophetic vision leaves Baal completely behind.

Hosea 3

In chapter 1 God instructed the prophet to take a harlotrous wife; here he calls him to love an adulterous wife. There the woman was identified as Gomer, the daughter of Diblaim; here she remains anonymous. It seems probable that the woman in chapter 3 is also Gomer, because the language does not suggest the initiation of a new marriage but rather a husband's loving constancy toward his wayward wife whose identity is taken for granted. Chapter 3 assumes chapter 1. In both chapters the larger reality of Yahweh's marriage to Israel is said to be symbolized through the human relationship, creating the presumption that only one marriage is in view. But the particular emphasis of chapter 3 lies upon the steadfast *love* of the husband. Hosea was not merely to accept an adulteress as his wife; he was to love her, and love her until he won her. The prophetic marriage of Hosea and Gomer assures Israel that her own violations of the covenant cannot sever the covenant, for Yahweh loves her with a love that will not let her go.

>[1]And the LORD said to me, 'Go again, love a woman who has a lover and is an adulteress, just as the LORD loves the people of Israel, though they turn to other gods and love raisin cakes.' [2]So I bought her for fifteen shekels of silver and a homer and a lethech of barley. [3]And I said to her, 'You must dwell as mine for many days; you shall not play the harlot, or belong to another man; so will I also act toward you.' [4]For the children of Israel shall dwell many days without king or prince, without sacrifice or pillar, without ephod or teraphim. [5]Afterward the children of Israel shall return and seek the LORD their God, and David their king; and they shall come in fear to the LORD and to his goodness in the latter days.

Yahweh calls Hosea to keep on loving Gomer,[77] even as she continues to run to the arms of another man,[78] with the same love that Yahweh is showing to Israel, even as they go on turning to the Baals.[79] The impulse underlying the faithfulness of Yahweh is a deep and undying love for his people. But what do they, for their part, love? Raisin cakes.[80] The abrupt mention of raisin cakes seems odd. And that is the point. Her love *is* oddly misplaced. No matter what she may tell herself, she does not love Yahweh. She loves Baal, for she 'has a lover and is an adulteress'. But the last clause of verse 1 makes the telling point that what attracts Israel to her false lover is a trivial and earthly pleasure. The nation is like a woman who leaves her royal husband in their palace to go drinking with some good-for-nothing in the bars. Sensate Israel does not hunger for the spiritual things Yahweh offers.

To sustain the commanded demonstration of faithful love, Hosea has to buy his wife.[81] Why this is necessary at all he leaves unexplained. The bare fact teases the imagination, and one can

---

[77] The syntactical function of *'ôḏ* is debatable. It modifies either the introductory 'said' or the command to 'go, love'. Usage could be cited in favour of either construal, *e.g.* Ex. 4:6, favouring the former, and Zc. 11:15, favouring the latter. The net meaning in the former case, however, seems insipid by comparison with a command to continue the loving pursuit of a woman whom one would be inclined to detest. The adverb is front-loaded for emphasis.

[78] According to GKC § 125 c, the indeterminate status of *'iššâ(h)* is meant to amplify suggestively the character of the woman, *i.e.* 'such a woman (as has a lover . . .)'. God emphasizes to Hosea the salient point of his obedience.

[79] The participial form of *pōnîm* conveys the sense that their turning to other gods occurs even as Yahweh continues to love them. *Cf.* Gibson § 113, Rem. 1. The language of 'turning' to other gods means that Israel rejects Yahweh, regards him lightly, sees little in him to desire or hope in, and instead invests those affections in others. *Cf.* Dt. 31:20. Burroughs (*Hos*: 182) comments in typically Puritan style, 'Where the heart is, there is the eye.'

[80] *Cf.* 2 Sa. 6:19 [1 Ch. 16:3]; Song 2:5; Is. 16:7. The LXX reads 'cakes with raisins', the Vulgate 'wine-cups of grapes', the Syriac 'cakes of raisins'. Rashi quotes Menahem ben Saruk, the tenth-century lexicographer, who understands the *'ašîšê 'anāḇîm* to be 'cups of wine' (*cf.* the AV's 'flagons of wine'). Ibn Ezra and Radak comment similarly, the latter explaining, 'They loved the pleasures of the world.' The Samuel reference gives the impression that such cuisine, whatever it was, was regarded as appropriate for a special occasion, which the genitive *'anāḇîm* corroborates.

[81] The form ואכרה is problematic. The apparently doubled radical leads one to expect a first-nun root, but √*nkr* does not occur in the qal elsewhere in the

only speculate as to how Gomer's lifestyle took her where Hosea has to pay a price for her.[82] That price seems a modest one,[83] implying that Gomer was not worth much to anyone by then.

Having bought her back fair and square, Hosea dictates in verse 3 the terms under which their marriage, now resumed, will continue. With the larger prophetic vision in mind, he prescribes that for an indefinitely long period of time Gomer will live faithfully with him, avoiding all inappropriate contact with other men. For his part, Hosea will reply to her self-possession by keeping himself from her.[84] She will live 'like a widow' (La. 1:1). The lengthy, but not permanent, duration of this harsh existence implies that they will eventually come together again for the full joys of marriage.

The reason for the austere measures is that Hosea and Gomer's human marriage is to project on to the screen of the human imagination the ultimate reality of Yahweh's severe mercies toward Israel, according to verses 4–5. For an analogously indefinite period of time, Israel will live without the familiar structures of human government and divine worship which she has abused.[85] The fact that the list of religious objects in verse 4 mixes together both lawful and pagan items is

---

Hebrew Bible and the semantics of that root do not suit the remainder of the verse, *pace* Ibn Ezra. Ibn Janaḥ, *Book of Roots, s.v.* √*krh*, is doubtless correct when he compares this usage with the sense of √*qnh* in Ru. 4:10. According to GKC § 20 h, the first radical is marked with *dagesh forte dirimens* (separating dagesh forte), rendering the shewa more audible. Radak writes that the dagesh is for euphony, that the root is √*krh* and that the sense is 'to buy'.

[82] Wolff (1974b: 61) comments, 'Hosea's report is limited to that which is decisive for the symbolic act.'

[83] *Cf.* Gn. 37:28; Ex. 21:32; Lv. 27:4; Dt. 22:28–29.

[84] The sense of *wᵉgan ᵃnî ᵓēlāyiḵ* is particularly obscure. The larger logical equation of verses 3–5, however, seems to require that Hosea's policy toward Gomer be one of deprivation, even as Yahweh withdraws Israel's privileges in the exile while remaining her heavenly husband. Since Gomer is required to be sexually inactive, one presumes that the deprivation imposed by Hosea is also sexual. The ellipse is filled in by both Ibn Ezra and Radak as follows: 'And I also will not come in to you.'

[85] Radak comments on verse 4, 'Now these are the days of the exile in which we are today. We have no king and no prince from Israel, but we are in the power of the nations and in the power of their kings and their princes. There is no sacrifice to God, and neither is there a pillar for idolatry. There is no ephod to God, which makes known future things by Urim and Thummim; and there are no teraphim for idolatry, which make known future things for the knowledge of them that believe in them.'

significant, for that is precisely the situation Israel has tolerated thus far. But God, in love, will not allow it to continue. For a long time, Israel will suffer exile, with all the deprivation and discipline entailed.[86] Yahweh will seem remote and life will be hard to bear. But when her affliction is complete, she will return to Yahweh her true God with wholehearted repentance. She will tolerate no more rival thrones, and the tribes will be reunited under the Davidic crown. She will worship no more golden calves, but will come trembling back to Yahweh, humbled for the unbelief with which she once dismissed his all-sufficient goodness and now fully convinced of it and yearning for it.

What eventually developed between Hosea and Gomer, the text does not reveal. That is not the point. The human marriage serves merely as the point of departure for the prophetic declarations to the nation concerning its current moral condition, its short-term discipline in exile and its long-term hope in the latter days. The life of whoredom she has chosen must be purged from her national soul; but through all the agony required for the cleansing to be thorough, nothing will be able to separate her from the love of Yahweh.

---

[86] Calvin (*Hos: ad loc.*) comments, 'He says "For many days" that they might prepare themselves for long endurance and be not dispirited through weariness, though the Lord should not soon free them from their calamities. "Though then your exile should be long, still cherish," he says, "strong hope in your hearts; for so long a trial must necessarily be made of your repentance, as you have very often pretended to return to the Lord, and soon after your hypocrisy was discovered; and then ye became hardened in your wilful obstinacy. It is therefore necessary that the Lord should subdue you by a long chastisement" . . . if he had stretched out his hand to them immediately, there would have been in them no repentance; but when thoroughly cleansed by long correction, they would then truly and sincerely confess their God.'

Chapter Four

Under every green tree

The vision of Israel as an unfaithful wife is developed by Jeremiah and especially Ezekiel into elaborate images. Hosea's contemporaries Isaiah and Micah, however, make a smaller but still noteworthy contribution to the emerging theological message.

Isaiah

The whoredom which formed the centrepiece of Hosea's message shrinks to two allusions in the written remains of the prophet Isaiah.[1] The first reference is featured in the introductory chapter. Isaiah 1:21 reads:

> How the faithful city
> has become a harlot,
> she that was full of justice!
> Righteousness lodged in her –
> but now murderers (RSV).

Surveying the Jerusalem of his day, Isaiah cries out in astonishment and anguish over its condition, much as one today would grieve over a once beautiful and safe neighbourhood now degenerated into rows of drug dens patrolled by corrupt police and overseen by judges for sale. Formerly

---

[1] In Is. 50:1, 54:4–6 and 62:5 marital language is used, but the theme of Israel's harlotry is not developed. Tyre is branded as a harlot in 23:15–17, presumably because, for Tyrian merchants, everything had its price, including moral principle. As elsewhere in the prophets, nations not covenanted to Yahweh are nevertheless required to adhere to a universal standard of justice. *Cf.* Na. 3:4–5. As for the question of Isaianic authorship, the reader is referred to Motyer (1993: 25–30).

constant in their observances of the ways of Yahweh,[2] the people of Jerusalem[3] have sunk to the level of whoredom. Their corporate life had shown visible evidence of having been marked by God's moral order, being full of justice.[4] The standard of righteousness had dignified her social intercourse, finding a welcome in her heart and in her ways.[5] But now? Walk the streets of this city, and anything could happen. One could even lose one's life.[6] The great ideals of the covenant have been

[2] The participial form of √'mn in this context, set in opposition to a harlot, suggests the profile of a faithful wife; but the sense of this word can also be appreciated from other usage, such as one who does God's will (1 Sa. 2:35), one who is steadfast toward God (Ps. 78:8, 37), one who walks in God's ways (Ps. 101:6) and one who rejects deceit (Ho. 12:1 [EVV 11:12]).

[3] The LXX includes the gloss Σιων after 'faithful city', which is dubious textually but convincing interpretatively in view of 1:1, 8, 27 and the record of Isaiah's ministry generally.

[4] The -î suffix in $m^e l\bar{e}^{'a} t\hat{i}$ is compared by Rashi with rabbāṭî 'amin La. 1:1 and by Ibn Ezra with $g^e nu\underline{b}t\hat{i}$ yôm $\hat{u}g^e nu\underline{b}t\hat{i}$ lāylâ(h) in Gn. 31:39, which modern grammarians call the hireq compaginis (the hireq of connection), usually marking a construct-genitive connection. Cf. GKC § 90 1; Jouon § 93 m.

[5] This use of √lyn is striking. The LXX handles it rather clumsily with ἐκοιμήθη, while Jerome finesses it with habitavit. Rashi takes the curious view that the verb implies a constant absolution of sin – the sins of the night forgiven at dawn and the sins of the day between dawn and dusk. He notes another interpretation which construes this as a reference to the courts of former times, which followed due process, in contrast with the courts of Isaiah's day, which commit murder by their hasty judgments. Radak comments, 'yālîn is not in reality an expression of spending the night but an expression of effort and diligence in a matter'. The sense, however, is simply that righteousness 'dwelt' or 'lodged' in Jerusalem. Cf. Jb. 17:2. Ibn Ezra properly notes that the yqtl form implies ongoing action, here in the past.

[6] The stichometry of the verse, misrepresented by the RSV and NRSV, draws attention to the last line. Moreover, the piel participle $m^e ra\underline{s}\underline{s}^e\underline{h}\hat{i}m$, rather than an unmarked qal, adds flavour to the text. The qal participle is used in Nu. 35, Dt. 4 and Jos. 20 – 21 in connection with the cities of refuge, referring to one liable for manslaughter as well as one who commits murder. The only other piel participle of this root in the Hebrew Bible is found in 2 Ki. 6:32, where an assassin is sent to murder Elisha. One could posit the professional sense of the piel participle here, as explained in WO'C 24.5c. But it is possible to overinterpret the qal/piel distinction. Cf. ibid., 24.3a–c. The other piel uses of √rṣḥ (Ps. 94:6 and Ho. 6:9 – the text of Ps. 62:4 appears to be corrupt) may evoke the cold-blooded character of the crime. In any case, Jerusalem has reached a point where no-one would mistake it for a city of refuge! No unfortunate manslayer is safe here. No-one is safe here. Finally, 'murderers' is probably synecdoche for all varieties of criminals, the worst being mentioned to imply all lesser ones. The irony may be that these murderers are not low-life

replaced by the hard reality of bloodshed in the streets.[7] And this, Isaiah laments, is how the faithful wife of Yahweh has become a harlot. Tragic, painful incongruity.

In this verse spiritual whoredom is seen to translate into social meltdown, for the offences decried in verses 21–23 are not religious but moral and social in nature.[8] The very fact that such outward wrongs are included within the portrayal of a harlotrous city, however, reveals that they spring ultimately from deeply personal defection from Yahweh.

The second reference, in Isaiah 57:3, reads:

> But you, come here,
>   you sons of a sorceress,
>   you offspring of an adulterer and a harlot.[9]

---

thugs but the very officials who bear responsibility for upholding justice and righteousness, perpetrating their crimes through 'legal' avenues. *Cf.* verse 23.

[7] One notes with interest the abstractions in the first two cola of the line, matched by the concrete 'murderers' in the last colon. Perhaps Isaiah is hinting at a cynical pragmatism quenching loftier impulses in the mentality of the times.

[8] Duhm (1968: 33) comments, 'Das Bild mag von Hosea beeinflußt sein, wird aber doch anders gewendet, da vom Abhuren des Weibes Zion von dem göttlichen Ehegemahl zu anderen Göttern mit keiner Silbe gesprochen wird; die Hurerei bestecht in dem Aufgeben der sittlichen Eigenschaften, durch die Zion allein Jahwe wert und mit ihm im Bunde war.' [The image may be influenced by Hosea, but is nevertheless used differently, since not a syllable is said about the harlotry of the wife, Zion, from the divine husband to other gods; the whoredom consists in the surrender of moral qualities, through which Zion valued Yahweh alone and was in covenant with him.]

[9] The traditional form *wattizneh*, 'and she committed harlotry', appears to be corrupt for three reasons. First, the form is probably 3 f s rather than 2 m s, because the initial verb in the verse is 2 m p. For this reason, one looks for a feminine antecedent. The nearer antecedent has to do with sexual sin but is masculine; the further antecedent (*'ōnᵉnâ(h)*), although feminine, concerns a different kind of offence. The received form appears to lack a referent to integrate it into the coherence of the text. Secondly, the sense 'and she committed harlotry' intrudes inelegantly into the literary texture of the verse. The prophet calls idolaters, as one discovers in due course, to draw near to God for judgment. The larger structure of the verse as a whole directs this summons to two classes of offenders, *viz.* 'sons of a sorceress' and 'offspring of an adulterer and [some form of √*znh*]'. A narrative *wyqtl* at the climax of this structure fractures the artistry of the whole. Thirdly, the twofold description of the addressees here in verse 3 is matched in verse 4 with 'children of transgression' and 'offspring of deceit', referring to the same persons but categorizing them with moral abstractions rather than according to the

The prophet contrasts the persecuted righteous who rest at peace in their beds (verses 1–2) with the popular idolaters who pursue a wildly orgiastic and ultimately futile worship of false gods (verses 3–13).[10] God confronts the idolaters directly in verse 3, exposing their true moral character via lineage. They are 'sons of a sorceress'[11] and 'offspring of an adulterer and a harlot',[12] personifying the nation as a whole. The prophet may

---

character of their parents. And this parallel component in the context includes nothing analogous to a verbal *wattizneh*. I therefore accept the emendation proposed in *BHS*, as do both the RSV and NRSV, which also achieves a more delicate balance with two participles in sequence. The LXX reads σπέρμα μοιχῶν καὶ πόρνης, apparently echoed in Jerome's *semen adulteri et fornicariae*. Symmachus' πορνευσάσης is more ambiguous as to his Vorlage. Gibson § 12, Rem. 3, suggests that the traditional text illustrates an asyndetic relative clause; but the *wyqtl* form functioning in that syntactical structure seems to be without analogy. Radak assumes an ellipse in the text: 'And *your mother* committed harlotry.' But even if another emendation should be posited – or no emendation at all – there is still no uncertainty as to a reference to harlotry here. The textual question only fine-tunes the particular force of the statement.

[10] The Palestinian setting of this passage, scarred with pre-exilic idolatrous practices alluded to already in Is. 1:29, is agreeable with the unity of the book as 'The vision of Isaiah the son of Amoz' (1:1). One need not accept Isaianic unity, however, to locate this passage in the pre-exilic era. Along with others, Westermann (1969: 301f., 319, 325) argues that the (in his view) three oracles contained in 56:9 – 57:13 constitute pieces of pre-exilic prophetic tradition incorporated into Trito-Isaiah's message.

[11] The LXX ('lawless sons') and Targum ('people of a generation whose deeds are bad') mistakenly connect the form *ōnᵉnâ(h)* with *'āwôn*, 'iniquity'. The Vulgate correctly interprets the phrase as *filii auguratricis*, 'sons of a (female) soothsayer'. The Syriac incorrectly forms a participle of √*mkk*, as if the Hebrew form were derived from III √*'nh*, 'to be afflicted, bowed down'. Rashi explains that the phrase means 'sons of sorceries'. Ibn Ezra appeals to Is. 2:6 ('soothsayers like the Philistines'). Radak comments, 'For your mothers were soothsayers and sorceresses, for sorcery is found mainly among women.' Foreirius, in *Critici Sacri, ad loc.*, construes *ōnᵉnâ(h)* as witches who harm others with their eyes, as if the Hebrew form were related to *'ayin*, 'eye'. Vitringa (1732: II:748) interprets the reference as one to pagan soothsayers. Biblical usage links the activity suggested by II √*'nn* with other forms of occult involvement. *Cf.* Lv. 19:26; Dt. 18:10, 14; 2 Ki. 21:6 [2 Ch. 33:6]; Mi. 5:11 [EVV 12].

[12] The adulterer is the male partner, Judah's 'father', and the harlot is their 'mother'. Radak takes it literally, commenting, 'Your fathers are adulterers and your mothers are harlots; so how will *you* be good?' Is. 1:21, however, identifies Jerusalem as the harlot. But who is the adulterous father? Verse 4b corroborates the view that in some sense the generation addressed is illegitimate and that their questionable origins have marred their own moral character, which

have chosen two abhorrent forms of human sin conspicuous in his times and thrown them together without intending a logical connection between them beyond the depth of each one's depravity, thereby suggesting that his people are stained with all forms of evil, even to this degree.[13] By tracing their moral flaw back into their origins, the prophet shows how inescapable is their degraded condition. They are doomed, without new parentage and a new nature. The passage goes on to expose their own enthusiastic participation in the evils of previous generations, however, so that personal responsibility cannot be evaded.

Grotius captures the net force of the accusation in the verse when he summarizes, 'In character you belong no more to Israel than ones who belong by nature to their so-called father, whom an adulterous mother begat from an adulterous man.'[14] Claiming Abraham as their father will not do, for they show not that family resemblance but quite another. As the ugly details unfold in the following verses, their condemnation is seen to be warranted.

Micah

The destruction of Samaria is decreed in 1:6 as the consequence of 'the transgression of Jacob' (1:5). Verse 7 aims the coming destruction more particularly at the idols of Samaria, which are

---

explains why they themselves are now to be found in bed with the idols (verses 7–8). Isaiah brands this generation of the nation with the same evils in which they were 'raised'. If that is so, then the adulterous 'father' may stand for the idols as a collective whole. *Cf.* Vitringa 1732: II:754.

[13] Note the unevenness of the insults, one identifying the mother only and the other both parents, as if the prophet were spitting the words out as quickly as they entered his mind. It is not impossible that an actual mixture of sorcery with idolatry is in view (2 Ki. 9:22 and Mal. 3:5?), but the following context elaborates only upon the image of idolatry as whoredom.

[14] Grotius, in *Critici Sacri, ad loc.*: '. . . moribus non magis ad Israelem pertinetis quam natura ad dictum patrem pertinent quos mater adultera ex adultero genuit.' Vitringa (1732: II:748) broadens the field of reference: 'Potest autem hic respici corruptio doctrinae, cultus, regiminis, morum, et quidem in semine perfecte adultero, haec omnia simul ἐν συμπλοκῇ.' [It is possible, however, that in view here is a corrupting of teaching, of worship, of government, of character, and indeed in a completely adulterous seed, all these things at the same time in combination.]

'the real target of YHWH's action and the crime which he punishes' (Mays 1976: 47):

> All her images shall be beaten to pieces,
>   and all her wages shall be burned with fire,
>   and all her idols I will lay waste;
> for from the wages of a harlot she gathered them,
>   and to the wages of a harlot they shall return.

The operative word in the first half of the verse is 'all', occurring three times to emphasize the thoroughness with which Yahweh will devastate Israel's idolatrous institutions. His opposition is radical, and their destruction will be complete. The word 'wages' (in 'all her wages shall be burned with fire') seems to clash with both the parallel references to images and idols and the verbal idea of being burned with fire. One expects instead to find here another reference to the physical images of false worship.[15] But that very expectation triggers the association desired by the prophet. 'Wages', as a harlot's pay,[16] is metonymy for the idolatrous images, implying their true meaning. They stand, condemned and condemning, as witnessing symbols of the dirty business to which Israel has reduced her worship. What Israel paid dearly to achieve was in fact something disgraceful. Even literally, the proceeds from her harlotrous idolatry financed the images. The connection is not casual but meaningful and even obvious.

What verse 7a intimates, viz. idols as the 'currency' of prostitution, is made fully explicit in verse 7b. Why will the images be utterly destroyed? Because they have been established in Israel's life through whoredom, so that meretricious exchange is the only thing they are good for and what they are properly doomed to. They are irredeemable. They came out of whoredom and they deserve to remain at that degraded level. The army of Assyria will loot Samaria's precious idols to fulfil the decree of Yahweh, so that all she has carefully accumulated and richly adorned will revert even after her own destruction to

---

[15] With others, Mays (1976: 46) emends and translates, 'All her Ashera shall be burned by fire.' This would perhaps require the further emendation of the 3 m p verb to a 3 f p form. But cf. Is. 27:9.

[16] See exposition at Ho. 2:12.

idolatrous use in Assyria.[17] The venom with which Yahweh detests the images, which Israel has so lavished with costly affection, drips from the very words.

The relevance of this prophetic utterance to our study is premised in the persuasion that the harlotry referred to here is not only the literal sex act at the high places but also, and more searchingly, spiritual whoredom in violation of the covenant with Yahweh. The figure of speech and the literal reality merge as one in the prophetic vision, the visible sin incarnating symbolically the deeper spiritual reality.[18] Spiritual adultery and physical adultery go together.

Jeremiah

Chapters 2 – 3 of Jeremiah's prophecy, bounded by references to the nation's youthful love for and defection from Yahweh, are pervaded with marital language.[19] This study will limit itself to the three passages in these chapters which develop the theme of spiritual harlotry most fully.

First, in 2:1–19, the prophet recalls to the people of God in his generation their original purity and privilege, now squandered for the sake of worthless alternatives to Yahweh. In verse 20, the prophet exposes the long-standing and widely practised extent of their apostasy:[20]

---

[17] *Cf.* Targum, Ibn Ezra, Radak, Vatable, Drusius, *et al.*

[18] *Cf.* Is. 57:7–8; Ho. 4:13–14. Stienstra (1993: 163), referring to Je. 2:20, argues that 'the actual situation, involving cultic prostitution, interacts with the metaphorical concept. The fact that idolatrous practices actually consisted of sexual acts made the marriage metaphor all the more appropriate for telling the people how badly they behaved with respect to YHWH.' The figure of speech is suggested by the literal reality, and the figure in turn invests the reality with deeper meaning. Perhaps it should be noted as well that, while there is no question as to licentious behaviour in connection with idolatrous worship, scholars are not universally agreed that 'cultic prostitution' functioned as such. *Cf. ABD, s.v.* 'Prostitution (Cultic)'.

[19] *Cf.* also Je. 4:30; 5:7–8; 9:2; 12:7; 22:20; 29:23. The language of adultery in 23:10 and 14 may or may not be figurative.

[20] The connection with the preceding context, signalled by the particle $k\hat{\imath}$, is ambiguous. Holladay (1986: 52) translates, 'Look, long ago you broke your yoke . . .' On p. 98, he comments, 'The verse continues with a second כִּי: the three occurrences of this conjunction in vv 20 and 22 are correlative, ticking off one by one the metaphors of covenant breaking. "Item: long ago you broke your yoke . . .; item: on every high hill . . ." '

For long ago you[21] broke your yoke
and burst your bonds,
and you said, 'I will not serve!'
On every high hill
and under every green tree
you bowed down as a harlot.

The text exploits two figures of speech for its effectiveness. First, Israel is compared with a stubborn, restless animal breaking out of its yoke and harness to run free. The 'yoke' and 'bonds' are the moral requirements entailed in the covenant which seem to Israel more like chains and slavery than meaningful and wise disciplines, worthy of her glad compliance.[22] Israel asserts, 'I will not serve!'[23] I will set my own terms and determine my own course.'[24]

Secondly, renouncing allegiance to Yahweh (or to anyone

---

[21] The MT construes the suffixed verbs in the first line of the verse as 1 c s forms, but the LXX (συνέτριψας) and Vulgate (confregisti) are doubtless correct in implying a 2 f s Vorlage. The consonantal text preserves an archaic 2 f s form, as in Je. 3:4, et passim. Cf. GKC § 44 h.

[22] Volz (1928: 25) comments, 'עלך: die ernste Religion Jahwes, die durch ihr Gesetz den Willen bilden wollte, erschien dem Volk als Joch.' [עלך: the stern religion of Yahweh, which through its law aimed to shape the will, seemed to the people like a yoke.]

[23] Reading the Kethib, which uses the unmarked yqtl form to express firm resolve; cf. Joüon § 114 c (3). The Qere is premised upon a fallacious understanding of the first half of the verse. According to this reading, Yahweh declares (following the AV), 'For of old time I have broken thy yoke, and burst thy bands, and thou saidst; I will not transgresse: when upon every high hill, and under every greene tree thou wandrest, playing the harlot.' In other words, 'I broke your yoke of Egyptian slavery, and you declared to me that you would no longer transgress my commandments; but you have broken your promise to the fullest extent.' Cf. Targum, Rashi, Radak. But it appears instead to be an accusation of defiant self-will rather than an affirmation of compliant submission, with the second half of the verse corroborating (with kî) the validity of the charge. The net force of the verse is that throughout Israel's history (me'ōlam) she has demonstrated a persistent inclination to commit whoredom with other gods out of a rebellious refusal to live under the rule of Yahweh.

[24] In fact, however, Israel wore either the yoke of Yahweh's rule or that of Babylon's. Autonomy proved a conceit incapable of realization in fact. It was Yahweh who placed the yoke of Babylon upon Israel's neck, and it was Yahweh who would eventually remove that burden. Cf. Je. 27 – 28; 30:8.

else, for that matter) and throwing off all restraint, Israel ventures forth into the libertine excesses of a degraded whore. She does not refuse any opportunity ('*every* high hill . . . *every* green tree') to explore the possibilities of the surrounding religious cultures, with their mingling of the spiritual with the visceral.[25] She abandons herself to the full experience they offer.[26]

Yahweh churns in anguish over Israel's original purity now turned rotten, in verse 21, and asserts her indelibly stained moral character, in verse 22. The prophet returns in verses 23–25 to the implied brutish and explicitly sexual images of verse 20. The theology of the covenant naturally offers marital

---

[25] Weiser(1969: 20) distinguishes Yahwism from the paganism alluded to by the verse in the following terms: 'Wenn Jeremia im Blick auf den im Bild des Ehebundes dargestellten Jahwebund, aber auch angesichts der an den Heiligtümern bräuchlichen Riten sexueller Ausschweifung diese Art Religion als "Hurerei" bezeichnet, so vollzieht er damit wie Hosea, der dieselben Bilder verwendet, die klare Scheidung zwischen der auf geistig-sittlichen Fundamenten ruhenden Religion des Jahwebundes und dem religiösen Typus jener Naturreligion, die dem dionysischen Lebensgefühl entspringt und entspricht; sie unterscheiden sich voneinander wie die Ehe von der Hurerei. Es ist der grundsätzliche Unterschied des verschiedenen Ausgangspunktes im Selbstverständnis des Menschen: Das Volk sucht sich von sich selbst und seiner Natur her zu begreifen, der Prophet von Gott und seiner Heilsgeschichte her.' [When Jeremiah, in view of the covenant with Yahweh represented in the image of marriage, but also considering the customary rites of sexual debauchery at the shrines, characterizes this kind of religion as 'whoredom', he thus accomplishes thereby – as does Hosea, who uses the same images – clear separation between the religion of the covenant with Yahweh resting on spiritual-ethical bases and the religious type of such nature worship as originates in and corresponds to Dionysian sensuality; they differ from one another as marriage differs from whoredom. It is the fundamental difference of the distinct point of departure in man's self-understanding: the people seek to understand themselves out of themselves and their nature, the prophet from God and his *Heilsgeschichte*.]

[26] The unusual *'att ṣoʻâ(h) zōnâ(h)* ('you bowed down as a harlot') seems to be a play on words. The word normally used for reverent prostration ($\sqrt{hwh}$) is not employed. The root $\sqrt{ṣ'h}$ instead denotes the act of bending over. *Cf.* the transitive piel, 'to tilt, tip over', in Je. 48:12. The point is that Israel bows down, or bends over, in worship at pagan shrines, and at the same time engages in harlotry. Carroll (1986: 130) suggests, 'The reader's imagination will serve better than a translation.' The NRSV ('you sprawled and played the whore') fails to evoke the scene hinted at by the text. Rudolph (1947: 15) heads his comments on verses 20–28 with the apt rubric, 'Und das nennt sich Jahwedienst!' [And that calls itself the worship of Yahweh!]

metaphors to convey its vision of Yahweh and Israel together. Idolatry, heavily flavoured with sexuality, exposes itself to prophetic attack from this very angle. Now, however, Jeremiah's prophetic imagination spins off the more outlandish figures of the young camel and the wild ass, in verses 23–25. But the animalian images are enfolded within introductory and concluding quotations of self-incrimination by the people which indicate that these figures are subordinated to and intended to put an even more unflattering spin on the harlot metaphor:

> [23]How can you say, 'I am not defiled,
>   I have not gone after the Baals'?
> Look at your way in the valley;
>   know what you have done –
> a restive young camel interlacing her tracks,
>   [24]a wild ass at home in the wilderness,
> in her heat sniffing the wind!
>   Who can restrain her lust?
> None who seek her need weary themselves;
>   in her month they will find her.
> [25]Keep your feet from going unshod
>   and your throat from thirst.
> But you said, 'It is hopeless,
>   for I have loved strangers,
>   and after them I will go' (RSV/NRSV).

When confronted with reproof, the hardened people evade self-examination, as verse 23 reveals.[27] Presumably, they defend and deceive themselves with appeals to their orthodoxy, the Solomonic temple, the functioning Levitical ministries. They perceive themselves as respectable Yahwists, and they resent the prophetic challenges to their integrity. And so Jeremiah 'dissipates the clouds of the hypocrites', under which they conceal themselves in 'supine self-security' (Calvin *Jer–Lam*: I:115).[28]

---

[27] The word order may nuance the people's assertion as follows: 'I have not gone after *the Baals*!'

[28] Grotius, in *Critici Sacri*, *ad loc.*, draws an illuminating parallel: 'Sicut inter Christianos quidam εἰδωλόθυτα manducantes negabant se esse εἰδωλολάτρας, sic et inter Judaeos qui de mensa Daemoniorum participaverant, credi volebant

The prophet brings forth their inconsistent toleration of and even fondness for the Baals. They have attended the pagan observances on 'every high hill' (verse 20) so regularly that they have worn a path in the valley beneath.[29] The prophet points to that well-worn track, marked by their own footprints, and challenges them to acknowledge its obvious meaning. They *have* gone after the defiling Baals.

Jeremiah then combines the idea of travel or movement with that of sexuality to portray the people's flirtations with the Baals in the most graphic terms. Yahweh's defiled wife is, first, a 'restive young camel'[30] running to and fro, doubling back time and again,[31] leaving wildly criss-crossed lines of tracks as she goes frantically after one Baal and then another and yet another, controlled by blind impulse, without a consistent pattern or meaning – apart from the unmeaning of rebellion itself. In real terms, Jeremiah sees the people of God as faddish and insecure, nervously searching the latest offerings from neomania, for they do not grasp the true meaning and abiding claim of the covenant.

Secondly, in verse 24, the harlot of Judah is 'a wild ass', such as roams untamed in the wilderness.[32] Restlessly sniffing for the

---

nihil mali fecisse.' [Just as among Christians certain ones eating foods offered to idols were denying that they were idolaters, so also among the Jews who partook from the table of demons, they wanted to be believed to have done no evil.]

[29] *Cf.* Radak. Alternatively, their 'way in the valley' may refer to their behaviour in a literal valley, *e.g.* Hinnom (*cf.* LXX 'in the graveyard'), where they practised idolatry in gruesome forms. Targum, Rashi and Radak propose Peor as the location.

[30] *Cf.* Is. 60:6. The adjective *qallâ(h)* suggests her skittish readiness to move quickly (*cf.* 2 Sa. 2:18; Is. 30:16; La. 4:19), insinuating Judah's fickle instability. *Cf.* Bailey & Holladay (1968: 256–260).

[31] The frequentative piel participle *mᵉśāreket*, which BDB defines as 'twist', is explained by Radak in connection with *sᵉrôk naʿal*, 'thong of a sandal', in Gn. 14:23, for thongs bind the sandal several times, laced back and forth.

[32] The noun *pereh* (alternative spelling to *pereʾ(ʾ)*, according to Radak) is masculine (Jb. 39:5), with which the adjective *limmud* is consistent. The subsequent references to gender (reading the Qere *napšāh*) clash with this. The discrepancy is tolerated, even exploited, however, as a quiet reminder to the reader of the larger image, behind the more immediate one, of the harlot. The wild ass portrays the harlot directly, and the people of God figure into the equation indirectly as the reality behind that figure. The grammatical problem has a positive exegetical function. Radak's interpretation of the form as epicene (*cf.* GKC § 122 d) explains the text away without illuminating its idiosyncratic expression.

scent of a male, her lust is out of control.[33] The males of the species may spare themselves any effort, for when she is in heat she is the one who initiates the pursuit.[34] The disgusting image of the covenant people driven with an animal craving to be sexually satisfied by someone, anyone, shocks and offends. It was meant to. The people of God are open, even eager, to find new aspects of Baalism to explore and enjoy. They cannot get enough. But they do not realize that, in so doing, they are degrading themselves to the level of the bestial. Yahweh's treasured possession, his kingdom of priests and holy nation of Exodus 19:5–6, has so declined from her uniquely dignifying privileges as to be fit for comparison with a ruttish donkey. Yahwism may seem boring and trite, its potential exhausted and its appeal passé, its scope confining and its tone severe, its priests predictably narrow and its prophets irritatingly strident; but fortunately (in asinine Judah's view) the Baals are always there for relief, spicing up the wearying routine, titillating the senses, offering a more life-related and relevant message, reinvigorating the empty life and granting a reassuring sense of identification with the surrounding nations.

Verse 25 opens with an admonition that the people stop wearying themselves in their pursuit of the Baals, wearing out their shoes and parching their throats.[35] But rather than a realistic appeal for moral amendment, the imperative is a

---

[33] The hapax *ta'ᵃnâ(h)* is misunderstood by LXX as if from √*ntn*. Jerome, connecting it syntactically with the preceding clause, comes closer nevertheless to what must be the sense with *in desiderio animae suae adtraxit ventum amoris sui*. The surrounding clauses conjure up an image of this animal as one eager to mate. If, with Radak (referring to Ex. 21:13), one connects this word with III √*'nh*, as does BDB, then the semantics must hover around the idea of 'encounter opportunely', to use BDB's definition. The referent would then be the animal's season of heat. Holladay (1986: 101) observes, 'If the young camel cannot walk straight, then the female wild ass in heat walks only too straight, so impetuously that one cannot deal with her. Both animals in their different ways are perfect symbols for Israel's tracks to Baal . . .'

[34] *Cf.* Holladay (1986: 102): 'The word to potential mates is, "Relax, you will have your chance!"'

[35] Rashi discerns the irony within the prophet's call when he comments, '*Keep your feet from going unshod.* This is your wont, like the wild ass which loves to wander. My prophets say to you, "Keep yourself from idolatry, lest you go unshod into exile, and keep your neck from dying of thirst."' If they refuse to ease themselves of the burden of Baalism, the deprivations of exile will be forced upon them.

statement of the obvious to highlight the cry of despair in the second half of the verse.[36] What they ought to do is clearly evident. It is even in their own interests. But they are addicted. While verse 23 records the people's denial that they have gone after the Baals, verse 25 complements that denial with their frankly contradictory and pitiably weak confession of acquiescence to that very course.[37] They live at the mercy of their desires; and, with a sigh, they admit it. The people who refused the service of Yahweh (verse 20) discover servitude in Baalism.

What future, then, does Jeremiah's generation of the covenant community have with Yahweh? Is restoration even possible any more? Jeremiah exploits the occasion of a drought to challenge the nation's superficial repentance, in 3:1–3, the second text in chapters 2 – 3 which calls for special attention here. His purpose is to confront the people with the depth of their long-standing involvement in idolatry, a condition which defies easy treatment and jeopardizes their security with God:[38]

> [1]If a man divorces his wife
>   and she goes from him
>   and becomes another man's wife,

[36] Cf. McKane 1972: 88. On p. 87, McKane writes, 'The appeal to Israel in v. 25 is that she should not persist in a fever of activity which is destructive of her well-being, which reduces her to misery and exposes her to extreme dangers. Israel's answer is not a denial that this is so, but an admission that she is impelled by an uncontrollable desire towards the rites of Baal worship.'

[37] Cf. Je. 18:12. Radak paraphrases, 'My heart despairs from walking after God. I will no longer walk after him but after foreigners, for I see that they are successful. I love them, and after them will I go.' Targum connects the foreigners with their idols: 'Because I loved to associate with the nations, so after the worship of their idols will I go.' Weiser (1969: 21) dissects the psychology of the verse in terms of 'ein rätselhaftes, aber gerade in seinem Widerspruch lebenswirkliches Eingeständnis der Macht der Sünde, die allem, was von Gott kommt, das "Umsonst" des Zweifels und das "Nein" des Ungehorsams entgegensetzt!' [. . . a puzzling, but exactly in its contradiction a genuine, confession of the power of sins, which, for everything that comes from God, juxtaposes the 'Futility!' of doubt and the 'No!' of disobedience.]

[38] The lē(')mōr introducing verse 1, relegated to a footnote in both the RSV and NRSV, does not dovetail with the last line of 2:37, as if chapter 3 opened with a continuation of the condemnation of Judah but now in her own words. Radak connects it with 'For the LORD has rejected those in whom you trust' in 2:37. It may be a scrap left from a more formal introductory formula, on the analogy of Hg. 2:11–12. Cf. Fishbane 1985: 307.

will he return to her?
Would not such a land[39] be greatly polluted?
You have played the harlot with many partners;
   and would you return to me?
                                                says the LORD.
[2]Lift up your eyes to the bare heights and see!
   Where have you not been violated?
By the waysides you have sat waiting for them
   like an Arab in the wilderness.
You have polluted the land
   with your vile harlotry.
[3]Therefore the showers have been withheld,
   and the spring rain has not come;
yet you have a harlot's brow,
   you refuse to be ashamed.

   Yahweh reasons with his people. In verse 1, it is as if he unrolls a Torah scroll, locates Deuteronomy 24:1–4, sets it before them and explains its implications for their situation together. 'Think about it,' Yahweh says. 'What if a man follows the divorce law here in Deuteronomy 24 because he discovers after the knot is tied some sexual offence in his wife,[40] they split up, and his ex-wife remarries? Now, is it possible under any circumstances for that man ever to become her husband again?[41] Would not such a

---

[39] With others, McKane (1986: 1:58) emends $hā'āreṣ\ hahî(')$ to $hā'iššâ(h)\ hahî(')$, following the LXX (ἡ γυνὴ ἐκείνη) and the Vulgate (*mulier illa*). This modest emendation has the advantage of postponing the referent, the land (the nation), until its more timely appearance in verse 2. Moreover, the emended text makes clear the inference to be drawn from the legal question set before the people. This way, the application of the law comes with full force in verse 2 rather than prematurely, it would seem, in verse 1. Finally, the emendation has the virtue of providing a smooth transition from the theoretical wife posited in the Deuteronomic law to the woman (personifying the nation) having sex with multiple partners in the last line of verse 1. It is not impossible, however, for the biblical author to move rapidly and unevenly from his premises to his conclusions. Perhaps the Greek translators, followed by Jerome, were smoothing over a tension in the text which was nevertheless authentic. I reluctantly decline what is otherwise a highly attractive emendation.

[40] The '$erwaṭ\ dābār$ of Dt. 24:1 is a crux; but there is little question as to its sexual nature, whatever else may be said about it. Jeremiah assumes this as an essential component part of the overall logic of the case being set forth.

[41] The LXX reverses the roles, with the woman returning to the man. It may have seemed unlikely to the translators that Yahweh would come back to Israel,

violation greatly[42] pollute the land? What does this Deuteronomic law say?'

His questions bristle with disturbing implications. Judah has
belonged not to one other lover but to many, and these
relationships were morally invalid to begin with.[43] Given her
multitude of defiling liaisons, has Yahweh indeed divorced her?
And if so, what hope can there be of restoration to him? Does
not his own law exclude her now and for ever from his covenant
embrace? Yahweh himself insinuates the dreadful conclusion
with a final question: 'And would you return to me?'[44] How
feebly the people grasped the significance of their compromises
with Baalism. To them, it was inconsequential; to Yahweh, it was
inexcusable. Without realizing it, Judah has created an impossible situation, placing herself beyond redemption – at least
within the provisions of the law.

In verse 2, the prophet admonishes, 'If you think Yahweh's
assessment of your condition is unfair, look for yourself. Show
me one cultic site[45] where you have not been debauched!'[46] He

---

especially if, in their view, the verb √šwḇ in this metaphorical context bears
connotations of repentance. But the MT is certainly correct, as it is more
consistent with the language of Dt. 24:4 and raises a more profound question
here in Je. 3. *Cf.* Targum, Vulgate.

[42] The infinite absolute strengthens the passion of the question, according to
GKC § 113 q.

[43] Rashi supplies the preposition, *ad sensum*, commenting, '*With* many lovers'.
The verb √znh is construed with a direct object, without the preposition, also in
Ezk. 16:28.

[44] The force of the infinitive absolute here is paraphrased in GKC § 113 ee as
'and thinkest thou to return again to me?' The interrogative force of this
statement is evident in the connection with the preceding *hᵃyāšûḇ 'ēleyhā 'ôd*
within the logic of the verse as a whole.

[45] Radak interprets the *šᵉpāim* as 'high places, like the lofty mountains and
exalted hills, for thus was the way of idolaters at that time'.

[46] Attempting to read the Kethib. The Qere, 'you have been lain with', shows
the Masoretes' desire to sanitize the public reading of Scripture of indelicate
expressions. Radak names it a euphemism. One sympathizes, however, with the
Masoretes' concern as soon as one contemplates the use of a modern
equivalent to the sense of the Kethib. One ends up searching for one's own
'Qere' reading. The verb √šgl appears only four times in the Hebrew Bible (Dt.
28:30; Is. 13:16; Je. 3:2; Zc. 14:2), having to do with sexual violence (Münster, in
Critici Sacri: 'mulierem humiliare'), in each case concealed behind a Qere
reading with √škb. *Cf.* Ginsburg 1966: 346. If one were to venture a plain
translation, it might be something like 'You have been screwed'; but we find
that wording as problematic for public reading as the rabbis found the Hebrew

compares Israel with a common whore, waiting for customers at a commercial intersection like a Bedouin merchant,[47] available to passers-by.[48] What was raised as a theoretical possibility in verse 1, *viz.* that such behaviour in a marital context would pollute the land morally, is now asserted plainly in verse 2, and Judah is identified as the culprit.[49] She has indeed defiled the land with her harlotry – and that, not as the victim of male whim (such as may be the concern lying behind the law of Deuteronomy 24) but by her own preoccupation with harlotry and evil.[50]

This explains, according to verse 3, why the nation is suffering a drought at the time of this utterance. The Baal rites are worthless. Far from triggering abundant rains, they only antagonize the true Lord of the harvest and draw the curse of sterility down upon the land.[51] Judah has been degrading herself for nothing. And yet she has become so hardened that her heart is impervious to the whispers of love, the deliberations of reason and even the sufferings of affliction. The impertinent wilfulness evident in her national countenance is not for show; it exposes the truth of her soul.[52] She has lost the capacity to reflect, to respond, or even to care.[53]

---

text. In any case, such language implies that the Baals were not gentlemen with Lady Judah.

[47] Radak comments, 'For thus is the way of the Arabs who dwell in the wilderness. They sit for them by the roads, waiting for caravans passing through, to sell to them and to buy from them.' The image of an easy 'pick-up' availing herself at a truck stop may translate it into modern terms.

[48] *Cf.* Gn. 38:13–19; Ezk. 16:25; Pr. 7:12. The ambiguous *lāhem* is amplified by the RSV and NRSV into 'lovers', derived out of the passive *šuggalt* in the preceding line. 'Lovers' is not entirely satisfying, however, in view of the rough treatment that verb implies. Moreover, 'lovers' connotes a reference to the idols, whereas the intended reference here may be to idolaters, as Radak interprets. Perhaps the anonymous *lāhem* is meant to suggest just that, *viz.* the anonymity of those for whom she waits.

[49] Calvin (*Jer–Lam: ad loc.*) comments, 'The Jews were not led away by the enticement of others to violate the conjugal pledge which they had given to God, but were, on the contrary, moved by their own wantonness, so that they of themselves sought base and filthy gratifications.'

[50] The RSV construes *biznûṭayik ûb⁽rā'āṯēk* as hendiadys, while the NRSV ('with your whoring and wickedness') treats each noun as having its own discrete function.

[51] *Cf.* Lv. 26:18–19; Dt. 28:22–23.

[52] *Cf.* Is. 48:4; Ezk. 3:7–8.

[53] The verb √*m'n* construed with an infinitive, but without the preposition *l⁽*, finds analogies in Je. 5:3 and 9:5. Calvin comments, 'The object is to show that

Having wrecked their marriage with Yahweh and gone off to many others, the people may not expect restoration to their first husband. And even if, legally, that were a conceivable possibility, their own continuing brazenness renders their desolation fitting. There is no going back for Jeremiah's generation.

Whatever outward show of repentance the nation might muster in this season of adversity lacks convincing authenticity, as verses 4–5 reveal. It is vitiated by their practical unwillingness to change their lives. And this is not the first time Judah's hypocrisy has neutralized her credibility with Yahweh, as verses 6–10, the third passage calling for attention here, draw out. Even under the leadership of her most courageous reforming king, Judah still did not mean business with God:

> [6]The LORD said to me in the days of King Josiah: 'Have you seen what Apostasy Israel did, how she went up on every high hill and under every green tree, and played the harlot there? [7]And I thought, "After she has done all this she will return to me"; but she did not return, and Betrayal, her sister Judah, saw it. [8]She saw[54] that for all the adulteries of Apostasy Israel I divorced her and gave her a decree of divorce; yet Betrayal, Judah her sister, did not fear, but she too went and played the harlot. [9]Because she took her harlotry so lightly, she polluted the land,[55] committing adultery with stone and tree. [10]Yet for all this Betrayal, her sister Judah, did not return to me with her whole heart, but only in pretence, says the LORD.'

God had from heaven given to the Jews manifest tokens of his displeasure, and yet without any benefit; for they had the front of a harlot and felt no shame; that is, they were moved by no judgments of God and could not bear to be corrected.' Cf. Pr. 30:20

[54] With the RSV and NRSV, I accept the emendation as proposed in *BHS* text footnote 8[a], which the coherence of the passage surely requires. The burden of the passage at this point is not what God saw but what Judah saw and should have learned from. Radak, retaining the MT (of course), must argue that its 'And I saw' is connected logically with 'but only in pretence' at the end of verse 10, making the point that God saw what human eyes could not perceive.

[55] The RSV and NRSV emend the intransitive qal *watteḥᵉnap* to a transitive hiphil because of the object marker in *'eṭ hā'āreṣ*. The hiphil in verse 2 warrants this change.

The days of King Josiah of Judah witnessed aggressive reformation initiated by the king and supported by the people.[56] But the judgment of God still looms over Judah, for, unlike Josiah himself, the people only pretended to repent. Their harlotrous routines remained comfortably intact. Lest the people miss the sharpness of his message, Jeremiah insists that they see the true import of their idolatry and the full extent of its consequences. He does so by putting Judah's national sins against the backdrop of Israel's, continuing with the terms and images of verses 1–3.

In verse 6, the prophetic vision perceives the northern kingdom as apostasy incarnate,[57] frequenting the pagan sites of worship in spiritual harlotry.[58] God was patient, however, according to verse 7. He waited to see whether she would return to him, but she persisted in her course. And her sister-state to the south, Betrayal,[59] observed what Israel was doing even as

---

[56] *Cf.* 2 Ki. 22:1 – 23:30, especially 23:1–3 and 25.

[57] 'That faithless one, Israel' of the RSV and NRSV does not capture the force of *m^ešubâ(h) yiśrā'ēl*, in which the abstract noun does more than merely describe Israel; it identifies her as apostasy itself. Jerome renders it as *aversatrix Israhel. Cf.* Rudolph (1947: 20): 'Israel ist die leibhaftige Abtrünnigkeit.' [Israel is apostasy incarnate.]

[58] Rashi notes that the form *wattiznî* is equivalent to the expected *wattizen*, which appears in verse 8. *Cf.* GKC § 75 ii. Radak regards the yod as in the place of a he', such as occurs at times in the third radical position, citing Dt. 32:18 and Je. 18:23. The participial *hōl^ekâ(h)*, between the *qtl 'āś^eṯâ(h)* and the *wyqtl wattiznî*, refers to action in the past but marks that action as spread out over the course of time.

[59] Functioning much like *m^ešubâ(h)* in verse 6, the indefinite adjective standing before its noun carries substantival force. *Cf.* GKC § 132 b; Gibson § 42, Rem. 1. Again, Jerome draws out the sense with *praevaricatrix soror eius Juda*. The sense of √*bgḏ* is illustrated in verse 20, where a woman betrays her husband. Rashi comments, ' "Betrayal" is harsher than "Apostasy". Israel, since they were the first to become corrupt and did not see punishment, to learn from it and to repent, are called Apostasy. Judah, since they saw that [Israel] went into exile but did not receive correction, is called Betrayal.' Volz (1928: 44) writes, 'Die beiden Reiche erscheinen als Personen, als Schwestern, und haben wie die Kinder einer Familie auch ihre Namen; Israel heißt Meschuba, Juda Bagoda; als Nomina propria ohne Artikel . . . Die Namen sind (wie die der Kinder Hoseas oder Jesajas Hos 1; Jes 7,3; 8,3) symbolisch und stellen den Charakter dar. Schon in den Namen drückt sich aus, daß Juda mehr Schuld hat; בגודה ist schärfer und deutet auf eine niedrige Gesinnung.' [Both kingdoms appear as persons, as sisters, and as the children of a family even have their names. Israel is called Meshuba, Judah Bagoda, as proper names without an article . . . The names are (as those of the children of Hosea or Isaiah – Ho. 1; Is. 7:3; 8:3)

Yahweh also was contemplating it. If Israel was unrepentant, would Judah be instructed, alerted and warned so that she at least might repent?

She had ample opportunity, according to verse 8. She saw all the adulterous provocations[60] which led eventually to Yahweh's divorce from Apostasy. In real terms, this divorce took the form of foreign exile in 722 BC. But Betrayal, looking on at the national pattern of apostasy in the north and its final outcome, remained unmoved.[61] The fear of God never entered her heart even as these events passed before her eyes. Indeed, she repeated the harlotry of her sister.

One might have thought that the very harlotry which sent Apostasy into historical oblivion would have sobered Betrayal with the great consequences hanging in the balance of her national ethos and behaviour. But astonishingly, to Judah spiritual adultery was a casual matter, according to verse 9.[62] Not only did she follow Israel's example in spite of the screaming warning of the exile, she also thought little of doing so. She trivialized her moral character. As a result, the last virgin territory preserving spiritual integrity in this world was finally polluted with the defiling worship of sticks and stones.

Alarmed with the threats of God's law, Josiah did initiate

---

symbolic and represent their nature. Already in the names it is expressed that Judah bears more guilt; בגודה is sharper and points to a base disposition.]

[60] The unusual syntactical contrivance consisting of *'al kol 'oḏôṯ* *"ᵃšer* is paraphrased in GKC § 158 b as 'for this very cause that . . .' The compound connective has the force of emphasizing the numerous occasions of Israel's adultery. The *kî* clause is interrupted, then, until *sillaḥtîhā*, so that the full moral warrant for the divorce may be set forth before the divorce itself is declared.

[61] Radak comments, 'She saw all that Apostasy, Israel, did but did not lay it to heart. What is written lacks the point, but what is not written is discernible from what is written.'

[62] GKC § 112 ss interprets *wᵉhāyâ(h)* as indicating 'a longer or constant continuance in a past state'. How that interpretation inheres in the syntax as syntax seems problematic. More convincingly, Gibson § 84 (b) proposes that this simple waw with *qtl* 'identifies an event as going on at roughly the same time as a previous event'. If this construal is valid, the point is that her frivolous assessment of her covenant bond with Yahweh pervaded and explained (*min*) her life of harlotry, with its dreadful consequences as declared in the rest of verse 9. Radak expounds *qōl*: 'The sense is lightness. And the Masorah [Parva] says of it, "Unique and defective; in the sense of lightness."' Targum paraphrases, 'And it happened that, because her idolatry was trivial in her eyes . . .'

attempts to purify the land of the contaminants of idolatry. And he found a measure of popular co-operation in his efforts. But Jeremiah reveals that, underlying that appearance, a debilitating hypocrisy crippled the inward power that Josiah's outward reforms might otherwise have shown. The people went along with him to some extent, and perhaps their solemn assemblies prompted a kind of dewy-eyed sentimentality toward the nation's venerable religious traditions. But there were no eyes gouged out and no hands chopped off. Betrayal, therefore, refused to repent even as she repented. She thought she could get by with an appearance of repentance, so that she could persist in a life of carnality minimally disturbed, as verse 10 implies.

Therefore, in God's moral calculus Judah is *worse* than Israel, according to verse 11, for she sinned against greater light. And the appeal to Israel in the north, in verses 12–14, calling for repentance with a promise of mercy, is not so much meant to restore a nation already removed from history as it is to reproach Judah by speaking past her, offering her nothing. For Judah, the door of mercy closes.

Beyond Jeremiah 2 – 3, one other passage calls for our attention here. In 13:20–27, the prophet announces that the very one whose friendship Judah has courted will come out of the north to expose her to national humiliation. Her own sinful choices are pulling this judgment down upon her, and she is by now beyond recovery and incapable of repentance. Verses 25–27 conclude the oracle:

> [25]This is your lot,
>> the portion I have measured out to you, says the LORD,
> because you have forgotten me
>> and trusted in lies.
> [26]I myself will lift up your skirts over your face,
>> and your shame will be seen.
> [27]Your adulteries and your neighings, your lewd harlotries
>> on the hills in the countryside –
> I have seen your abominations.
> Woe to you, O Jerusalem!
>> You are unclean.
>> After, how much longer?

According to verse 25, the judgment coming upon Judah is divinely appointed and therefore proportionate, fair and inescapable.[63] She has squandered her inheritance in the land, which she once received as her lot,[64] so that now all she can claim is a place in exile. Yahweh asserts his own will over Judah's statecraft and idolatry. She answers to him alone.

The reason why Yahweh has decided to abandon his people is that they have already abandoned him.[65] Looking over the social landscape, the prophetic eye discovers a scene of massive God-neglect. The people do not include Yahweh meaningfully in the practical reality of their lives, where real faith is tested. Instead, they have staked their lives on the Baals, discarding the reality of God and embracing the unreality of counterfeit gods.[66]

In verse 26, Yahweh intrudes himself abruptly back into Judah's equation of life.[67] He intends the purposeful exposure of her infidelities through the palpable demonstration of his

---

[63] The demonstrative *zeh* presumably refers back to the judgments described in verses 20–22 and 24 rather than forward to what follows. Although verses 26–27 return to the adversities assigned to Judah, their descriptions have the function not of informing the nation of what is coming at them but of juxtaposing Yahweh's sovereign judgment with the clear moral warrant for that divine determination. The very fact that verse 26 repeats the threat of verse 22 suggests that it serves a different purpose. Moreover, verse 25 itself does not develop what the determined punishment is but only that it is answerable to Judah's abuse of God.

[64] *E.g.* Nu. 36:2–3; Jos. 17:14; 18:11. The RSV's and NRSV's 'the portion I have measured out to you' is an acceptable paraphrase of the Hebrew, emphasizing Yahweh as the determiner of what Judah will receive in the course of future providences. Rashi paraphrases the *mᵉnāṭ middayiḵ* as 'the portion of your measures [*heleq middôṭayiḵ*]', implying that *miḏ* does indeed bear the sense of 'measure'. *Cf.* Vulgate.

[65] The *'ᵃšer* linker functions causally. *Cf.* WO'C, 38.4a. Rashi describes the logic of the text as 'measure for measure' punishment. Radak comments, 'With the measure which you have measured I have measured to you. You have forgotten me, and I have forgotten you. You turned your back and not your face to me, and I have hidden my face from you. And you are to be devoured, and many evil sorrows have found you. This is your lot and measure from me.'

[66] *Cf.* Je. 10:14; 16:19. Mesudath David makes explicit what is surely intended by *baššāqer*: 'Because you have forgotten me and have trusted in idols, which are a lie, therefore I too will forget you.'

[67] The introductory *wᵉgam 'ᵃnî*, signalling reciprocal action, does not correspond with *gam 'attem* in verse 23 but rather answers the people's deliberate ignoring of God in 25b with his own self-assertion.

effectual reality.[68] There will be no more ignoring of the word of Yahweh when Babylonian invasion explodes the pleasant lies in which the people have invested their hopes. Baal will avail nothing, and the people's love affair with him will be seen to be the wretched thing that it is – and that, by *Yahweh's* doing.

Verse 27 details *how* Judah has forgotten Yahweh and trusted in a lie.[69] What was it that attracted her confident regard, crowding Yahweh from her heart? Jeremiah heaps term upon term to pour out vituperative condemnation upon all that he loathes in the popular religion of his day.[70] The easy-going Baalism infecting the nation is nothing but the furtive caroming of adultery and the nasal blare of randy horses,[71] together

[68] With the RSV and NSRV, I take the *qtl* verbal forms in verse 26 to function with prophetic certainty and vividness. The figurative language in the verse does not describe a rape of the nation, *pace* some commentators, but rather the public humiliation of being openly confronted with one's wrong. Calvin (*Jer–Lam*: II:197f.) comments, '. . . it is as though a vile woman was condemned to bear the disgrace of being stripped of her garments and exposed to the public, that all might abhor a spectacle so base and disgraceful. God, as we have before seen, assumed the character of a husband to his people; as then he had been so shamefully despised, he now says that he had in readiness the punishment of casting the skirts of his people over their faces, that their reproach or baseness might appear by exposing their uncomely parts.' Judah's humiliation was effected through the agency of the Babylonian conqueror; but Yahweh's purpose here is to draw attention to his own ultimacy behind it all. That purpose does not require him to portray himself as the raping Babylonian soldier; the language rather suggests that he is the indignant husband putting an end to his wife's abuse of him. The burden of the verse lies simply on the shame of exposure, as the disambiguating B line makes plain. The same kind of meaning operates in Na. 3:5. *Cf.* Ezk. 16:35–38; 23:10, 29; Ho. 2:5 [EVV 3]. Human sexuality, while a good creation of a good God, nevertheless, if exposed under certain conditions, violates that delicate sense of dignity instinctive to the human soul.

[69] The RSV and NRSV fail to show that the direct objects of the verb 'I have seen' are front-loaded. 'Your adulteries and your neighings' are together judged to be 'your lewd harlotries', the asyndetic element at the end of the first line. That entire line constitutes the direct object of the eventual 'I have seen'. And the compound direct object is judged again with the supplementary 'your abominations' after the verb. This unusual syntax presumably manifests the emotional intensity of the author.

[70] Calvin (*Jer–Lam*: *ad loc.*) comments, '. . . the prophet, I have no doubt, meant here to wipe off a colour with which the Jews painted themselves; for they said that they intended to worship God, while they accumulated rites which were not prescribed in the law.'

[71] Rashi glosses, 'Like the neighing of adulterous horses.' *Cf.* Je. 5:8.

denounced as 'your lewd harlotries'.[72] What she has paraded out in the open, on the hills in the countryside, and yet without true perception, has not been lost on Yahweh. The clarity of his eye discerns the true inner character of her religious life. He sees it all as detestable 'abominations'.[73]

Jeremiah's passionate distress breaks out in verse 27b with a cry of woe. Jerusalem is filthy beyond cleansing with her idolatries. And in broken cadences difficult to interpret and translate, the tender-hearted prophet agonizes over how much longer she may remain in her degraded condition.[74]

A wounded God and a wounded prophet collaborate to wound the heart of an unresponsive nation. The people do not know who they are or whose they are. The reality of their marital union with Yahweh makes astonishingly little impression on them. The prophet Ezekiel must appear before them, therefore, to stretch the harlot metaphor in new and startling directions.

[72] The 'lewd harlotries' of the RSV is a valid paraphrase for the compound *zimmaṭ zᵉnûṯek*, concerning which Holladay (1986: 416) writes, 'The noun זמה may mean a 'plan' in general but became a technical term in cultic law for indecent conduct, especially of sexual misdeeds . . .' *Cf.* KB, s.v. The emphasis of the construct-genitive chain falls upon 'the *lewdness* of your harlotry', as Jeremiah searches for language to convey the depth of Judah's obscenity.

[73] In Lv. 11:43 the verbal form of √*šqṣ* is coupled with √*ṭm'* (hithpael), 'to defile oneself', in Dt. 7:26 with √*t'ḇ*, 'to abhor', and in Ps. 22:25 [EVV 24] with √*bzh*, 'to despise'. A *šiqqûṣ* is something to be detested as idolatrous in Dt. 29:16 [EVV 17], 2 Ki. 23:13 (concerning Josiah's reforms, and paralleling *šiqqûṣ* with *tô'ēḇâ(h)*, Je. 7:30; Ezk. 7:20; and elsewhere.

[74] The strange collocation *'aḥᵃrê māṭay 'ōḏ* defies interpretation. BDB, *s.v.* *māṭay*, renders it as 'after how long yet?' The phrase consists of the preposition 'after' plus the interrogative adverb 'when?' plus the adverbial 'still, yet'. The sense must have to do with continuance through time, and the middle element turns the whole in an interrogative direction. The apparent incoherence of the collocation may be due to the emotion energizing it, as if the prophet struggled to utter his thoughts with his usual elegance and clarity. Perhaps the sense is 'After [this], how much longer [will you remain unclean]?' Targum paraphrases, 'Woe to you, Jerusalem! You shall not be clean. Until now you have had an extension for many days,' suggesting that Jerusalem has been spared judgment for some time. Radak expands as follows, 'You will not be clean after ('aḥᵃrê) you have been defiled. And if you say that you will be clean, when (māṭay) will it yet ('ōḏ) be, seeing that you will not be clean before you go into exile?' He construes it as a cancellation of their vain hopes for restoration, which is congenial with the force of the pericope as a whole. Rashi draws out the sense by inserting the verb, as if it read, 'After when will you yet be clean?' Both the LXX and Vulgate mistake the unpointed preposition as containing a 1 c s suffix.

Chapter Five

In every public square

The eager readiness of the human heart to welcome affirmation is exceeded only by its quick weariness with sustained confrontation. It is a universal mark of our natural moral imbalance. So, after the sobering messages of Hosea, Isaiah, Micah and Jeremiah, it would be understandable if the follower of the biblical story were to flinch at yet another prophetic encounter. But it is the false prophets who heal the wound of God's people lightly. Their diagnosis is superficial, and their prescription ineffective. The serious reader of the Bible, turning to the true prophets, takes courage from the fact that the biblical drama is not only a story of outrageous betrayal, but also one of costly redemption bringing infinite ecstasy. If prophetic censure takes us down very deep into our present condition, prophetic promise also lifts us up very high into our ultimate destination. With that hope in view, therefore, the story proceeds, resolute in purpose, through Ezekiel's frank exposure of Israel's spiritual whoredom toward the eventual restoration of the covenant community in the New Testament.

Ezekiel 16

The controlling purpose energizing Ezekiel 16 is, according to verse 2, to 'make known to Jerusalem her abominations'.[1] The exiled prophet, writing antecedently to the final downfall of the city, spreads before the people of God a picture of the harlotries which are drawing down upon them a judgment no longer remotely theoretical but now pressingly apparent. He addresses the people with a passionately graphic sermonic

---

[1] The theme of spiritual harlotry is most fully exploited in Ezk. 16 and 23. Forms of $\sqrt{znh}$ for spiritual harlotry also appear in 6:9; 20:30; 43:7 and 9, but without further development.

embellishment of the messages of Hosea and Jeremiah. His prophetic vision corresponds so nearly to the concrete realities of their corporate life that the literal and the figurative at times blend together.

The prophet reviews the nation's history not to mark major events but rather to sting the public conscience with an ugly portrait of their true moral quality,[2] as that is undeniably evident in broad patterns of behaviour through the centuries toward pagan deities and pagan powers. They have demonstrated a consistent bias against Yahweh and have treated his bestowments not as incentives to love him the more but as currency with which they may court the favour of his rivals.

The word of the Lord sets the scene, in verses 3–14, by directing the covenant community's attention to their unpromising origins. They were like an unwanted newborn girl, exposed to die by her pagan parents. Yahweh happened by, rescued her and moved on. Years later he passed that way again only to find the girl now grown into a beautiful young woman, but primitively naked. Yahweh clothed her, married her and lavished upon her extravagant gifts, so that she was much admired by others. All that has exalted Israel as a special nation, all that has dignified her in the eyes of other nations, has been the bestowment of Yahweh, who loved Israel with a covenant generosity not shown to any other people. She owes him everything.

Verses 15–43a then tell the story of Jerusalem's whoredom. Verses 15–34 accuse the people of a harlotry which manifested itself in two forms: idolatry (verses 16–22), and foreign alliances (verses 23–34), while verses 35–43a announce the punishment decreed for them by Yahweh.

> [15]But you trusted in your beauty, and played the harlot because of your fame, and lavished your harlotries on any passer-by. [16]You took some of your garments, and made for yourself patchwork shrines, and on them played the harlot; nothing like this has

---

[2] It would take coarsened sensibilities not to agree with Cooke (1936: 160), who confesses, 'There is much in this chapter which is repulsive to our taste.' Tragically, that was the necessary and appropriate purpose, for Israel's sin was itself repulsive.

ever been or ever shall be. *[17]*You also took your beautiful jewellery of my gold and of my silver, which I had given you, and made for yourself male images, and with them played the harlot; *[18]*and you took your embroidered garments to cover them, and set[3] my oil and my incense before them. *[19]*Also my food which I gave you – I fed you with choice flour and oil and honey – you set it before them as a pleasing aroma; and so it was,[4] says the Lord GOD. *[20]*And you took your sons and your daughters, whom you had borne to me, and these you sacrificed to them to be devoured. Was there too little of your harlotries? *[21]*And you slaughtered my children and delivered them up as an offering to them. *[22]*And in[5] all your abominations and your harlotries you did not remember the days of your youth, when you were naked and bare, flailing about in your blood.

The prophetic eye detects the nation's seminal error in their reliance upon the power of their own beauty, in verse 15. The people twisted their God-given privilege and prosperity into opportunities for immodest self-display.[6] Seduced not by others but by their own love of reputation, charting their national

---

[3] The Kethib *nāṭattî*, if accepted, may yet be 2 f s. *Cf.* GKC § 44 h.

[4] The NRSV's 'and so it was', omitted by the RSV, represents with less than lucid meaning the less than lucid text *wayyehî*. It seems improbable that this reading would have arisen through a mistaken repetition of *nîḥōᵃḥ*. Its very incongruity, but not impossibility, in this place creates the presumption of authenticity. Its exegetical function is a separate and difficult question. Calvin (*Ezek*: II:117f.) proposes, 'Here God takes away all occasion for their turning aside, when he says *it was so*, for we know that men always have various pretences by which they lay the blame on some other parties, or soften it off, or cover it with some disguise. But God here says that there is no occasion for dispute, since the matter is perfectly plain.'

[5] The emendation of *wᵉēṭ* to *zō(')ṭ*, corroborated by the LXX, is attractive because of the ambiguity of the Hebrew. The Vulgate shows a preposition, however. Targum construes the Hebrew as containing two definite direct objects. The preposition *'ēṭ* functions in connection with expressions of cognition in Is. 59:12 and Je. 12:3. This may explain the RSV's/NRSV's rendering, 'And in all your abominations . . . you did not remember . . .'

[6] The preposition in *wattiznî 'al šᵉmēḵ* is causal, which coheres with the idea of trusting in one's beauty in the first clause of the verse and with the general import of verse 14 as well.

course not with the discrimination entailed in loyalty to Yahweh but with recklessly self-assured openness to the flattering attentions of others, the nation's self-admiration drew them into harlotries with all comers.[7] Pride went before their fall.[8]

With a repetitive directness pounding with intensity, in verses 16–21, Yahweh lists the generous gifts which he had bestowed upon his bride and which she in turn parlayed into the worship of other gods, betraying her lawful husband.[9] The beautiful

[7] The gushing enthusiasm of this worldly young woman is suggested by the verb $\sqrt{špk}$ and by her openness to any interested partner ('*any* passer-by'). Fairbairn (1960: 169) renders salient the force of the prophet's accusation: 'Instead of seeking, as in duty bound, to promote [her husband's] credit and renown in the world, [the unfaithful wife] acts rather as if her object were to show how low a place he held in her esteem and how much she preferred others before him.'

[8] The obscure *lô yehî* at the end of verse 15 is handled variously in the Greek tradition, Vaticanus omitting it but Hexaplaric fragments corroborating the currency, if not the meaning, of the Hebrew text. Targum regards the prepositional *lô* as if it were the negative particle *lô(')* and expands the sense into 'But it was not right for you to do so'. Jerome renders *ut eius fieres*, 'so that you became his', which provides *ad sensum* a connective particle and does not match the 3 m s form of the Hebrew verb. Rashi, accepting the MT as a given, glosses, 'And from the time that they desired you, you declared yourself available to them; and to every one who requested your harlotry, his it was.' Radak comments, 'His is your desire and your favour. Like a harlot who offers herself to all, for she does not have enough with the men of her own city so that she offers herself to strangers passing by on the road by her, so you have not had enough with one idol or with two or with three, for "As many as your cities are your gods, O Judah" [Je. 2:28; 11:13]. If any idolater from the nations afar off passes by and an idol is in his hand, your desire would be for it with the result that you would manufacture it in your own land.' If *lô yehî* is authentic, it may be a parenthetical quotation intended to mock Jerusalem's unbounded eagerness to share her beauty and fame with any potential lover passing by: 'Let it be his!' The shortened *yqtl* form may also be equivalent in force to the imperfect. *Cf.* GKC § 109 k.

[9] It seems likely that Ezekiel's florid imagery is meant to conjure up a general recollection of the various privileges of Israel's covenant status. It is not as though one can draw a convincing connection between one aspect of the covenant and, say, Israel's 'beautiful jewellery'. Instead, Ezekiel weaves a general record of the nation's relationship with Yahweh into an elaborate image of a wife lavishly provided for by her doting husband but who returns his kindness by stabbing him in the back with ungrateful treachery and adultery. 'The gift replaces the giver' in the affections of the nation, to quote Zimmerli (1979: 342).

garments he provided for her she sewed into 'patchwork shrines'[10] equipped with a bed for her harlotries (verse 16).[11] Her beautiful jewellery,[12] crafted from Yahweh's personal treasures,[13] she fabricated into metallic images of male deities

[10] The *bāmôṯ ṭᵉluʾôṯ* become εἴδωλα ῥαπτά, 'embroidered idols', in the LXX and *excelsa hinc inde consuta*, 'heights stitched from here and there', in the Vulgate. Rashi explains, 'Covered with striped garments of various kinds of colours.' Radak writes, 'The way of the harlot is to beautify her house and to enlarge it with lovely garments, with colourful garments, in order to attract the heart of whoremongers to gather [them] into her house. The interpretation of *bāmôṯ ṭᵉluʾôṯ* is, "You have made patches [*ṭᵉluʾôṯ*] from garments compounded and large, this one upon that one, until mounds [*bāmôṯ*] were made of them." And those garments were coloured . . . And this is the interpretation of *ṭᵉluʾôṯ*, like "spotted" or "patched", which show variously in each section bright colours, with wool washed black and white or yellow, and so on.' Usage of √*ṭlʾ* in Gn. 30:32–39 and Jos. 9:2 corroborates the view that these tented high places are of a patchwork nature. 2 Ki. 23:7 may allude to their manufacture. The net force of Ezekiel's description is to insult these shrines as bizarre, gaudy concoctions, perhaps attracting popular attention but certainly misusing the elegant materials from which they were made. They are not even tasteful, much less morally legitimate.

[11] *lō(ʾ) ḇāʾôṯ wᵉlō(ʾ) yihyeh* at the end of verse 16 resists interpretation. The LXX's καὶ οὐ μὴ εἰσέλθῃς οὐδὲ μὴ γένηται, 'and you will not enter nor will it come to be', takes a stab at the unpointed Hebrew text, while Jerome's *sicut non est factum neque futurum est*, 'as it was not done nor will be done', offers a more elegant but still, relative to the Hebrew text, a problematic version. Targum's 'not according to that which is fitting and not according to that which is proper' sheds no light on the Hebrew. Rashi comments, 'It was inappropriate for this to happen.' Radak writes, 'High places like these are not coming, that is, they are not about to come and there will be no man or people who will make them like these in abundance.' The interpretative proposal of the RSV and NRSV is presumably premised upon the Vulgate's testimony, perhaps corroborated by the logic of Ex. 10:14; but the structure and vocabulary of that utterance provide an inexact parallel to this one.

[12] The RSV's 'fair jewels' and the NRSV's 'beautiful jewels' might connote precious stones; but these items, whatever they may have been, were of gold and silver. *Cf.* similar language in Gn. 24:53; Ex. 3:22; 11:2; 12:35; Ezk. 16:39; 23:36; Pr. 20:15. Radak connects the prophet's figurative portrait with the literal history of the nation when he comments, 'Out of love for idols they were making from the beautiful objects of silver and gold that they had – they were making from them images, as it says in connection with the event of the calf, "And all the people removed the golden rings which were in their ears" (Ex. 32:3).'

[13] '. . . *my* gold and *my* silver, *which I had given you* . . .' We note with interest the same point reinforced in verse 18 ('my oil and my incense'), 19 ('my bread which I gave you, I fed you'), 20 ('whom you had borne to me') and 21 ('my children').

for harlotrous use (verse 17).[14] The richly woven garments with which Yahweh had adorned his wife she fitted on to her idolatrous images, setting before these manufactured gods objects of devotion intended for her communion with Yahweh (verse 18). The fine foods[15] which he had given her she offered to her male images – offerings which had the especially perverse feature of mimicking worship truly pleasing to Yahweh[16] (verse 19).

Yahweh then thunders his most damning accusation in verses 20–21, *viz.* his wife sacrificed his very children to be devoured in the rites of idol worship.[17] And when he demands, 'Was there too little of your harlotries?', his reproach implies the superlatively hideous nature of this final betrayal.[18] Not even the

[14] Unless the prophet intends the reader to imagine actual phallic devices used for sexual self-play, the harlotry in this case functions as a figure within a figure, the male images being male idols such as Baal. But Ezekiel chooses his language in such a way that a more disgusting possibility is hinted at, conveying his utter revulsion at the nation's idolatry. He *hates* the Baal images as things with which the wife of Yahweh has degraded herself. Radak identifies them as images of Baal and interprets the reference as figurative for 'the way of harlots, who make male images for an object of sexual intercourse'.

[15] The generic *laḥmî* is explicated by the appositional *sōleṭ wāšemen ûḏ*e*baš*, in turn followed by a relative clause *he*e*ḵaltîḵ* without the connective *'*a*šer*, which does appear in the preceding relative clause modifying *laḥmî*. The appositional phrase is added to show the superior quality of Yahweh's provision for his people and therefore the wickedness of their own ingratitude and abuse. The entire syntactical structure suspended from *w*e*laḥmî* is a *casus pendens*, resumed in the suffix in *ûn*e*ṭaṭṭîhû* in the main clause.

[16] The phrase *l*e*rê*a*ḥ nîḥō*a*ḥ* alludes to the propitiatory aroma offered to Yahweh, *e.g.* Lv. 1:9.

[17] With boldly marital language, Yahweh claims the paternity of the children of the nation: 'whom you had borne *to me . . . my* children . . .' The uses of $\sqrt{zbḥ}$ (20), $\sqrt{šḥṭ}$ (21) and hiphil $\sqrt{'br}$ (21) indicate that the children's being 'devoured' took the form of religious ritual. The use of $\sqrt{'br}$ may suggest Molech worship, 'by fire' to be supplied mentally – which indeed is included in the RSV. *Cf.* 2 Ki. 16:3; 17:17; 21:6; 23:10; Ezk. 20:31. Radak makes explicit the connection with Molech worship, 'a more severe worship than others'. Cooke (1936: 169) suggests the mentality of the times: '. . . in the desperate days before the capture of Jerusalem, a revival of deep-seated superstitions took place; ordinary sacrifices were unavailing; the only hope seemed to lie in a more powerful and costly kind of offering.'

[18] The RSV construes *ham'aṭ mittaznuṯāyiḵ* (Qere) as an interrogative bridge into verse 21, the force of which is to put the wife's child-abuse into perspective as even worse in her husband's eyes than her harlotries: 'Were your harlotries so small a matter that you slaughtered my children . . .?' The NRSV agrees with that logic but not with that syntax, rendering the clause as an exclamation: 'As if

children escaped her raging lusts, as she sank to the level of Canaanite paganism. But because she had trivialized her previous harlotries, she could not see or feel the degraded enormity of the child-sacrifice she eventually dared to commit.

Finally, in verse 22, running his finger down the whole list, as it were, Yahweh emphasizes the shockingly thoughtless ingratitude underlying Israel's entire history of abominations and harlotries. Had the people pondered their former helplessness and destitution, they would perhaps have moderated their impulses. But as it was, overflowing with Yahweh-given luxury, forgetful Israel heaped devotion upon the idols. They received the grace of God in vain.[19]

The nation's harlotries also took the form of entanglements with foreign powers, a *de facto* denial of Yahweh as Israel's all-

---

your whorings were not enough!' Both the LXX's awkward ὡς μικρὰ ἐξεπόρνευσας ('As trifling things did you fornicate!') and Jerome's *numquid parva est fornicatio tua* ('Your fornication is small?!') do not quite represent the force of the Hebrew. Targum paraphrases with 'Was your error a small thing in your eyes?' Other uses of interrogative $m^e{}^c at$ + *min* + object (Nu. 16:9; Jb. 15:11; Is. 7:13; Ezk. 34:18) favour the sense, 'Was there too little of your harlotries?' That is, 'Did you feel that your harlotries were so small a thing that you added the sin of child-sacrifice?' The question is asked in incredulity and reproach.

[19] Fairbairn (1960: 170) opens up the inner spiritual reality operative here: 'It may possibly appear as if the picture were somewhat overdrawn, when Israel is represented as courting the attention of those foul divinities, and, for that purpose, turning to account her beautiful ornaments and stores of plenty. But a deep truth lies at the bottom of this representation. For what were the false gods in question but the personification of those carnal desires and affections which the good things so amply poured into Israel's lot had but served to feed? Deified human nature in its manifold varieties of lust and earthliness? So that their zeal in worshipping such gods, and lavishing on them costly tokens of their regard, very much resolves itself into an anxiety to have the countenance of Heaven upon the gratification of their own grovelling and earthly propensities. And hence it was that, when replenished with a fulness of worldly comforts, Israel so naturally preferred the worship of idols to that of Jehovah, and, like a treacherous spouse, breaking loose from the holy restraints of wedlock, yielded themselves to the service of these impure rivals; for thus they could give freer play to the corrupt affections of nature. Their conduct in this was simply an example of the native effect of the world upon the heart, according to the circumstances of the time; and when our Lord, speaking for all times, sets before us the prodigal son, selfishly coveting his portion of goods, and going to spend them in alienation from his father's house, he but presents us with another exhibition, differently modified, of the same great truth. Let the heart of nature be fed to the full with gifts, and there will never fail to appear, in one form or another, the idolatry of self and the world.'

sufficient resource for life. Her culpable rejection of him is presented in vivid and provocative language, in verses 23–34. The burden of verses 23–29 is the unashamedly public display of her harlotry:[20]

> [23]And after all your wickedness (woe, woe to you! says the Lord GOD), [24]you built yourself a platform, and made yourself a lofty place in every public square; [25]at the head of every street you built your lofty place and prostituted your beauty, spreading your legs[21] to any passer-by, and multiplying your harlotry. [26]You also played the harlot with the Egyptians, your neighbours large of flesh, multiplying your harlotry, to provoke me to anger. [27]Behold, therefore, I stretched out my hand against you, and diminished your allotted portion, and delivered you to the desire of your enemies, the daughters of the Philistines, who were ashamed of your lewd behaviour. [28]You played the harlot also with the Assyrians, because you were insatiable; you played the harlot with them, and still you were not satisfied. [29]You multiplied your harlotry also with Chaldea, the land of merchants; and even with this you were not satisfied.

The introductory clause of verse 23 links this section with the preceding one. Before moving on, however, Lord Yahweh casts an eye back at the wickedness exposed in verses 15–22 and

---

[20] Eichrodt (1970: 208) explains how foreign alliances and idolatry were not unrelated developments: '. . . the political self-abandonment of the people of God . . . would well be likened to the immodest self-abandonment of a harlot, seeing that such political manoeuvring always worked in favour of importing the state-cult of the great power concerned and other foreign religious customs, and thus infringed the exclusive right of the covenant God.'

[21] It is exegetically arbitrary and unnecessarily fastidious to efface the plain sense of *watt᷄paśś᷄qî 'et raglayik*, as do both the RSV and NRSV ('offering yourself'). Euphemism evades the graphic portrayal deliberately chosen by the prophet for its offensiveness. If one accepts in principle the figure of harlotry as a legitimate prophetic metaphor, then the entailments must also be accepted. Rashi is plain-speaking: 'As he compares her to a harlot, he speaks with the language of sexual intercourse, for [in intercourse] there is a spreading of the legs.' The AV translates, 'Thou . . . hast opened thy feet to every one that passed by.'

thunders a double 'woe'. Intruded into the flow of verses 23–24, this utterance reveals the vehemence of Yahweh's accusations and the certainty of the nation's doom. Their guilt is not forgotten as the story progresses; it is compounded.

In addition to idolatrous harlotry, Jerusalem's apostasy led to open political harlotry as well. The covenanted nation made conspicuous[22] their availability to such political intercourse with other nations as violated the prerogatives of Yahweh (verses 24–25).[23] A nationwide mentality, taking for granted the political 'realism' of soliciting the protection of foreign powers, was the

[22] The prophet notes her 'platforms' and 'lofty places' in all the public squares. The *geb* (or *gāb* in other manuscripts) which she built has been variously interpreted. The LXX reads οἴκημα πορνικόν ('whore house'), and the Vulgate *lupanar* ('brothel'). Targum suggests 'heathen altars'. Rashi interprets it as 'a height, in the sense of a pedestal or an altar'. Radak wisely observes that the verse is repetitious, the *geb* and the *rāmâ(h)* functioning analogously. He interprets both as altars. The word is used in Ezk. 43:13 of the 'height' of the altar there, in Ps. 129:3 of a man's back, and variously elsewhere. The etymological sense offered by BDB is 'be curved, convex, elevated'. The RSV's 'vaulted chamber' overinterprets the word, while the NRSV's 'platform' strikes a persuasive balance by suggesting the idea of height while allowing for ambiguity as to the precise nature of the building. The structure of the verse favours this judgment. As Radak noted, the two clauses repeat one another, drawing *geb* and *rāmâ(h)* into close semantic proximity, with *bᵉkol rᵉḥôb* modifying both verbal clauses. The fact that the first clause of verse 25 refers again to the *rāmâ(h)* but omits the *geb* corroborates their identification. The discrete force of that clause is to emphasize the nationwide extent of their sin ('at the head of every street') rather than to imply a contrast between the *geb* and the *rāmâ(h)*. As for the latter, it may be a play upon *bāmâ(h)*, 'high place', but the political nature of the sin in view here renders that word less apt. The prophet's image is that of a house of prostitution, not a shrine.

[23] Calvin (*Ezek: ad loc.*) comments, '. . . the Jews were condemned not only for vitiating the worship of God by their perverse fictions, but for flying, now to the Egyptians, now to the Assyrians, and thus involving themselves in unlawful covenants. It is a very common method with the Prophets to call such covenants fornications; for as a wife ought to lie under the shadow of her husband, so God wished the Jews to be content under his protection. But as soon as any danger frightened them, they fled tremblingly to either Egypt, Assyria, or Chaldea. We see, then, that they had in some sense renounced God's help, since they could not rest under his protection, but were hurried hither and thither by vague impulse . . . when the Lord placed the people in the land of Canaan on the condition of defending them there, of protecting them on all sides, and of opposing all their foes, we see them enclosed, as it were, by his protection, so as to render all treaties useless, since they could not treat with either the Egyptians or the Assyrians without at the same time withdrawing themselves from God's aid.'

moral equivalent to a popular franchise network of bordellos on the high street of every Judean village. 'Cinderella' prostituted the beauty of her status as holy to Yahweh,[24] returning to him as many harlotries as privileges he had bestowed.[25]

Yahweh specifies the Egyptians, 'large of flesh',[26] as the first[27] among the passers-by to whom his wife spread her legs and thereby multiplied her harlotry to provoke him to anger (verse 26). In response, Yahweh disciplined her with adverse providences, so that she suffered economic and political loss[28] at the hands of the opportunistic Philistines[29] and failed to fulfill her potential as possessor of the promised land (verse 27). The pagan Philistines, however, blushing at Israel's lewdness,[30] would not have had the nerve to sin as boldly as

[24] Targum paraphrases, 'You desecrated your holiness.'

[25] The 'multiplying' of Israel's harlotries in verse 25 corresponds to the multiple bestowments of her gracious husband in verses 8–14.

[26] The RSV and NRSV render $\check{s}^e\underline{k}\bar{e}nayi\underline{k}$ $gi\underline{d}l\hat{e}$ $\underline{b}\bar{a}\check{s}\bar{a}r$ as 'your lustful neighbours'. But the text should be allowed to speak its own language rather than be muted by an understandable but unnecessary reticence. Rashi glosses, 'possessors of a [large] sexual organ'. Radak comments, 'The sexual organ he calls flesh; "his flesh flows or his flesh stops" [Lv. 15:3]. And thus it says concerning the Egyptians, "whose flesh was the flesh of donkeys" [Ezk. 23:20].' Cooke (1936: 170) calls this 'a coarse fling at the power of Egypt'.

[27] Verse 26 shows verbal $\sqrt{znh}$ construed with the preposition 'el followed by the 'sons of Egypt', verse 28 the same syntax with 'the sons of Assyria', and verse 29 the heighened element of verbal $\sqrt{rbh}$ with the nominal object $taznu\underline{t}$ followed by the rest of the equation concerning the Babylonians. This threefold registration of international partners suggests that Israel's whoredom was a persistent pattern compromising the integrity of her foreign policy.

[28] The noun $h\bar{o}q$ is used in the sense of a certain allowance or ration of food in Gn. 47:22 and Pr. 30:8. Radak comments, 'The allotted portion of your food, which I gave you – the fine flour and oil and honey – I diminished it and took it from you.' Cooke (1936: 170f.) comments, 'It may well be that the prophet refers to what happened in 701 B.C., at the time of the Assyrian invasion, as Sennacherib records it: "his [Hezekiah's] cities which I had plundered I separated from his land, and gave them to Mitinti king of Ashdod, Padi king of Ekron, and Silbel king of Gaza, and diminished his land".' Cf. ANET: 288.

[29] Targum interprets the 'daughters' of the Philistines as their villages, quoted approvingly by Radak. Grotius, in Critici Sacri (1698 edn), explains, 'Femininum nomen usurpat, ut melius continuet allegoriam.' [He uses a feminine noun, better to render the allegory coherent.]

[30] The syntax of middarkē̱k zimmâ(h) at the end of verse 27 is explained by GKC § 131 r as a case of apposition in which the second, defining noun functions as a kind of adverbial accusative. They paraphrase, 'of thy conduct in lewdness'. It

Israel did. But still, even with Yahweh's hand actively warning and opposing her, Israel did not restrain her desires.

Addicted to ever more harlotries, the people of God turned eastward to whore, secondly, with the Assyrians (verse 28).[31] The repetitious nature of the verse emphasizes that, even after their harlotry with the Egyptians and the Assyrians, their nymphomaniacal desire was still not sated.[32] Israel sought the Assyrians because their liaison with the Egyptians left them unsatisfied (28a); then, even after their affair with the Assyrians, they still craved for more (28b). They never got out of their system an eagerness for conformist submission to unlawful allegiances. They never came to the point of declaring their distaste for the tawdriness of it all.

In verse 29, Yahweh declares that Israel 'multiplied their harlotry', thirdly, with the Babylonians, perhaps partly motivated by a meretricious commercial incentive in this case.[33] Like an unquenchable appetite, their whoredom was a long-standing, aggressive social trend out of all control.[34]

---

may, however, more simply mean 'of thy conduct [which is] lewdness'. *Cf.* Gibson § 39, Rem 1.

[31] The *min* prefix in *mibbiltî soḇ'atēk* is causal, and the pronominal suffix is a subjective genitive. *Cf.* Rashi; Joüon § 170 i.

[32] *BHS* proposes that the pronominal suffix in *wattiznîm* be omitted; but that would dull the point, for the antecedent Assyrians must reappear here for the prophet's message to carry its full force. It is not just that Israel committed harlotry; it is that they did this with the Egyptians, and then with the Assyrians, and even then (*wᵉgam* signalling emphatic climax in the sentence) they still wanted more. *Cf.* verse 29. Radak suggests that *wattiznîm* is the equivalent to *wattiznî 'immām.*

[33] Rashi comments on *'el 'ereṣ kᵉna'an kaśdîmâ(h)*, 'To me it seems that "Canaan" is like "trader", like "a merchant [kᵉna'an] in whose hand is a deceptive scale" (Ho. 12:8 [EVV 7]), for thus he calls the land of the Chaldeans a land of traders, as it is said *infra*, "And he brought it to a land of merchants [kᵉna'an], and set it in a city of traffickers" (Ezk. 17:4).' The appositional *kaśdîmâ(h)* epexegetes the potentially ambiguous *'ereṣ kᵉna'an.*

[34] Three times in the paragraph (verses 25, 26 and 29) Yahweh accuses the nation of 'multiplying her harlotries'. Calvin (*Ezek. ad loc.*) comments, 'The sum of the whole is, that the Jews were seized with such a furious impulse that they manifested no moderation in their wickedness. For they had not revolted from God once only, or in one direction, but wherever occasion offered, they were accustomed to seize it too eagerly, so that they showed in this way that not even a drop of piety remained in their minds. Let us learn then from this passage to put the bridle on our lusts in time; for when the fire is lighted up, it is not easily extinguished, and the devil is always supplying wood or adding oil to the

But neither the chastisement of God (verse 27) nor the unprofitability of her foreign allegiances (verses 30–34) could turn Israel back from trifling herself away:

> [30]How sick is your heart, says the Lord GOD, that you did all these things, the deeds of a brazen harlot; [31]building your platform at the head of every street, and making your lofty place in every public square. Yet you were not like a harlot, because you scorned payment.[35] [32]Adulterous wife, who receives strangers instead of her husband! [33]To all harlots gifts are given; but you gave your gifts to all your lovers, bribing them to come to you from all around for your harlotries. [34]So you were different from other women in your harlotries: no one solicited you to play the harlot; and you gave payment, while no payment was given to you; you were different.

The anguished cry of verse 30 declares the unpleasant truth about Israel's moral condition and identifies the inner source of the behaviour portrayed in verses 15–29. (Verse 31a summarizes the more immediate context in verses 23–29.) Her national soul

---

furnace, as the phrase is. Let us then prevent the evil which is here condemned in the Jews, and let us restrain ourselves, lest the devil seize upon us with insane fury.' No Christian is so wilfully undiscerning, although perhaps inventive of sophisticated rationalizations, as the one determined to win the favour of the Christ-denying world. Restraint and self-awareness are crushed under the drive to conform.

[35] I accept the textual emendation proposed in *BHS* at 16:31[a]. Rashi's gloss shows how obvious the sense must be, whether one emends the text to conform to conventional morphology or allows for an unconventional form. Radak maintains that the plural ending is attested in the infinitive; *cf.* Chomsky (1952: § 78 c). The other textual proposal, however, at 16:31[b], is less convincing. 'To collect' payment is sensible, and for that very reason it renders banal the prophet's more trenchant accusation. Here is a harlot who not only declines to collect payment; she despises payment. She not only refuses it in practice; this high-minded whore rejects it in principle. Wonderfully absurd, and true to life. The verb $\sqrt{qls}$ is used in the sense of 'despise, mock, scoff at' in 2 Ki. 2:23; Ezk. 22:5 and Hab. 1:10. Radak, in both his commentary and his *Book of Roots, s.v.* $\sqrt{qls}$, interprets the word as an expression of contempt, despising. The infinitive with l^e functions epexegetically, explaining *how* Israel is not like a harlot. *Cf.* WO'C 36.2.3e.

is sick.[36] Only that can explain how she has gone so far as a brazen harlot.[37] And yet here is prostitution with a difference – a whore who refuses payment (verse 31). Verse 32 briefly interrupts the development of the paragraph's primary thrust while the prophetic voice pauses in sorrow to lament how things stand, flavouring the accusations with shock and grief. The woman reducing herself to this low level is in fact married and provided for. Israel's national disgrace is entirely unnecessary. She commits adultery not because Yahweh has failed her but for the thrill of it.[38] She sins for the sake of sinning. Verse 33 resumes the thought that, customarily, harlots are paid for their services. But not Israel. She bribes men to come to her. She gives all and gets nothing. A common whore at least has the incentive of monetary gain for submitting herself to degradation. But here is a harlot who seeks no advantage for herself. Compelled by appetite alone, she has no motivation but sheer desire. If she gains nothing, she does not care. She is glad to be possessed for its own sake. Uncommon harlotry (verse 34)![39] The kingdom of priests and holy nation, God's own possession, *did* distinguish

---

[36] The LXX and Vulgate are confused at *mâ(h) ʾamulâ(h) libbāṭēk*. Targum's 'How powerful was the wickedness of your heart!' is at least identifiable as a rendering of the Hebrew tradition. Ibn Janaḥ defines the sense of the adjective as 'weakened'. Rashi glosses, 'Morally degenerate, like "the feeble Jews" (Ne. 3:34 [EVV 4:2]) and like "for I am feeble" (Ps. 6:3 [EVV 2]).' The RSV and NRSV read 'sick', presumably on the analogy of Arabic *malla*, 'to be wearied, feverish'. *Cf.* KB, *s.v.* II.√'*ml*. The unusual *libbâ(h)* may be 'a feminine by-form of לב', according to Zimmerli (1979: 328); *cf.* Rashi.

[37] The strong-willed determination of the harlot is made plain with the adjective *šallāṭet*, from √*šlṭ*, 'to domineer'. The LXX misreads the root, but Jerome captures the sense with *opera mulieris meretricis et procacis*. Targum reads, 'like the deeds of a woman, a female prostitute, who has control within herself'. Rashi explains, 'For her evil desire is powerful over her'; but, more aptly, Radak comments, 'The deeds which you did were deeds of a harlot, who is domineering within herself, so that she does all that she wants.' Zimmerli (1979: 328) translates the phrase as 'arch-harlot'. Thus the prophet sums up his evaluation of all of her behaviour narrated thus far.

[38] Mezudath David comments, 'You are an authentic adulteress, who commits adultery out of a love for adultery.'

[39] Zimmerli (1979: 349) captures the power of the paragraph: 'Another redactor of the prophet's school has noted in vv 30–34 how senseless this sinful disobedience towards the Creator appears in the eyes of natural man, even though the people themselves do not notice this. In its blindness it sacrifices its possessions even where others, calculating more soberly, expect to be paid. Thus it is even more despised by them. The world in fact would have to

herself from other nations – by out-debauching herself, compared with them,[40] into a 'caricature of subhuman vileness' (Eichrodt 1970: 212).

Yahweh's beloved has antagonized him to such an extent that his jealous anger stirs him to act with redemptive punishment, according to verses 35–43a. He will orchestrate events in such a way as to turn against Israel the very nations she has made love with, shaming her before them, so that she turns from her disgraceful course:

[35]Therefore, O harlot, hear the word of the LORD: [36]Thus says the Lord GOD, Because your lust was poured out[41] and your nakedness uncovered in your

---

question whether it had ever seen anything like the disgraceful disobedience of the people of God and shake its head in incomprehension. The perverseness of God's people in acting in their own way had become something completely strange in the world's history, even to worldly eyes – *corruptio optimi pessima.*' Fairbairn (1985: 171) applies the warning to the church: '. . . the cutting remark is brought in, that none of these nations followed her – the treacherous and wanton dealing was all on Israel's part – she conceded everything to them, they yielded back nothing in return to her – her wickedness was gratuitous and unrequited folly. A solemn and pregnant truth, which the Church of God should never forget. She loses all, and the world gains all, when she foolishly stoops to impair the testimony of God, or adjust the claims and services of religion to the tastes and practices of the carnal mind. A nominal advance or apparent reconciliation may possibly be achieved by the manoeuvre, but it can be no more than nominal and apparent; the interests that really profit by such a policy are those of the flesh and the world. It is only when the Church is faithful to her testimony – when she stands in the truth of Christ, and in that truth shines forth "bright as the sun, clear as the moon," that she is found also, in her conflict with evil, "terrible as an army with banners."'

[40] Interestingly, the text assumes, for the sake of argument, the understandability, if not the legitimacy, of ordinary prostitution, in order to show how far Israel has gone. The conspicuous noun *ḥepek* appearing at the beginning and the end of the verse to accent its importance, makes explicit the author's interest in the 'unnatural inversion of the human order' (Zimmerli 1979: 329) illustrated by the history of Israel. The RSV's 'no one solicited you to play the harlot' for *weaḥᵃrayik lō(') zûnnâ(h)* may be a fair paraphrase of the force of the unusual Hebrew clause. But the sense may also be (more literally), 'and after you harlotry was not committed', that is, 'Following your pattern of harlotry, there has never been another case like yours.' The point then goes beyond Israel's solicitation of her lovers – an accusation already levelled – by establishing her behaviour as the extreme of harlotry. *Cf.* Targum, Rashi, Radak.

[41] The RSV's 'your shame was laid bare' assumes the emendation of *ḥiššāpēk* to *ḥospēk*, perhaps corroborated by Targum. This reading also assumes an

harlotries with your lovers, and because of all your abominable idols, and because of[42] the blood of your children that you gave to them, [37]therefore, behold, I will gather all your lovers with whom you took pleasure, all those you loved and all those you loathed; I will gather them against you from all around, and will uncover your nakedness to them, so that they may see all your nakedness. [38]And I will judge you as women who commit adultery and shed blood are judged, and bring upon you the blood of wrath and jealousy. [39]And I will give you into the hand of your lovers, and they shall throw down your platform and break down your lofty places; and they shall strip you of your clothes and take your beautiful jewellery, and leave you naked and bare. [40]They shall bring up a mob against you, and they shall stone you and cut you to pieces with their swords. [41]And they shall burn your houses and execute judgments upon you in the sight of many women; I will make you stop playing the harlot, and you shall also make no more payments. [42]So will I satisfy my fury on you, and my jealousy shall turn away from you; I will be calm, and will be angry no longer. [43]Because you have not remembered the days of your youth, but have enraged me with all these things; therefore, behold, I

---

interpretation of the etymologically problematic $n^e\dot{h}u\check{s}t\bar{e}k$ in close semantic alignment with 'your nakedness was uncovered'. This is not unreasonable. The LXX reads 'you poured out your copper', and the Vulgate, 'your copper was poured out' – both of which witness to the authenticity of the MT's √*špk* but also give the appearance of guesswork in their rendering of $n^e\dot{h}u\check{s}t\bar{e}k$ in this context. Rashi interprets the latter as 'lower part', on the analogy of Mishnaic $n^e\dot{h}\hat{o}\check{s}e\underline{t}$, 'bottom (of a stove)'. He paraphrases the resultant sense ('Your bottom was poured out') as 'From a greatness of desire for harlotry, your "fountain" flowed', hinting perhaps at discharge from a venereal disease. Radak also interprets the word as 'bottom', that is, female genitalia, which this woman showed to all. He interprets the sense of niphal √*špk* here as 'uncovered, visible'. Clearly, the sense may be construed in various ways. The NRSV's 'your lust was poured out' has the virtue of working from the received text with an arguable interpretation of $n^e\dot{h}u\check{s}t\bar{e}k$ in this sexually oriented context.

[42] The causal sense evident in the RSV and NRSV implies the emendation of the MT's $w^e\underline{k}idm\hat{e}\ \underline{b}\bar{a}nayi\underline{k}$ to $\hat{u}\underline{b}idm\hat{e}\ \underline{b}\bar{a}nayi\underline{k}$, as noted in BHS 16:36[f]. The traditional reading is not, however, impossible, as it correlates their shedding of the children's blood with their own coming miseries. Cf. Rashi (who glosses with ובעון דמי בניך (דמי בניך)), Radak.

have returned your deeds upon your head,[43] says the
Lord GOD.

Verse 35 announces a divinely decreed consequence accruing
from Israel's harlotry. The moral warrants for the punishment,
which have already been set forth in lurid detail, are summar-
ized in verse 36. The reasons given are her unrestrained lust
poured out in shameful self-display with her lovers, her many
abominable idols,[44] and the bloody child-sacrifices which she
offered the idols. Verses 37–41 pronounce the sentence of
punishment, mingling literal with figurative portrayals of her
afflictions.[45] Yahweh is gathering against his wife all whom she
had formerly admired and trusted, so that he may shame her
before them with punishments due to a wife guilty of adultery
and murder. Yahweh's wrath and jealousy will compel him to
deliver his covenanted people over to invading armies to be
plundered and savaged,[46] bringing their harlotries to an end

---

[43] The unusual particle $h\bar{e}(')$, attested otherwise only in Gn. 47:23 and
interpreted here by the LXX as ἰδού, reappears in post-biblical Hebrew
meaning 'Behold!' *Cf.* Segal 1958: § 304. Rashi glosses, 'Like *hinneh.*' The
heavily marked $w^egam\ ^{'a}n\hat{i}\ h\bar{e}(')$ followed by the direct object, a prepositional
phrase and finally the verb labours to draw attention to each word with
atomically weighted force and solemnity.

[44] The foully detestable character of the idols is insinuated by the doubly
pejorative Ezekielian $gill\hat{u}l\hat{e}\ t\hat{o}^{'a}b\hat{o}tayik$. On the former term, see Zimmerli 1979:
187. The filthiness of the idols lies at the heart of the prophetic reproach.

[45] Eichrodt (1970: 209) comments, 'The punishment is that usual in ancient
law, but behind it stands God himself. It is he who gathers the lovers to the trial,
he who reveals the shame of the adulterous wife, he who sees that she is
condemned to suffer the legal penalty for her adultery. In choosing this woman
to be his wife he was not amusing himself, but fully committing himself to put
his love into effect by founding a community, within which it was his will to
enter into an intimate relationship with his people, and through it with all
mankind. So the retribution demanded by such light-hearted disregard of his
unheard-of graciousness is not merely a chilly withdrawal, nor yet a penalty
enforced according to the letter of the law independently of any inward feeling,
but a solemn act of calling to account, carried out in a fit of blazing indignation,
to bring about a realization of what a grave thing it is to put his holy will to
shame, and at the same time to show how seriously he takes his human partner.'

[46] The ambiguous $\hat{u}n^e tatt\hat{i}k\ dam\ h\bar{e}m\hat{a}(h)\ w^eqin'\hat{a}(h)$ at the end of verse 38 may
be intentionally so, implying that Yahweh's wrath and jealousy are operative in
the invaders' fury. *Cf.* Rashi with Radak. Stienstra (1993: 151) argues, 'If YHWH
were not upset, unhappy, jealous and angry on account of His wife's behaviour,
the metaphor would utterly fail. Even if the main idea of the metaphor, as it is

before a watching world.[47] Verse 42 assures the people that there will be an end to their miseries when Yahweh's holy anger, finally assuaged, no longer burns against them. And verse 43 summarizes the moral logic of the whole: Israel's unthinking ingratitude, her trivializing of his gracious bestowments, her discontented itch for the world's favour, has enraged Yahweh, prompting him to initiate a measure-for-measure requital upon her head.[48] The sentence is just.

The remainder of the chapter, verses 43b–63, continues the female personification of Jerusalem but takes it in a different direction. Jerusalem has two sisters, Samaria and Sodom. But 'evangelical' Jerusalem has sunk so low that she makes 'liberal' Samaria and 'pagan' Sodom look good by comparison. Given all the grace Yahweh has extended to her, therefore, how could he refuse it to her sisters? All three will ultimately be restored. And self-righteous Jerusalem will never again look down with scorn on morally 'inferior' Samaria and Sodom, for she will see herself in a true light. She did not earn or deserve Yahweh's favour in her pathetic infancy, and neither can she claim it now. It was freely given then; it will be freely given again, and she will finally view herself not with pride (verse 15) but with shame (verse 63).

---

developed by various prophets, is to show up the unfaithfulness, ingratitude and disobedience of the people of Israel with respect to YHWH, there is no way in which the metaphor could be successful, if YHWH were unmoved by the behaviour of His wife. The punishment He inflicts on her is not just retribution in order to do justice, the judgment He passes is not the balanced pronouncement of an impartial, uninvolved judge. YHWH is the husband who has been betrayed in His love for His wife, and His feelings are accordingly human.'

[47] Targum paraphrases 'in the sight of many women' in verse 41 with 'in the sight of many countries'. Radak, quoting Targum, glosses, 'That is, the men of the countries; but he calls the countries women in keeping with the parable.' Calvin (*Ezek. ad loc.*) comments, 'He understands the neighbouring people under the name of women . . . This is very bitter, when not only we must perish, but the cruelty of enemies must be satiated while many behold us.'

[48] Israel reveals her nakedness in seduction (36), for which Yahweh reveals her nakedness in shame (37). She bribed her lovers to come to her for romance (33), for which Yahweh gathers them for violence (37, 39–41). She slaughtered Yahweh's children for her idols (20–21), for which bloodshed she will answer to Yahweh (36). The platforms and high places she built for her open prostitution (24–25, 31) her ex-lovers will destroy (39). She used her beautiful jewellery for idolatry (17), for which her ex-lovers will take it away (39). She will be cruelly returned to the primitive crudity in which Yahweh had first found her and from which he had raised her (7, 39).

117

Ezekiel 23

Ezekiel 23 strikes a note similar to the conclusion to chapter 16. Jerusalem has manifested comparatively deeper moral depravity, calling for greater reproach. She fully deserves the cup of doom being forced to her lips. Samaria, which at this moment in history no longer exists as such, is brought into the picture primarily as a foil to Jerusalem. It is Jerusalem's exceeding harlotries which the prophet insists upon. As in chapter 16, one would be wrong to seek one-for-one correspondence between textual detail and historical reality. The passage offers a large and imaginative prophetic vision of the covenanted people in their actual (as opposed to their professed) relationship with Yahweh, reworking their history into an extended tale of harlotry so as to pronounce moral evaluation rather than narrate events in chronological succession. But unlike chapter 16, this prophetic word bears down upon the people of God with not a single syllable of consolation or hope.

The prophet sees in the eventual historical character of both north and south a moral stain which can be traced back to their remotest national origins without material change. They have been marked by spiritual harlotry from the beginning. The depth of their whoredom never allowed for a honeymoon of purity to offer their husband Yahweh, while the full extent of their readiness for sinful entanglements has been unveiled by the centuries of debauchery since that time. All along, they have been governed not by covenant principle and constancy toward Yahweh but by a burning lust for harlotrous alliances with foreign powers, Jerusalem's grovelling dependencies being the more opprobrious.

Verses 1–4 introduce the *dramatis personae* of the parable:

> [1]The word of the LORD came to me: [2]'Son of man, there were two women, the daughters of one mother; [3]they played the harlot in Egypt; they played the harlot in their youth; there their breasts were caressed, and there their virgin bosoms were fondled. [4]Oholah was the name of the elder and Oholibah the name of her sister. They became mine, and they bore sons and daughters. As for their names, Oholah is Samaria, and Oholibah is Jerusalem.'

Israel learned early the pleasures to be had in seductive approaches by foreigners. The prophet's anachronistic identification of two Israelite national entities in Egypt, albeit united in their origins,[49] resembles the imaginative portrayal by a political cartoonist of a public figure in his childhood but with adult features for immediate recognition. But the portrait would also insinuate an underlying continuity between the child and the adult with regard to the issue at point, as here. The eventual politics of Israel and Judah only made visible the promiscuity within the nation's soul active from its beginning. To the prophetic eye, what later emerged as two adulterous kingdoms is clearly discernible already in Egypt, when as girls they began their careers of easy availability for casual sex.[50] They had always hankered after debased and debasing pleasures. But still, Yahweh graciously took the sisters to be his wives and raised up children by them.[51]

[49] The 'one mother' represents their shared family line. Rashi explains, 'The two of them from one nation were divided in two in the days of Rehoboam.' Radak comments, 'He compares the unified nation to a mother. And when they were divided, they were sisters. In Egypt they were one assembly, and thus until the kingdom of the house of David was divided.' Radak does not allow for Ezekiel's more radical analysis of the nation's moral history, however.

[50] Verse 3a makes clear that they 'played the harlot' in Egypt; 3b describes mere foreplay, suggesting their first experiences with harlotry and their unresisting loss of virginity.

[51] Strikingly, the same prophet who beheld an astonishing vision of Yahweh in his mysterious otherness (chapter 1) also dares to present Yahweh as a husband with two wives, having children by each. Targum expunges the anthropomorphic imagery with, 'And they were serving before me, and they prospered with sons and daughters' – which may identify the referent but does not really interpret the language. Such language as this has prompted some to posit a traceable connection between the vision of Yahweh as the husband of Israel and similar motifs in pagan mythology, e.g. MacLaurin 1964: 15. This line of reasoning explains nothing, however, for the exegete, and is ultimately as evasive and unsatisfying in its own way as is Targum's circumlocutory expedient. The most authentic explanation of this theology in general is to be found in the Old Testament's own historicized thought-world, and the most convincing key to this verse in particular lies in Je. 3:6–11. Ezekiel's interest here is the consanguinity of the two kingdoms and their covenantal bond with Yahweh, on account of which privilege they grew in numbers and strength. In using metaphorical language, the prophet expects the reader to select from all the possible entailments of the metaphor only those which are consistent with his known assumptions and appropriate to his contextual purpose. It would be unfair to the author for the reader to pour every conceivable entailment into

The sisters' names hint at the most conspicuous feature in
their national identity, *viz.* their relationship with Yahweh, as his
nearness to his people is made institutionally incarnate. The
similarity between the girls' names causes the reader immediately to expect that one may find closely twin moral characters in
these two. The difference between the names offers a complementary nuance. 'Oholah' connotes the northern kingdom's
defiant religious autonomy, while 'Oholibah' affirms the southern kingdom's privileged religious authenticity[52] – which, when
betrayed, makes Oholibah all the more culpable.

Verses 5–10 narrate the history of the big sister, Oholah:

> 5'Oholah played the harlot while she was mine; and
> she lusted after her lovers the Assyrians, warriors
> 6clothed in blue, governors and commanders, all of

the author's language, heedless of his theological parameters and local
intention. Moreover, the chaste language of this verse contrasts markedly with
the explicit imagery in Canaanite mythology, *e.g.* Gibson 1978: 123–127. The
very modesty of Ezekiel's language shows how strictly limited his intention is,
while the graphic detail of the Ugaritic myth shows how unrestrained its
theology is willing to be. Even if – *if* – Yahweh's marital relationship with Israel
derived ultimately from pagan concepts, still, it was disciplined severely by the
inner logic of Yahwism itself. Eichrodt (1970: 322f.) observes, 'There is not a
single hint of goddesses with whom a divine husband enters into wedlock. The
whole stress is laid upon two female figures which personify two kingdoms
clearly defined politically, which are chosen by Yahweh to be his instruments
and owe everything to him, but which fail to do their duty.' Rather than corrupt
the biblical vision of Yahweh, this language enhances one's sense of his
personal love and generous care for his people.

[52] Unlike 'Not My People' of Ho. 1:9 and other prophetic names, these
symbolic names should probably not be interpreted in English explicitly as
'[She has] her [own] tent' and 'My tent [is] in her' – that is, the tent of
meeting. The lack of the mappiq in each creates the presumption that the
names are not intended to translate directly into predications. But still, the
outward form of the names cannot but imply a deeper meaning in each,
especially in a passage which depends for its effectiveness upon the suggestive
value of symbols, thereby inviting the reader to scrutinize the text for subtle
messages. Radak comments, 'And the interpretation of Oholah is "the tent
which is hers"; I had no share in it; and they are the calves which Jeroboam
made. And Oholibah is Jerusalem; that is to say that "my tent is in her"; and
there I am dwelling, for in her is the sanctuary, which is the dwelling place of
my glory.' If the names *as names* are incidental to the message of the text, then
why are they provided at all? The sisters could easily have been identified
merely as Samaria and Jerusalem without this distracting complication. It
invites interpretation.

them desirable young men, mounted horsemen. ⁷She
bestowed her harlotries upon them, the choicest men
of Assyria all of them; and she defiled herself with all
the idols of everyone for whom she lusted. ⁸She did
not give up her harlotries which she had practised
since Egypt; for in her youth men had lain with her
and fondled her virgin bosom and poured out their
lust upon her. ⁹Therefore I delivered her into the
hands of her lovers, into the hands of the Assyrians, for
whom she lusted. ¹⁰These uncovered her nakedness;
her sons and her daughters they seized; and her they
slew with the sword; and she became a byword among
women, when judgment had been executed upon her.'

Rejecting the loving protection of her divine husband,
Oholah was attracted[53] to Assyria's military élite, according to
verses 5–6, like a naïve girl love-struck by a group of gallant
young officers.[54] A preference for impressive-appearing foreigners rather than contentment with Yahweh lay at the root of her
harlotry.[55] Awed by Assyria's imperial power and drawn toward it
by her own worldly heart, her political leanings predisposed her
as well to accept with an insufficiently radical critique the idols
of the Assyrians, according to verse 7. And verse 8 makes the
point that her history showed no evidence of improvement or
amendment subsequent to her early experiences. She never did
learn. Therefore, according to verses 9–10, God set in motion

[53] Rashi glosses *watta'gab* as 'And she desired'. Radak, *Book of Roots*, s.v., defines
the meaning as 'to be stirred up with desire and love'. In his commentary he
writes, 'And my revered father [Joseph Kimchi], of blessed memory, wrote that
all [usage] found with this expression is in the sense of harlotrous desire;
therefore, they were licentious.'

[54] The RSV and NRSV are almost certainly correct to interpret *qᵉrôbîm* at the
end of verse 5 as 'warriors', rather than as the appositional adjective 'near', in
view of the military description of these men in verse 6 and the presumed
cognate *qᵉrāb*, 'battle'.

[55] One notes with interest that the outward appearance is all that the prophet
describes, presumably because that is all that Oholah thinks of, demonstrating
a superficiality unworthy of a covenanted nation. This surface-level perspective
blinds her to the terrible potential Assyria represents, which will appear all too
really in verses 9–10 after it is too late. One also notes that the prophet
dismissively declines to interact with any of her professed rationales for her
alliances with the Assyrians; he only declares his total condemnation of her
insecure desire for Assyria's favour.

his law of Fearful Symmetry, whereby the morally necessary but consciously unintended consequences revert to the offender.[56] The very ones Oholah lusted after did indeed come to her, but with violent intent.[57] One envisions a breathless Oholah eagerly awaiting her sexy Assyrian boyfriends, only to be raped by them when they arrive. Tragic, gullible Israel – now the topic of ridicule among the nations.[58]

Witnessing her northern sister's catastrophe, little sister Oholibah had reason to take solemn warning. But, sinning against greater light, against obvious self-interest, she outdid her sister in fawning sycophancy before foreign powers, according to verses 11–21:

> [11]'Her sister Oholibah saw this, yet she was more corrupt than she in her lusting and in her harlotries, which were worse than the harlotries of her sister. [12]She lusted after the Assyrians, governors and commanders, warriors clothed in full armour, mounted horsemen, all of them desirable young men. [13]And I saw that she was defiled; they both took the same way. [14]But she carried her harlotries further; she saw male figures carved on the wall, images of the Chaldeans portrayed in vermilion, [15]with belts around their waists, with flowing turbans on their heads, all of them looking like officers – a picture of Babylonians whose native land

[56] Zimmerli (1979: 489f.) observes wisely, 'God needs no angel from heaven; he judges men through that which they have chosen for themselves in their own godless love.' The objects of Israel's misplaced confidence God turned into the agents of her own ruin. Truly, God is not mocked.

[57] Eichrodt (1970: 324) helps one to enter into the real-life referent: 'Cool calculations on the relativities of political power cause disregard of Yahweh's claim to exclusive possession. Not only has Assyria the best expectations of a promising future, but that also holds out a hope of the overthrow of dangerous neighbours like Damascus. A price must be paid, however, for this self-surrender; the great king makes vassals who are disloyal feel how ruthless his vengeance can be. Or, expressed in allegorical terms, the earlier lovers make the harlot pay for the faithless way in which she has jilted them. The judgment executed upon her gives a picture of the bloody overthrow of Samaria, the punishment of her leaders, the deportation of her inhabitants, and her removal from the category of politically independent nations.'

[58] Targum interprets accurately when it renders, 'And she was a byword for the nations.' Rashi listens in, as it were, to the comments: 'See what has arisen for Mrs So-and-So because of her lewdness!' Contrast Ezk. 16:14.

was Chaldea. [16]When she saw them she lusted after them, and sent messengers to them in Chaldea. [17]And the Babylonians came to her into the bed of love, and they defiled her with their lust; and after she defiled herself with them, she turned from them in disgust. [18]When she carried on her harlotries so openly and flaunted her nakedness, I turned in disgust from her, as I had turned from her sister. [19]Yet she increased her harlotries, remembering the days of her youth, when she played the harlot in the land of Egypt. [20]And she lusted after their paramours, whose flesh was the flesh of donkeys and whose emission was the emission of horses. [21]Thus you longed for the lewdness of your youth, when the Egyptians fondled your bosom and caressed your young breasts.'[59]

The burden of the oracle as a whole is the greater guilt of Jerusalem, which now unfolds before the reader in both plain declaration (verse 11) and subsequent narrative (verses 12–21). But *how* did Oholibah's harlotries exceed those of her sister? The prophet declares a threefold indictment.[60] First, in verses 12–13, Jerusalem followed the same faithless and humiliating path of flirting with the Assyrians, and even for the same reason, *viz.* their outward pomp. The language of verse 12 closely resembles that of verses 5–6.[61] This is not a pedantic, post-Ezekielian scribal intrusion but a purposeful insisting upon the

---

[59] The RSV and NRSV appear to emend the problematic *ba'sôt mimmiṣrayim daddayik l^ema'an* to *b^e'aśśôt miṣrayim daddayik l^ema'ēk*, which are likely necessary reconstructions of a more meaningful and authentic text.

[60] One notes the charge in verse 11 that Oholibah's harlotries were worse than those of her sister, and then in verse 14 that she carried her harlotries further and finally in verse 19 that she increased her harlotries.

[61] The one significant difference is *l^ebuśê miklôl* in 12 versus *l^ebuśê t^ekēlet* in 6. The parallelism leads one to expect in *miklôl* a reference to colour, but the root I √kll does not favour that interpretation. The phrase appears again in Ezk. 38:4, but with the same ambiguity as here. The 'full armour' of the RSV and NRSV is a guess, based upon the sense of the root, and may be accurate. But one can sympathize as well with the AV's 'clothed most gorgeously', taking *miklôl* in the sense of 'completion, perfection'. The LXX reads ἐνδεδυκότας εὐπάρυφα, 'clothed with fine garments', and the Vulgate *indutis veste varia*, 'clothed with variegated clothing'. Interestingly, Targum renders both quite similarly with 'clothed to perfection', as if *t^ekēlet* were also from I √kll. Radak glosses, 'With all kinds of beautiful clothing.'

point that Oholibah repeated the folly of Oholah, as the end of verse 13 makes clear, even though she had seen with her eyes the disastrous consequences of foreign defilement.

Secondly, in verses 14–18, Jerusalem shared her harlotries with the Babylonians. The prophet emphasizes the striking fact that Oholibah became involved with them through an absurd kind of emotional attachment. It was a case of love at first sight[62] – with bas reliefs.[63] Like a teenage girl fantasizing in rapturous love with a movie star projected on the screen who neither knows her nor would care if he did, Oholibah's affections were kindled by something not only inferior to the glory of Yahweh but even one step removed from literal human reality. Again, it is the appearance of dashing magnificence that captures the fancy of her shallow personality (verses 14–15). Roused to desire[64] by this striking display of virile manhood wielding awesome military power, she invites the Babylonians to be her lovers; but they prove loathsome, she feels degraded and her emotions swing from infatuation to disgust (verses 16–17).[65] Observing the brazen openness of her harlotries, her husband finds in his heart a reaction not dissimilar to her own loathing (verse 18).[66] But this does not evoke his sympathy. It presages

[62] In verse 16, $l^{e}mar'\bar{e}(h)$ $'\hat{e}neyh\bar{a}$ is included to emphasize that it was the very sight, the look, which enflamed her lust. Radak comments, 'As soon as she saw them, she lusted after them; and this is why it says, "At the sight of her eyes."'

[63] Rashi comments, '"She carried her harlotries further" by being seized with desire for images which she had not seen [in living reality] but [only] their likeness engraved on the wall.' The sort of thing envisaged is illustrated in Du Ry (1969: 101, 106–108) – although those particular specimens happen to be Assyrian in provenance.

[64] According to GKC § 48 d, the longer, cohortative-like form of the $yqtl$ 3 f s in the Qere of verse 16 and the text of verse 20 stands 'without any effect on the meaning'.

[65] In real terms, Judah solicits the favour of the aggressive, up-and-coming Neo-Babylonian empire. But their protections become as oppressive as the Assyrians' had been, and 'disillusionment took the place of overconfident expectations', according to Eichrodt (1970: 326). He also proposes that this political policy may have been accompanied at a popular level by 'a craze for everything foreign' (p. 325) in the lifestyles of the Jerusalemite aristocracy. Changing with the times in all the wrong ways, Judah happily shed her watchman mentality for a cosmopolitan image.

[66] Radak comments on 'I turned in disgust from her': 'That is to say, I removed my Shekinah from her, so that she was free for the king of Babylon, her lover.'

her doom, for her husband sees what she does not see. She perceives the Babylonians as disgusting, but she does not see that she bears the same contemptible guilt for which Oholah has already suffered. Given the history of the north, Yahweh would be wrong not to judge the south.

Thirdly, in verse 19–21, oblivious to self-discovery and impervious to self-reproach, Oholibah returns to the vomit of her earliest harlotries with the Egyptians,[67] who are infamous for their lasciviousness. The text, uncensored by squeamish sensibilities, portrays this scene: the royal wife of Yahweh – Yahweh, the human form seated on the throne in Ezekiel 1:26ff., of gleaming bronze, like the appearance of fire with a brightness round about him like a colourful bow – the glorious Yahweh is forsaken by his wife whose cravings drive her to Egypt. For what? For a repulsive caricature of womanish, sybaritic lechers[68] with gigantic penises overflowing with semen.[69] One need not ask, What is wrong with this picture? No subtlety is intended.[70]

One conclusion is inescapable: she is incorrigible. She has never learned, and she never will. She will *never* be faithful to her husband. Covenant loyalty is alien to her soul. So, mercy accomplishes nothing. Judah's privileges are pearls cast before swine. She has never been crucified to the world and the world to her.[71] What really compels her is vulgar, worldly spectacle, not the sublimity of Yahweh's all-sufficiency.

[67] The RSV and NRSV inexplicably read '*her* paramours' for *pilagšêhem*. The antecedent to the pronominal suffix, however, is doubtless implied in the reference to 'Egypt' at the end of verse 19.

[68] Egypt's 'paramours' in verse 20 are, literally, '[male] concubines', for the word *pilegeš* is used uniformly elsewhere for a female concubine, but the description above is otherwise male. The word here may be 'a defamatory heightening of מאהבים', to quote Zimmerli (1979: 487). This choice of terms suggests in these persons nothing even of the glamour offered by Oholibah's eastern lovers. '[Male] concubines' connotes instead a perverse mingling of male with female characteristics in a person identified primarily by easy sexual availability.

[69] Rashi explains that the 'flesh' of verse 20 is 'the sex organ' and that 'emission' is 'the spouting forth of seed'.

[70] I apologize to the reader, if offence is taken from this exposition. I sympathize. But my exposition represents what the text of Scripture either states or implies, and my conscience is bound to the text – as sacred as it is shocking.

[71] Zimmerli (1979: 489) observes, 'The community is remorselessly faced with its crime in which it has, from the very beginning, repeatedly given its love to

Judah's consecutive pro-Assyrian, then pro-Babylonian and
then pro-Egyptian policies, playing one overlord off against
another as expediency directs, have consistently demonstrated
her cynical disregard for Yahweh as her rightful husband. That
attitude is now confronted, in verses 22–35, Yahweh's declaration of recompense in four movements:

> [22]Therefore, O Oholibah, thus says the Lord GOD:
> 'Behold, I will rouse against you your lovers from
> whom you turned in disgust, and I will bring them
> against you from every side: [23]the Babylonians and all
> the Chaldeans, Pekod and Shoa and Koa, and all the
> Assyrians with them,[72] desirable young men, governors
> and commanders all of them, officers and warriors,[73]
> all of them riding on horses. [24]And they shall come
> against you from the north[74] with chariots and wagons
> and a host of peoples; they shall set themselves against
> you on every side with buckler, shield, and helmet, and
> I will commit the judgment to them, and they shall
> judge you according to their judgments. [25]And I will
> direct my jealousy against you, that they may deal with
> you in fury. They shall cut off your nose and your ears,
> and your survivors shall fall by the sword. They shall
> seize your sons and your daughters, and your survivors
> shall be devoured by fire. [26]They shall also strip you of
> your clothes and take your beautiful jewellery. [27]Thus I

---

what has a reputation on earth because it is resplendent with weapons and
appears to be youthful and vital.'

[72]Joüon § 103 j explains that in Ezekiel, and elsewhere, the form of the
preposition 'et was at times mistaken for the marker of the definite direct object,
as one observes here and in verses 25 and 29.

[73]The RSV and NRSV have emended ûqᵉrûîm to ûqᵉrôbîm in verse 23, favoured
by the coherence of the passage, despite the fact that the LXX, Targum and
Vulgate all assume the traditional Hebrew text as Vorlage. Cf. verses 5–6, 12.

[74]The MT hōṣen does not savour of authenticity. The RSV and NRSV have
followed the LXX's ἀπὸ βορρᾶ in emending to miṣṣāpôn, 'from the north', the
direction from which Mesopotamian invaders would probably come. Cf. Ezk.
26:7. Jerome reads instructi curru, 'equipped with chariotry', for hōṣen reḵeḇ.
Targum suggests '(with) implements of war', Rashi 'the surroundings of
camps', Radak 'the name of one kind of chariot' or, preferring to follow
Targum, 'a weapon of war', noting this word's uniqueness in the Bible.
Everyone is guessing.

will put an end to your lewdness and your harlotry
brought from the land of Egypt; you shall not lift up
your eyes to them or remember Egypt any more.'

First, according to verses 22–27, Oholibah will look again
upon her darling cavaliers, but this time in dread.[75] They will
march against her with all their impressive power in full display,
and Yahweh will stand aside to let them have their way. Indeed,
rather than punish her by the humane standards of his own
covenant household, he will give her up to the barbaric savagery
of her lovers' foreign customs.[76] Having sinned as a pagan, she
will suffer as one. And while she is being mutilated, stripped,
plundered, and her children murdered by the gleeful victors,
verse 25a prepares her to feel the very jealousy of Yahweh
himself in every lash of the whip and every slice of the knife. Her
agonies will not be meaningless or accidental but unambiguous
acts of God effected through human agency. Only this extremity
of misery will suffice to cure her of her craving for the harlotries
of Egypt, where it all began, as verse 27 declares.[77]

[75] The alliance of Babylonians, Chaldeans and Assyrians shows that Judah's
past will come back to haunt her. But the addition of the heretofore
unmentioned forces of Pekod, Shoa and Koa intimates that opportunistic
minor players, like vultures, will also take advantage of the situation to exploit
fallen Judah.
[76] Verse 24 removes from every Judahite heart any lingering hope for
mitigating mercy. Not only will Jerusalem fall, but the people will be abandoned
to the whimsy of their conquerors who have never been ennobled by the
restraint which distinguishes the Mosaic law. Eichrodt (1961: I:78f.) writes, 'A
further very noteworthy characteristic of Israelite law is *the abolition of gross
brutality* in the punishment of the guilty. Not only is the rule "one crime, one
punishment" accepted, whereas the Assyrian law, for example, provides for a
wide range of physical and monetary penalties, but there is an absence of those
pernicious bodily mutilations so general elsewhere, such as the cutting off of
the hands, the cropping of the nose or ears, the plucking out of the tongue,
branding, cutting off the breasts. In the Code of Hammurabi such mutilations
are not at all uncommon; while in the Assyrian law from the period c. 1100 B.C.,
that is to say some hundred years after Moses, they are multiplied in the most
repulsive manner.' (Italics his.)
[77] Eichrodt (1970: 330) draws out the fuller significance of the reference to
Egypt: 'The kingdom of the Nile is not the dark background against which
Israel's slavery and her liberation by Yahweh shines out brightly, providing the
people as it were with a halo as the object of divine election. She is the tempter,
whom Israel was only too ready to welcome, who deprived her right from the
beginning not only of her natural innocence but also of the further honour

²⁸For thus says the Lord GOD: 'Behold, I will deliver you into the hands of those whom you hate, into the hands of those from whom you turned in disgust; ²⁹and they shall deal with you in hatred, and take away all the fruit of your labour, and leave you naked and bare, and the nakedness of your harlotries shall be exposed.⁷⁸ Your lewdness and your harlotries ³⁰have brought⁷⁹ this upon you, when you played the harlot after the nations, because you polluted yourself with their idols. ³¹You have gone the way of your sister; therefore, I will put her cup into your hand.'

The second oracle of doom, in verses 28–31, abandons Oholibah to her former lovers – 'those whom you [now] hate',⁸⁰ and who will 'deal with you in hatred'. Having become disillusioned with her foreign allies, she will not be able to walk away from them, come back to Yahweh and be received as if nothing had happened. He will give his adulterous wife over to her ex-lovers, so that her desire (to expose herself) becomes her fate (as they strip her naked). The land will be denuded by her marauding enemies, making it obvious that her gamble on their affections was a huge miscalculation. And what verses 29b–30 insist upon is that her final demise is not due to her failure with foreign powers but rather to her very success. No honing of the skills of statecraft could have averted her downfall; the whole effort was wrong to begin with. It was, to Yahweh, 'lewdness and harlotries'. Only that can explain what she must now suffer.

---

imparted to her by God. So recollection of the times of bondage is also recollection of shame and scandal and brings to light a general similarity with her present condition; the history of salvation is transformed into a history of ever-increasing dishonour and loss of self-respect and self-exposure to shame.'

⁷⁸ Joüon § 150 k allows that feminine singular forms are at times suppressed in favour of the masculine, although wᵉniglâ(h) is not listed as a possible illustration of this pattern. BHS considers the necessity of emendation to the 3 f s form probable. Zimmerli (1979: 476), however, considers the extant form a participle.

⁷⁹ Zimmerli, ibid., calls the infinitive absolute 'a vocalization of embarrassment' due to the mistaken division of the verse. He would emend to a qtl 3 c p form, which may be the wisest course. The Masoretic form is acknowledged, however, as functional in GKC § 113 f; Joüon § 123 w; Gibson § 103, Rem. 2.

⁸⁰ The relative marker functions 'independently'. Cf. WO'C 19.1d; GKC § 138 e.

Deep in her national soul, she has loved the paganism which the foreign nations had to offer,[81] as her older sister had done. As a result, the cup of sorrow passes now to her as well.

The third oracle, in verses 32–34, exploits and develops the image of the cup in verse 31:

> [32]Thus says the Lord GOD:
> 'You shall drink your sister's cup,
>   deep and large;
> it shall be for laughter and derision,
>   for it contains much;
> [33]you will be filled with drunkenness and sorrow.
> A cup of horror and desolation,
>   is the cup of your sister Samaria;
> [34]you shall drink it and drain it out,
>   and gnaw its sherds,
>   and tear out your breasts;
> for I have spoken, says the Lord GOD.'

The prophetic message rises to a level of extreme torment and devastation as the literary form rises to poetry. Layer upon layer, each additional misery compounds Jerusalem's suffering. The cup of divine wrath[82] which Oholah has already drunk is

---

[81] *Pace* the RSV and NRSV, it seems to me more forthcoming to construe *biznôtēk* in 30 as temporal and *'al '^{a}šer* as causal. The temporal clause reinforces that her 'lewdness and harlotries' were made manifest in her politics; and the causal clause in turn exposes to view the underlying reason for her compromising foreign policy, *viz.* she had become contaminated with their idols. The more profound defection, therefore, was religious, and the political grew out of that. Fairbairn (1960: 255) comments, 'The spirit of heathenish idolatry, situated as Israel was, naturally led to the copying after heathenish manners and the forming of heathenish alliances; and with every step taken in the one direction, the other was sure to follow.'

[82] The image is that of a cup filled to the brim with a powerful potion, to make the one who drinks it reel with an exaggerated drunkenness. Yahweh holds this cup in his hand and forces it to the lips of the nation to be judged. It represents, in real terms, the breakdown of order, the loss of control and good judgment, the panic and disarray, as a nation staggers like a drunk toward divinely ordained destruction. *Cf.* Ps. 75:9 [EVV 8]; Is. 51:17; Je. 25:15–16, 28; 51:7; La. 4:21; Hab. 2:16. The figure makes vividly clear to the Judahites 'the compulsion there is to accept destiny, the impossibility of rejecting it, the trepidation at its death-dealing effects, the bitterness of the suffering it involves, and how it has to be tasted to the full', to quote Eichrodt (1970: 331).

now set before Oholibah. It is filled, deep and large, with more than enough to leave her blind drunk, weaving, staggering, reeling in sorrow, horror and desolation, which provides a kind of perverse amusement for the watching world.[83] Judah will drink it dry, every last drop of 'the most unsparing visitations of wrath' (Fairbairn 1960: 257), imbibing the fullness and finality of Yahweh's abandonment with sufferings beyond all limit. Mad with pain, she will gnaw at the sherds of the empty, broken cup[84] and frantically tear at her own breasts in raging self-injury. Thus, Jerusalem, who deceived herself with pleasant assurances that 'It can't happen here', will find that she is no exception to the law of God. What held for Samaria holds no less for Jerusalem, with unutterably terrible reality.

Verse 35 contains the fourth and final oracle of doom:

> 'Therefore thus says the Lord GOD: Because you have forgotten me and cast me behind your back, therefore you also – bear the consequences of your lewdness and your harlotries!'

The verse summarizes and concludes the section by presenting Oholibah's apostasy with two new metaphors.[85] In her

---

[83] The RSV reads as if *tihyeh* were 2 f s: 'You shall be laughed at and held in derision.' So the NRSV: 'You shall be scorned and derided.' The phrase as a whole does not appear in the LXX but it is found in the Vulgate and Targum. It could be a parenthetical aside with a 3 f s form, 'She will be scorned and derided.' But the most satisfactory interpretation may be that of Radak, who comments, '*tihyeh*: The interpretation is that the cup will be for laughter and derision. The interpretation is that the nations will laugh at and deride the great punishment coming upon you' – taking the *kôs*, which the adjectives '*ᵃmuqqâ(h)* and *rᵉḥābâ(h)* mark as feminine, as the understood subject of *tihyeh*. The burden of distinctiveness, of standing alone with Yahweh, proved unbearable for emotionally immature Judah, who sought the acceptance and approval of the nations. But rather than the comforts of inclusion, she found oppression and ultimately derision.

[84] Radak comments, 'You will break the cup with your teeth to drain out its sherds.' The RSV reads, 'and pluck out your hair', based upon the Syriac version, noting the sense of the MT in the margin. The Hebrew text is both the more arresting and the more coherent with the immediate context, however, with its vision of an insane Oholibah not only drinking the cup dry but biting it to pieces and sucking on the sherds for the very last drops of the drink.

[85] *lāḵēn* heads the verse as an indication that a final conclusion is now to be drawn from the above. The moral warrants for the utterance of judgment are

lewdness and harlotries she has 'forgotten' Yahweh and 'cast [him] behind [her] back'. She has rejected him by a conscious, deliberate choice,[86] preferring to order her corporate life by standards other than those entailed in his law.[87] She therefore stands without excuse.[88] Yahweh and all he represents was presumably an embarrassment to Judah's pride, an impediment to the realization of her ambitions. Her selective Yahwism, retaining all that was comforting and conveniently 'forgetting' all that was contrary to carnal preference, will bear the consequences.[89] Reality is not optional. Even when Judah chose to disregard Yahweh, he was still there.

Finally, verses 36–49 summon the priest-prophet to adjudicate the offences of the two kingdoms, north and south, continuing the metaphor of the two sisters. Verses 36–45 rehearse the people's sins, while verses 46–49 insist that the punishment ordained will bring their lewdness to an end and Yahweh will be vindicated in their eyes. The emphasis of this concluding section lies upon the people coming to terms with God's judgment as a righteous judgment. The aim here is not restoration, for Oholah is long gone by now; the aim is rather to declare the perfect justice of their terrible sufferings at God's hand. Not only must they be disciplined; they must themselves concede that they deserve it, and then they will truly, personally know that 'I am the Lord GOD':

> [36]The LORD said to me: 'Son of man, will you judge Oholah and Oholibah? Then declare to them their abominable deeds. [37]For they have committed adultery, and blood is upon their hands; with their idols they have committed adultery; and they have even

---

introduced with *ya'an*, and the judgment itself is set forth in the *wᵉgam* clause. *Cf.* similar syntax in Ezk. 5:11; 16:43; 20:24–25.

[86] Targum paraphrases, 'Receive the guilt of the *counsel* of your sin and idolatry!' Rashi quotes approvingly. (Italics added.)

[87] *Cf.* 1 Ki. 14:9; Ne. 9:26.

[88] One hears, if only by a dim presentiment, the cries of 'Away with him! Crucify, crucify him!'

[89] The RSV and NRSV include, *ad sensum*, 'the consequences of' in the concluding clause, and doubtless they are correct to do so. Radak paraphrases, 'The punishment for your lewdness bear and endure!'

offered up to them for food the children whom they
had borne to me. [38]Moreover, this they have done to
me: they have defiled my sanctuary on the same day
and profaned my sabbaths. [39]For when they had
slaughtered their children for their idols, on the same
day they came into my sanctuary to profane it. And lo,
this is what they did in my house.'

What Oholah and Oholibah wished to recede from popular
view into an amorphous blur the prophet sets forth plainly.
The sisters have sinned in two ways. One, they have
committed adultery with idols. Two, they have shed the
blood of Yahweh's children in child-sacrifice.[90] Moreover,
verse 38a penetrates to the ultimate meaning of their ways,
viz. they have attacked Yahweh himself. The sisters do not
violate merely a theoretical code of ethics which might be
arguable several ways; they have done these things to their
own gracious husband. It was personal, unjustified and
obvious. But it was also hypocritical, for they continued with
the outward observances of orthodox Yahwism[91] even as their
lives denied its inner meaning.[92]

With relentless tenacity, the prophet forces the reader to
visualize the harlotry of God's people in such a way as to see it
clearly for what it is:

[40]'Moreover, they sent for men to come from far away,
to whom a messenger was sent, and lo, they came. For
them you bathed yourself, painted your eyes, and
decked yourself with ornaments; [41]you sat on a stately
couch, with a table spread before it on which you had
placed my incense and my oil. [42]The sound of a
carefree multitude was in her, with men of the rabble
brought in drunken from the wilderness; and they put

[90] Verse 37 does not list four offences but two, each one stated, then restated,
in an A–B–A'–B' form.

[91] *Cf.* Lv. 19:30; 26:2. Radak comments, 'They worshipped the idols to provoke
me, and on that very same day they came into my house to offer sacrifices.'

[92] The mingling of 3 f p suffixes (verses 36–38) with 3 m p suffixes (verse 39)
shows how thin and permeable was the membrane separating the author's
thought into the categories of the literal and the figurative.

bracelets upon the hands of the women, and beautiful crowns upon their heads.'

How Oholah and Oholibah doted on their lovers! Not only did the sisters violate their pledge to Yahweh; they did so with style, openly displaying their true feelings.[93] The paragraph sets the scene of a feast. In verse 40a, Oholah and Oholibah send out their invitations to the nations, who respond positively. The people of God initiated and welcomed unlawful connections with foreign powers. In 40b, Oholibah[94] prepares to present herself to her guests attractively. In so doing, she must adapt to their standards of cosmetic beauty rather than to Yahweh's law. In verse 41, she completes her arrangements for the feast,[95] offering her lovers the very articles with which she should have been honouring her husband Yahweh. The language of verse 42a seems intended to conjure up a scene of drunken revelry in Jerusalem, drawing in a mob who, if Jerusalem had been serving Yahweh faithfully, would not have come to celebrate her degradation but to bow in repentance before the Judge of all the earth.[96] In verse 42b, her foreign lovers present Oholah and

---

[93] The compound emphatic connective *w⁵ʾap kî* has the effect of heightening the accusation of verses 40ff., relative to 36–39. Rashi comments, 'And all the more serious than everything else was that they sent to bring to them some of the leaders of the nations, their lovers.'

[94] Interestingly, the 3 f p form of the verb in 40a is discontinued and the verbal forms resume in the 2 f s form, presumably narrowing the reference to Oholibah, the prophet's primary interest. So Radak: 'He says this with regard to Oholibah.' Later, in connection with verse 42b, he notes that 'the main object of the prophecy is concerning Oholibah.'

[95] Radak unpacks the connotative value of 'a table *spread*', commenting, 'The interpretation of *'ārûk* is "spread" with all kinds of good foods.'

[96] Every phrase of verse 42a in the Hebrew text is challenging. Through the s⁵golta, the language evokes the idea of a crowd of merry-makers cavorting within Jerusalem. Radak comments, 'He says that the sound of a multitude was heard in her, in Oholibah; and that multitude was carefree, that is, peaceable.' On through the zaqeph parvum, emendation seems necessary, either semantic or textual. Rashi interprets the preposition *'el* in the sense, 'for the sake of'. Radak construes it as equivalent in force to *'im*, 'with'. Alternatively, one could omit the preposition, resulting in an intelligible circumstantial clause through the athnach: 'with men from the generality of humankind brought in, drinking [Kethib]/drunkards [Qere], from the wilderness' – that is, vulgar rowdies, flocking in from the outback to drag royal Jerusalem down to their level, and that with her glad permission. The RSV and NRSV appear to have handled the text along this line.

Oholibah with flattering gifts, sealing their relationship. In real terms, Israel and Judah gained commercial advantage through the nations.

The guests having arrived and the orgy begun, Yahweh pronounces judgment, in verses 43–45:

> [43]'And I said of the one worn out with adulteries, "Now let them practise harlotry with her, and she with them." [44]For they[97] have gone in to her, as men go in to a harlot. Thus they went in to Oholah and to Oholibah, lewd women. [45]But righteous men shall pass judgment on them with the sentence of adulteresses, and with the sentence of women that shed blood; because they are adulteresses, and blood is upon their hands.'

Yahweh looks upon his wife now as one 'worn out with adulteries'.[98] She is wasted. Good for nothing better, she is given up to her debauchery, according to verse 43.[99] Now that she has exhausted her capacities in her adulterous binge, God gives her up to her lovers and to herself. The scene of foreign representatives entering Jerusalem is, to the prophetic eye, suggestive of unlawful sexual union, according to verse 44a. Indeed, both north and south have fallen to this level, marking them as 'lewd women'.[100] The 'men' of verses 40 and 42 reappear in verse 45, but now described as 'righteous'. They

[97] I accept the emendation registered in *BHS* at 23:44[a], reflected in the RSV and NRSV, which assumes the Qere reading *yiznû* in verse 43. The subject of the verb is the 'men' of verses 40 and 42.

[98] The substantival adjective in *labbālā(h)* is followed by an adverbial accusative *ni'ûpîm*, defining the particular sense in regard to which she is worn out. *Cf.* Rashi. The verbal root of the adjective is illustrated in Gn. 18:12, as Radak points out. The language suggests that her adulteries have gone to such an extent that she is now wearied by them, perhaps prematurely aged by her dissolute way of life. So Radak: 'He says, by way of the parable, that she has become aged through idolatry.' One also notes the functional equivalence of √*n'p* with √*znh* in the logic of the verse.

[99] After the 3 f p pronominal suffixes in 42b, the text reverts to feminine singular forms in 43–44a. Oholah and Oholibah are again mentioned in 44b, with plurals continuing through verse 45. Radak comments, 'When he speaks in the singular, he speaks concerning Oholibah.'

[100] Radak comments, 'This [the form *'iššot*] is unique. It comes from *'iššā(h)*. [He says] *'iššot* because he says the women are women of disgrace.'

are the foreign powers given a free hand to judge the people of God, according to verses 22–24.[101] However unwittingly, they participate in the righteous judgment of God.[102]

In the concluding paragraph, verses 46–49, Yahweh lets slip the dogs of war:

> [46]For thus says the Lord GOD: 'I will bring up an assembly against them, and make them an object of terror and of plunder. [47]And the assembly shall stone them and cut them down with their swords; they shall slay their sons and their daughters, and burn up their houses. [48]Thus will I put an end to lewdness in the land, so that all women may take warning and not commit lewdness as you have done. [49]And they shall repay you for your lewdness, and you shall bear the penalty for your idolatrous sins; and you shall know that I am the Lord GOD.'

Since Oholah has already suffered the judgment called for here, one may see this as a declaration of Yahweh's standing policy, his final word, for his people when they persist in harlotry. Such a course must lead to destruction. The very fact that Israel's history already bears out the seriousness of Yahweh's intentions should sober Judah all the more. He is bringing[103] against her a conquering invader to wreak such devastation as to make onlooking nations shudder with horror

---

[101] Rashi comments, 'The men are judges, the princes of the king of Babylon and the king of Assyria.' Radak nuances the adjective 'righteous': 'My revered father, of blessed memory, wrote that it is not saying that they are really righteous but that they are experts in legal arguments and apt to judge.' The most functional interpretation is to take the adjective in a relative sense (more 'righteous' than Israel and Judah) as an added criticism of Oholah and Oholibah, *viz.* that 'righteous' pagans will stand in judgment over the elect people of God. GKC § 135 o reckons that the masculine plural suffix in *'ôthem* is due to a weakened distinction in gender; and so in the following context.

[102] *Cf.* the language of verse 45 with that of 16:38.

[103] The infinitives absolute in verse 46 serve in the place of finite verbs, but which type of finite verbal function is a difficult question. The RSV and NRSV take them as virtual imperatives. But the 2 f p forms in verses 48–49 render that interpretation awkward. Radak comments, ' "Bring up" is an infinitive, and so is "make them an object of terror", as if he had said, "I will bring up and I will make".' This is consistent with verse 48.

at the sight and take warning.[104] The fierceness of the remedy
required to 'put an end to lewdness in the land' testifies to the
extreme measure necessary truly to reverse a social trend driven
by a pervasive spirit of harlotry controlling the tone and
direction of the nation. This wound is not lightly healed.

To visualize Jerusalem as a smouldering ruin, with its walls
broken down, its treasures looted, its people murdered and
deported, its sanctity violated, its mission defeated, the divine
Presence removed – to visualize this is to see in concrete form
the prophetic vision of the wreckage of Yahweh's marriage to
his adulterous wife. The story begs for completion. Yahweh's
own promises in Hosea encourage his people to look forward to
a new beginning. In some ultimate sense Yahweh will again
betroth his people to himself in perfection for ever. When and
how will this restoration materialize in real life? The New
Testament brings the story to consummation.

[104] The 'women' taking warning are other nations, as Radak explains,
consistent with the imagery throughout the chapter.

Chapter Six

The ultimate marriage as 'one spirit'

While the New Testament brings to ultimate resolution the moral tension of God's covenanted people fallen away from him into harlotry, it does not begin on an encouraging note. After the sufferings of the intervening centuries, long after flagrant idolatry had been banished from Jewish life, one cannot but wonder how much illumination the people of God have gained when Jesus responds to his contemporaries with denunciations not unlike those of the Old Testament prophets:

> Then some of the scribes and Pharisees said to him, 'Teacher, we wish to see a sign from you.' But he answered them, 'An evil and adulterous generation seeks for a sign' (Mt. 12:38–39a, RSV).

> And the Pharisees and Sadducees came, and to test him they asked him to show them a sign from heaven. He answered them, '. . . An evil and adulterous generation seeks for a sign' (Mt. 16:1–2a, 4a, RSV).

> 'For whoever is ashamed of me and of my words in this adulterous and sinful generation, of him will the Son of man also be ashamed, when he comes in the glory of his Father with the holy angels' (Mk. 8:38, RSV).

The crudities of old-time Baalism had been sublimated into subtle, even respectable, forms of God-evasion. In a profound sense, little progress had indeed been realized since prophetic times. Nor could it have been otherwise. As the rabbis themselves said, in every sin there is something of the golden calf (Snaith 1950: 289).[1] The perfect and eternal betrothal

---

[1] *Cf.* Sanhedrin, 102a.

137

prophesied by Hosea, however, was not to be defeated by the
little, or even by the large, golden calves of everyday human
sinning. As the New Testament opens, the divine husband
comes for his people, and the final events leading to the
consummation are set in motion.

This ultimate fulfilment is witnessed to by New Testament
authors not only in confident response to the Old Testament,
since the purpose of God cannot be defeated, but also as
prompted by Jesus himself. He went beyond condemning his
generation as adulterous. Jesus taught his church to perceive the
resolution of the unfinished work of God in terms of his own
mission:

> Then the disciples of John came to him, saying, 'Why
> do we and the Pharisees fast, but your disciples do not
> fast?' And Jesus said to them, 'Can the wedding guests
> mourn as long as the bridegroom is with them? The
> days will come, when the bridegroom is taken away
> from them, and then they will fast' (Mt. 9:14–15, RSV;
> cf. Mk. 2:18–20; Lk. 5:33–35).

> And again Jesus spoke to them in parables, saying,
> 'The kingdom of heaven may be compared to a king
> who gave a marriage feast for his son . . .' (Mt. 22:1–2,
> RSV).

> 'Then the kingdom of heaven shall be compared to
> ten maidens who took their lamps and went to meet
> the bridegroom . . .' (Mt. 25:1, RSV).

For those who joyfully recognize in Jesus the bridegroom of
the covenanted people, the deprivation of fasting is out of the
question. Celebration is the only meaningful response. And yet
Jesus himself hints that the wedding will be delayed while he is
taken away from them, and then they will mourn longingly for
him. He anticipates the irony of Israel's indifferent and even
hostile rejection of the wedding invitation. But they will not
succeed in spoiling the celebration. In fact, the wideness of
God's mercy will throw the invitation open to the nations,
bringing in the bad along with the good, so that the wedding
hall is filled with guests. But even for them, a note of warning is

sounded. Those who do accept the king's invitation must still be properly attired for the occasion or suffer painful expulsion. And finally, the imminent return of the bridegroom requires of God's people watchful attention to their personal readiness. Some will be unprepared and disqualified; others will be waiting in alertness and therefore received into the marriage feast, after which the door will shut.

Allowing for subtle variation of the basic marital metaphor in his discourses, Jesus clearly perceives and presents himself in the role of Yahweh in the divine marriage with the covenanted people.[2] John the Baptist confirms his testimony:

> 'You yourselves bear me witness, that I said, I am not the Christ, but I have been sent before him. He who has the bride is the bridegroom; the friend of the bridegroom, who stands and hears him, rejoices greatly at the bridegroom's voice; therefore this joy of mine is now full. He must increase, but I must decrease' (Jn. 3:28–30, RSV).

John welcomes with joy the bridegroom Jesus, whose visibility on the national scene he is eager to promote, even at the expense of his own.

The point is that the Old Testament expectation of the marriage of Yahweh with his people, to be restored and enjoyed for ever, comes into the framework of New Testament theology through the teaching of Jesus himself. The category is meaningfully operative in his self-understanding and public ministry. The light of Old Testament revelation shone through the prism of his theological imagination into the refracted glory of New Testament witness in its colourful variety. And our Lord's perception of his generation as adulterous and of himself as the bridegroom is one stream among others in the theological spectrum with which New Testament writers illuminate the present tension and the approaching consummation.

---

[2] Muirhead (1952: 181) observes, 'As far back as we can go in our sources we find the symbol of the Bridegroom understood as applied to Jesus by His own authority. He has placed Himself in the centre of the symbol. He is the Bridegroom, and the symbolism rearranges itself about Him.'

James 4:4[3]

The sharp admonition of James echoes the denunciation of our Lord upon his generation and the prophetic cries of the Old Testament. But while its burden evokes that of a Hosea or an Ezekiel, its categories are indigenous to the New Testament. The vision is broadened beyond specific manifestations of rivalry with God, such as the Assyrians or Babylonians (naturally) or even the Romans, and is lifted to the level of the axiomatic, with 'the world' as the enemy of God in the hearts of his people. The vision is also personalized. Not the covenanted nation but each particular individual is bidden to search himself for the adultery of desiring the friendship of the world:

> You adulteresses! Do you not know that friendship with
> the world is hostility toward God? Therefore whoever
> wishes to be a friend of the world makes himself an
> enemy of God.

In the course of exposing to view the passions of the soul which underlie and energize the outward conflicts of human society, James abruptly hurls at his readers the emphatic 'You adulteresses!'[4] This scornful epithet is calculated to awaken them to the dangerous sin into which they have fallen and the

[3] Whether or not James is the earliest New Testament document, the burden of this particular utterance provides a theological bridge from the Old Testament into the New. James 'lived in an age of transition' from a Jewish church to a wider Christian community and outlook, according to Guthrie (1990: 732). Guthrie also states that James's 'approach to ethical problems and his denunciations and warnings find striking parallels in the Old Testament prophetical books. He appears as a kind of Christian prophet' (p. 727). It seems appropriate that his text should appear first in order here. We will then proceed to Paul and finally to the Revelation.

[4] The RSV blurs the particularity of the language with its 'Unfaithful creatures!' And the NRSV misrepresents the plain sense of the Greek text with its 'Adulterers!' Perhaps the RSV's concern was how 'adulteresses' coheres with a context concerned with inner emotions generating conflict between Christians and compromising the Christian *vis-à-vis* the world. The NRSV may be interpreting the charge of adultery in a literal sense, in which case an accusation against women only seems odd. (The Byzantine reading, 'Adulterers and adulteresses!', may be similarly premised.) But, seen against the background of the Old Testament, James's language is most meaningful. Personal friendship with the world is his analogue to national alliances with Assyria, and

clarity of the choice they must make.[5] His categories are absolute, precluding compromise and evasive over-qualification. The choice is, in its essence, disturbingly simple. They have to choose between one allegiance and another, opposing allegiance.[6] This is stated principially in verse 4a.

And James' readers may not claim ignorance. 'Do you not know this?' he demands. They ought to know, surely they must know, that human society is pervaded with a bias against God. Fallen human beings centre their lives around anything but God. They console themselves with the comforting feeling that vast numbers share the same outlook, and 'How can everyone be wrong?' Massive God-neglect, veiling a deep God-hostility, is made to seem normal. And, James insists, 'How can one flirt with such a consensus without adulterating one's covenant with God?'[7]

---

others, in the Old Testament. But the sense is readily apparent even without appealing to the obvious Old Testament categories, as is evident in Grotius, *Critici Sacri* (1698 edn), *ad loc.*: 'Hic tamen hae voces sumendae in sensu figurato. Nam qui Deo uni non adhaerent, nec ei per omnia parere cupiunt, sed partim Deo, partim Mundo se accommodant, similes sunt iis conjugibus, qui suo suave conjuge non contenti externos amores admiscent.' [Here, however, these words are to be taken in a figurative sense. For they who do not adhere to the one God, nor wish to obey him in all things, but adapt themselves partly to God and partly to the world, are like the married who, unsatisfied with his or her own spouse, mix together alien loves.]

[5] Mußner (1975: 180) writes, 'Die scharf tadelne Anrede μοιχαλίδες braucht nach den vorhergehenden Ausführungen des Jak nicht weiter zu überraschen. In jenem Verhalten, das die "Lüste" zu befriedigen sucht, sieht Jak eine Art von Buhlerei mit der Welt (φιλία τοῦ κόσμου). Darum fordert er jetzt die Leser auf, sich von dieser falschen Weltliebe abzuwenden und sich ganz Gott zu unterwerfen.' [The sharply critical address μοιχαλίδες, after the foregoing statement of James, need not surprise further. In that behaviour which seeks to gratify 'lusts', James sees a kind of harlotry with the world (φιλία τοῦ κόσμου). For that reason he now summons the readers to turn away from this false love of the world and to submit themselves fully to God.]

[6] *Cf.* Henry (*Exp. ad loc*): '. . . he who sets his heart upon the world, who places his happiness in it, and will conform himself to it, and do any thing rather than lose its friendship, he is an enemy to God . . . Hence arise wars and fightings, even from this adulterous idolatrous love of the world, and serving of it; for what peace can there be among men, so long as there is enmity towards God?'

[7] *Cf.* Ropes (1916: 260): 'To be a "friend of the world" is to be on good terms with the persons and forces and things that are at least indifferent toward God, if not openly hostile to him.' More fully, to cherish a preference for all that is temporal, tangible, earthly, sensate, all that is 'highly esteemed among men'

A personal corollary is drawn in 4b ('Therefore'). If it is true that friendship with the world is hostility toward God, then one thing follows. Anyone wishing to cultivate friendship with this God-hating world makes himself an enemy of God. A Christian cannot have it both ways, giving his best affections to the world while also felicitating himself for his good standing with God. And it is merely the *desire* for friendship with the world – not total immersion in it, or complete identification with it, but merely the wish to be on good terms – which draws a frown from God.[8] Neither is it necessary for one positively to desire alienation from the favour of God. Violated moral laws operate irrespectively of human intentions.[9] To win the opposition of God it is only necessary that one bend one's soul around to wish friendship with the world.[10]

James is not seeking merely to guard his readers from worldly patterns of behaviour; he is calling them away from even the desire for worldly approval by defining the issue so clearly, strictly and finely that no-one wishing to be God's friend will allow himself to be drawn after the world, Demas-like, in his

---

(Lk. 16:15), 'the lust of the flesh and the lust of the eyes and the pride of life' (1 Jn. 2:16), to sympathize with serving Mammon rather than God (Mt. 6:24), to assume as valid the mind of the flesh rather than the mind of the Spirit (Rom. 8:5–8), to regard as impressive and promising the wisdom of man rather than the foolishness of God (1 Cor. 1:18 – 2:16), to be more exercised in favour of self-esteem than Christ-esteem, to salute the power of human politics more enthusiastically than the weakness of God's strategies (2 Cor. 10:3–4), to savour the approval of those who disregard God and as a result grant favour according to godless criteria and for God-neglecting reasons – this, and much more, is friendship with the world. *Cf.* Mt. 12:30.

[8] Davids (1982: 161) observes, 'Even the attempt (βουληθῇ indicates that the world may not accept such a person either!) to cultivate the world is disastrous, for that inner disposition constitutes (καθίσταται) one not just a compromiser or a poor Christian but an enemy of God!'

[9] The verb in ἐχθρὸς τοῦ θεοῦ καθίσταται accomplishes more than the simple equative verb might have conveyed. *Cf.* Rom. 5:19. It suggests that the change in one's relation to God is more objective than that which is conceived in one's own perhaps harmless intentions.

[10] Manton (*James*: 343, 346) properly observes, '*Will be the friend of the world.* – βουληθῇ noteth the aim and serious purpose. All do not find the world to favour them; do what they can, "the world is crucified to them"; but they are not as Paul was, "crucified to the world," Gal. vi. 14. Therefore the scripture taketh notice not of what is in the event, but the aim. Besides, the serious purpose and choice discovereth the state of the soul; he is also absolutely a worldly man that *will be* a friend of the world.'

affections and aspirations.[11] The Christian who understands and internalizes this warning will live outwardly with a kind of benevolent detachment from the world, enjoying the friendship of God so richly that the hostility of the world will be a small price to pay. Covenant faithfulness, then, is a deeply felt personal preference for the favour of God, at whatever the social cost. Spiritual adultery consists in the lingering wish to retain the world's favour even as one also wishes to enjoy the benefits of redemption. Such hypocrisy provokes God to jealousy, as James goes on to explain in verse 5.

Although the biblical drama is not greatly accelerated by this New Testament text, one nevertheless senses already a deeper, more personal, more searching penetration into the harlotry of soul which lies at the root of its outward manifestations. When this inner sickness is finally remedied, the perfect betrothal will have come.

1 Corinthians 6:15–17

Arguing for personal purity amid licentious Corinth requires Paul to explain to the Corinthian church the Christian view of the human body. The body is not the crowning human experience, but neither is it nothing. It has a legitimate place in God's scheme of things; it is 'for the Lord' (verse 13). In verses 15–17, Paul unfolds more fully the meaning and entailments of this perspective on the body:

> [15]Do you not know that your bodies are members of Christ? Shall I therefore take the members of Christ and make them members of a prostitute? Never! [16]Or do you not know that he who joins himself to a prostitute becomes one body with her? For, it says, 'The two shall become one flesh.' [17]But he who is united to the Lord is one spirit with him.

The Corinthian Christians must realize that their bodies have a significance greater perhaps than they have ever grasped. The human body is not only *for* the Lord, it is *of* the Lord, according

[11] According to Dibelius (1976: 220) '. . . relentless determination is demanded.'

to verse 15.[12] The union of the believer with Christ is all-encompassing; nothing of the believer's created being is so low as to fall outside the range of Christ's reclaiming grace.[13] Christian hands, eyes and feet are now Christ's hands, eyes and feet.

Paul then presses this axiom of Christian discipleship unhesitatingly all the way to sexual activity. It cannot be otherwise, if Christ is Lord and Saviour of the whole of life. Therefore, Paul asks rhetorically, shall I take my bodily members, which Christ has claimed for his own purposes and *all* of which (astonishingly) are included in his incarnational presence in the world through the Christian's participation in this mortal life – shall I take these bodily members and make them, as it were, members of a prostitute through the physical coupling of sexual intercourse? 'The members of Christ, the members of a prostitute?' The expression is startling, the thought revolting.[14] Spiritual harlotry takes on an even more shocking meaning than before, as involving the Christ.

[12] *Cf.* Godet (1893: I:308): 'As the Church in its totality is the body of Christ, that is to say, the organism which He animates with His Spirit, and by which He carries out His wishes on the earth, so every Christian is a member of this body, and consequently an organ of Christ himself. By means of the Spirit of Christ which dwells in his spirit [see verse 17], and by means of his spirit which directs his soul and thereby his body, this body becomes as it were the body of Christ, the executor of His thought; hence the practical conclusion: This organ of Christ must not be taken from Him to be given to a harlot.' In addition, Calvin (*1 Cor*: 130) shows his wonted insight: 'We should note that the spiritual union which we have with Christ is not a matter of the soul alone, but of the body also, so that we are flesh of His flesh etc. (Eph. 5:30). The hope of the resurrection would be faint, if our union with Him were not complete and total like that.'

[13] Robertson & Plummer (1914: 125) put the Christian doctrine into a larger perspective: 'The higher heathen view was that man's body is in common with the brutes, τὸ σῶμα κοινὸν πρὸς τὰ ζῷα, and only his reason and intelligence in common with the gods (Epict. *Dissert.* I. iii. I); but the Christian view is τὸ σῶμα μέλος τοῦ Χριστοῦ.'

[14] *Cf.* Chrysostom (*1 Cor*: 238): 'For supposing you had a daughter, and in extreme madness had let her out to a procurer for hire, and made her live a harlot's life, and then a king's son were to pass by, and free her from that slavery, and join her in marriage to himself; you could have no power thenceforth to bring her into the brothel. For you have given her up once for all, and sold her. Such as this is our case also. We let out our own flesh for hire unto the Devil, that grievous procurer: Christ saw and set it free, and withdrew it from that evil tyranny; it is not then ours any more, but His who delivered it. If you be willing to use it as a King's bride, there is none to hinder; but if you bring

And if that argument will not suffice to persuade the Corinthians to guard themselves strictly, Paul develops further, in verse 16, the true significance of the words 'members of a prostitute'. Paul anticipates that his readers might be tempted to dismiss his argument in verse 15 as too astounding to be taken with full seriousness. When Paul reasons his way from 'members of Christ' to 'members of a prostitute', is that not taking things a bit far? The Corinthians must understand that the one who joins himself to a prostitute enters into a 'one body' connection with her.[15] It falls short of, but nevertheless approaches, mimics and violates, the full, 'one flesh' union of marriage. It does not create 'one flesh', for all that that means; but it does draw a man and a woman into intimacy which properly belongs only to the marriage bond.[16] So then, sexual promiscuity is not a mini-marriage. It does not hijack the profound meaning of marriage. Paul's allusion to Genesis 2:24 is not intended to suggest that it does. But the Genesis 2:24 meaning of marriage does cast the shadow of its frown upon sexual promiscuity, as the latter encroaches upon its holy ground. Casual sex must not be trivialized through being compared with the satisfaction of one's hunger at a meal (verse 13). It is a sin of deep significance, as Paul explains further in verses 18–20.

But before he completes his pastoral admonition, Paul gives the Corinthians a brief glimpse, in verse 17, into the positive alternative which the believer may cherish and guard in a world crazed with sexual temptations. The Christian has been brought into spiritual union with the Lord, analogous to sexual union. Paul's language requires the analogy to be drawn. 'He who joins himself to a prostitute' and 'he who is united to the Lord', as the RSV renders, conceal the fact that the same linguistic structure

---

it where it was before, you will suffer just what they ought, who are guilty of such outrages.'

[15] Erasmus, in *Critici Sacri*, shows sensitivity to the text when he comments on the Vulgate's paraphrase, *unum corpus efficitur*. 'Est ἐστίν apud Graecos, *est* pro *efficitur*: quod est vehementius.' [*Is made one body*: It is ἐστίν among the Greeks, *is* for *is made*, which is more forceful.]

[16] *Pace* some commentators, I cannot dismiss Paul's change of language from 'one body', as his description of a relationship with a whore, to 'one flesh', which his allusion to Gn. 2:24 requires, because the marriage relationship of one flesh, bringing a man and woman together for life, is of another, higher order than a merely sexual encounter. Paul, the master theologian, chooses his words carefully.

occurs in each part of the equation.[17] The two unions, although radically incompatible, are nevertheless comparable. And the believer's spiritual union with the Lord is, for that reason, higher in nature and more fulfilling in effect than the momentary joining of merely sexual intercourse.[18]

Significantly, this spiritual reality puts not only the 'one body' union of promiscuity but also the 'one flesh' union of marriage into a less than ultimate perspective. The 'one body' and the 'one flesh' of verse 16 are both transcended by the 'one spirit' of verse 17. The difference is that 'one flesh' does not violate 'one spirit', while 'one body' does, because 'one flesh' unites two Christ-indwelt believers while 'one body' forges a monstrous connection between the believer, a 'member of Christ', and 'the members of a prostitute'. But the striking feature of this theological paradigm is that the believer is even more intimate with the Lord than with his or her spouse, for this is a union of spirit, and spirit always leads one more deeply into reality than does flesh. The 'cleaving to the Lord' of Deuteronomy 10:20 is now seen to be actualized through a joining of the believer's spirit with Christ. No more profound communion exists than that between the believer and the Lord,[19] and Paul's logic encourages the view that this communion is, as it were, super-marital in nature and already joined.

---

[17] Ὁ κολλώμενος τῇ πόρνῃ in verse 16 is paralleled by ὁ κολλώμενος τῷ κυρίῳ in 17, two very different but meaningful personal connections. The one creates 'one body', the other 'one spirit'. Let it be noted as well that this language points to the individual believer in marital union with the Lord, *contra* Muirhead (1952: 184): 'There seems no NT evidence for the use of the Bride as a mystical symbol, still less of its use as a symbol of a mystical relationship between Christ and the individual believer . . . In the NT the Bride is collective, never the individual Christian.'

[18] *Cf.* Hooker (*Laws*: V, 56): 'Seeing therefore that Christ is in us as a quickening Spirit, the first degree of communion with Christ must needs consist in the participation of his Spirit, which Cyprian in that respect well termeth *germanissimam societatem*, the highest and truest society that can be between man and him which is both God and man in one.'

[19] Scripture reserves language to describe the believer's union with the Lord which suggests its finality in human experience, *e.g.* Ps. 73:25; Jn. 15:1ff.; Gal. 2:20; Eph. 3:17, 19, *etc.*

2 Corinthians 11:1–3

Paul's intervention to save the Corinthian church, who were as naïve as they thought themselves sophisticated, from the 'false apostles, deceitful workmen, disguising themselves as apostles of Christ' (11:13) forces him into an awkward position. Unlike the false teachers, whose self-display is calculated to cultivate a personal following, the apostle submerges self so as to win converts to Christ. If Christ is proclaimed, in that he rejoices, irrespective of his own ratings. If he does call people to follow him, it is only because he himself is following Christ. For Paul, to live is Christ, not self.

But the dynamics of the situation in the Corinthian church tie his own personal status in with their faithfulness to Christ, because their wide-eyed fascination with the glamorous imposters endangers their allegiance to their Lord. Human leadership and divine authority have become entwined, in that Paul's rivals preach another Jesus, offer another spirit and proclaim another gospel (11:4). Moreover, the false teachers themselves have made Paul an issue, criticizing him for the very humility which sets him apart. Presumably, his example of selfless love for the church shone as an embarrassing exposé of their own self-advancing agendas. But in any case, Paul finds himself trapped into setting forth his credentials alongside those of his rivals, to re-establish his authority in the Corinthians' eyes, thereby appearing to legitimate criteria of 'success' which he himself does not even respect. He feels like a fool, perhaps even a hypocrite (10:12, 18). But what else can he do? Yielding reluctantly to necessity, Paul pleads with the Corinthians to try to understand and to make all due allowances in their perception of him:

> [1]I wish you would bear with me in a little foolishness. Do bear with me! [2]For I feel jealous for you with a divine jealousy, for I betrothed you to one husband, to present you as a pure virgin to Christ. [3]But I am afraid lest somehow, as the serpent deceived Eve by his cunning, your thoughts may be led astray from a sincere and pure devotion to Christ.

Writhing in embarrassment, Paul warns the Corinthians that

he must stoop to the foolishness of a little self-promotion, according to verse 1.[20] He fears that he may offend their sensitivities, even though they are broadly tolerant of his aggressive rivals. All he can do is ask them to suspend judgment long enough to hear him out.

Paul explains, in verse 2, that what compels him to engage in this nonsense is the watchful, protective, disinterested love that he cherishes for the Corinthians.[21] His motive is not wounded pride or envy or turf-protection but loving jealousy. They have nothing to fear, nothing to suspect, but only a friend to appreciate in the apostle; indeed, what energizes Paul is the very love of God.[22] He feels for them what God feels for them, and what God feels is a pure, intense, possessive desire to love

[20] Both the RSV and the NRSV construe ἀνέχεσθε as imperatival, although the form could be indicative. Erasmus, in *Critici Sacri*, comments, quoting the Vulgate: '*Supportate me*] Ἀνέχεσθε Graeca vox anceps est: at magis quadrat ut sit indicativi modi, *sustinetis*. Corrigit enim quod dixerat, *Utinam sustinuissetis*; imo, inᵩuit, *sustinetis, et quod opto factum, facitis*.' [*Bear me!* The Greek word Ἀνέχεσθε is ambiguous, and yet it is more fitting that it should be of the indicative mood, *you endure*. For he is correcting what he had said, *Oh that you would endure! Nay rather*, he says, *you do endure, and what I wish done, you do*.] But Calvin (*2 Cor*: 139) argues for the imperatival sense: 'But since the reasons that he adds are designed to induce the Corinthians to bear with him and later he will again take them to task for conceding him nothing, I have followed the Vulgate. By saying "Would that" etc. he had seemed to lose confidence but now, as if correcting his hesitation, he openly and freely commands.' The two interpretations are not greatly dissimilar in their net effect. If the verbal form is indicative, then ἀλλὰ καί is adversative with a heightening emphasis; but if imperatival, then the compound construction is copulative with a heightening emphasis. *Cf.* BDF § 448 (6). Turner (1963: 330) favours the imperatival sense, with ἀλλὰ καί 'introducing a strong addition', equivalent in force to 'yes, indeed'. The very fact that Paul begins the verse with an outburst of longing suggests that he fears he may be misunderstood, in which case the imperatival sense is the more functional.

[21] Chrysostom (*2 Cor.* 383) comments, 'He does not say, "For I love you," but uses a term far more vehement than this. For those souls are jealous which burn ardently for those they love, and jealousy can in no other way be begotten than out of a vehement affection. Then that they may not think that it is for the sake of power or honour or wealth or any other such like thing, that he desires their affection, he added, "with a jealousy of God".'

[22] *Cf.* Ex. 20:5; 34:14. The genitive in θεοῦ ζήλῳ is a genitive of attribute, properly rendered with an English adjective by the RSV and NRSV. Such a translation ought not, however, to obscure the person of God in one's understanding of this jealousy.

the Corinthians and to be loved by the Corinthians within the sanctity of an exclusive covenant of communion.

But of all the emotions that Paul might feel for the Corinthians, why is he energized with jealousy? And why is this jealousy 'divine'? Because the Pauline gospel calls the Corinthian church to a *marital* union with Christ. Acting as either father of the bride[23] or friend of the bridegroom[24] – the language could accommodate either image – Paul has betrothed[25] the Corinthian church to her one heavenly husband and to him only,[26] and the apostle bears a responsibility to present her to him on their wedding day a *virgo intacta.* The Corinthians' engagement to Christ came as a result of Paul's ministry, and he is the one to see the union consummated at the Parousia in purity.[27] While the false teachers wish to exploit the Corinthians, Paul's God-filled heart yearns to protect them and keep them for the ultimate human experience, *viz.* union with Christ alone.

It is this burden of pastoral responsibility which explains Paul's deep concern, expressed in verse 3. He knows that their

---

[23] *Cf.* 1 Cor. 4:14–15; 2 Cor. 12:14.

[24] On the analogy of John the Baptist in Jn. 3:29.

[25] According to BDF § 316 (1) the middle voice ἡρμοσάμην is the functional equivalent to the active voice. *Cf.* Turner 1963: 55. Chrysostom (*2 Cor*: 383) compares the role of Paul here to that of Abraham's servant in Gn. 24 negotiating a wife for Isaac: 'For he sent his faithful servant to seek a Gentile maiden in marriage; and in this case God sent His own servants to seek the Church in marriage for His son.'

[26] Hodge (1973: 252) writes, 'The marriage relation from its nature is exclusive. It can be sustained only to one man. So the relation of the church, or of the believer, to Christ is in like manner exclusive. We can have but one God and Saviour. Love to him of necessity excludes all love of the same kind to every other being. Hence the apostle says he had espoused (betrothed) them to *one* man.'

[27] Alford (1958: II:697) quotes the remark of Theophylact: ὁ μὲν οὖν παρὼν καιρὸς μνηστείας ἐστιν, ὁ δὲ μέλλων τῶν γάμων, ὅτε κραυγὴ γίνεται, ἰδοὺ ὁ νυμφίος. [The present time, then, is that of betrothal; but the time to come is that of the wedding feast when the shout will arise, 'Behold, the bridegroom!'] The operative words in verse 2 are 'a *pure* virgin', reinforced in verse 3 with 'a sincere and *pure* devotion to Christ'. Lapide (1876: XVIII:489, 492) quotes Augustine: 'Virginitas mentis est integra fides, solida spes, sincera charitas . . . Virginitas carnis, corpus intactum; virginitas animae, fides incorrupta.' [Virginity of the mind is an irreproachable faith, a firm hope, a genuine love . . . Virginity of the flesh, an untouched body; virginity of the spirit, an unspoiled faith.]

integrity toward Christ is under seductive attack. He is worried that their purity might somehow – and what an arsenal of evil devices is packed into that one word 'somehow'! – be sullied and Christ's conjugal rights violated. The issue will turn on whether they allow themselves to be duped with the alternative Jesus, the alternative spirit and the alternative gospel (verse 4) being offered them through the false apostles. If they open their minds to this deception,[28] they, like Eve, will fall from a sincere and pure[29] devotion to Christ.[30] In this instance, Paul is the only one who will guard the purity of the Corinthians for their rightful husband. And that is why he allows himself to compete for their attention and respect.

This passage makes two striking contributions to our unfolding biblical theme. First, the watchful jealousy of God, familiar to the Old Testament, is no less operative in the Christian church of the New. But now that divine jealousy burns for the perfect union of Christ with his bride. The passage intimates his deity

[28] Paul may have been familiar with the rabbinic tradition that the serpent seduced Eve and imparted to her sexual lust. *Cf.* Yebamoth, 103b. That cannot be Paul's view here, however, for it is not the Corinthians' bodies but their thoughts which are being targeted by the false teachers. *Cf.* verse 4 for the content of the deception. The point which Paul draws out of the parallel with Eve is the *deceptive* power of the temptation. It was perpetrated with 'cunning', not in 'lust', as is pointed out by Plummer (1915: 295). Calvin (*2 Cor*: 141), explains the apostle's reasoning: 'If false teachers have a show of wisdom to persuade us, if they are strong in their eloquence, if they can plausibly insinuate themselves into the minds of their hearers and instil their poison by quiet craftiness, then they work by the same methods that Satan employed to deceive Eve, for he did not openly declare himself her enemy, but crept in secretly under plausible excuses.'

[29] The text-critical problem at ἀπὸ τῆς ἁπλότητος [καὶ τῆς ἁγνότητος] is one in which each fact is patient of disparate explanations. The arguments are weighed in Metzger 1971: 583f. On balance, it seems likely that the longer reading is an authentic Pauline contrivance intended to echo, emphasize and amplify the ἁγνήν of verse 2. As a scribal intrusion, it is too apt, too elegant. Paul's point is the fullness, the depth, the unalloyed genuineness of the church's devoted commitment to Christ.

[30] Héring (1967: 78) writes, 'The Church which might be unfaithful is comparable to Eve led astray by the serpent (Gn. 3), a not very pertinent comparison, because she did not exactly betray her husband.' It is true that the parallel is inexact. Eve was drawn away from a pure faith in God, not from her husband Adam. But this alerts us to an important hermeneutical assumption operative behind the apostle's argument. Christ is both God, the second Adam and the husband of the people of God. All lines converge on him.

and ultimacy, for it is for Christ that the covenanted people are to be preserved faithful.[31]

Secondly, as the first Adam is typical of Christ, the last Adam,[32] so the first Eve is typical of the church, the last Eve.[33] If Paul's only intention in referring to Eve were to cite an Old Testament illustration of the danger of deception, he could have exploited other passages, *e.g.* Joshua 9. His reference to Eve requires a more searching explanation.[34] Paul assumes continuity between the covenanted peoples of the Old and New Testaments, such that Israel's destiny as the bride of God, frustrated through her

[31] This is evident not only within the larger biblical drama, but even the coherence of this passage itself favours the equation of θεοῦ with τῷ Χριστῷ in verse 2.

[32] *Cf.* Rom. 5:14; 1 Cor. 15:45. Christ is not another Adam; he is the *last* Adam. What the first Adam meant for the human race finds its ultimate resolution in Christ. *Cf.* Goppelt (1982: 129f.): 'In their acts and in the effect they have on others, Adam and Christ are related to one another as a photographic negative to its positive print or as a mold to the plastic shaped by it. "As the mold determines the shape of the casting, so from Adam's power over the human race comes Christ's mission and work, his death and his resurrection" [Schlatter] . . . For Paul, Adam is not simply an illustrative figure. He views Adam through Christ as a true type in redemptive history, as a prophetic personality placed in Scripture by God.'

[33] Typological theology perceives an Old Testament person, event or institution as an adumbration of the fuller revelation of God in Christ. This perspective affirms the meaning of the Old Testament text, declared in its own way and on its own terms; but it also permits the referent pointed to by the text to take on new colour as the sun of salvation rises in the appearing of Christ. This perspective is grounded in the persuasion that the subjects described in the Old Testament function as theological symbols of larger spiritual realities more fully revealed in the Christian gospel. Old Testament history therefore is not to be perceived as an incoherent series of unique and disconnected particulars; rather, it is a concatenated unity drawn together by its inner movement toward resolution in Christ as it presages later things, bearing symbolic witness to the consummation. Read this way, the Old Testament becomes one vast network of foreshadowings of Christ and his kingdom, the ultimate purpose of God. It invites the reader to look for Christ and his gospel in the timeless theological paradigms embodied in Old Testament history. A balanced treatment of this and related questions is to be found in Moo (1986: 179–211).

[34] Batey (1971: 12) calls Eve here 'a classic example of credulity'. Even if Eve were credulous, that would still fail to explain why *her* example, rather than another's, is chosen for this passage. For Paul, 'It is one of the great axioms of his theology that, with the Birth, Death, and Resurrection of Christ, the human race had a second start', to quote Chavasse (1939: 67f.). If that premise forms the theological substructure of Paul's admonition here, one may expect a more profound thought in Paul's reference to Eve.

own harlotry, is to be realized in the Christian church.[35] But even more, the fact that this passage goes back beyond historic Israel to the primeval events of Genesis 2 – 3 to find a precedent for the church, with Eve functioning as the analogue to the betrothed of Christ, creates the presumption of finality in the destiny of the Christian church. The biblical drama is coming full circle. With Christ, believers stand in a new Eden.

This explains Paul's urgency on behalf of the Corinthians. More is at stake in their direction than even they realize. They must learn to perceive themselves in connection with the remotest human origins of the past, when Eve was deceived, and forward into eternity future, when they will be presented to Christ. It is through Christ and his church that God is restoring sinners to purity, and the Corinthians have the privilege of participating in the great restoration. Sinners reunited with the Saviour by a new covenant find their lost virginity re-created[36] and the marriage for ever secured. But for now the temptations continue and costly decisions must be made by those who claim the betrothal, for the jealous love of God calls the bride to keep herself chaste for her coming bridegroom.[37]

There was no marriage before Adam and Eve, and there is none greater after Christ and his church. The fulfilment is coming increasingly into view.

Ephesians 5:31–32

Paul calls his Christian readers to treat one another reasonably, to co-operate with one another, to flex with one another's concerns and desires, out of deference to Christ (verse 21).[38] He

[35] This does not, however, exclude ethnic Israel. *Cf.* Rom. 11:25–36.

[36] The formerly 'immoral, idolaters, adulterers, sexual perverts, thieves, greedy, drunkards, revilers and robbers' (1 Cor. 6:9–11) of the Corinthian membership would have felt special power in this aspect of Paul's teaching.

[37] One notes that in 1 Cor. 6:17 Paul addresses the church as already joined to Christ *via* spirit, but here he views them as betrothed and yet to be presented to their bridegroom. Both perspectives are valid and consistent with the larger, 'already/not yet' dialectic operative in New Testament theology. Paul addresses each pastoral need with the emphasis within that tension which is most pertinent to the given case.

[38] The Pauline authorship of Ephesians, a debated question, is accepted here. Both sides of the issue are reviewed and assessed in Carson, Moo & Morris (1992: 305–309).

then explains what this attitude looks like in the case of a Christian wife (verses 22–24) and of a Christian husband (verses 25–30). Throughout his instructions Paul develops sublime parallels between a Christian marriage of man and wife and the ultimate marriage of Christ and the church, so that the type of marriage set forth in Ephesians 5 will be a sort of living gospel made visible before the world. The word is to be made flesh again.

In verse 31, Paul draws somewhat freely upon the Septuagint of Genesis 2:24[39] to define from Old Testament law[40] the meaning of Christian marriage:

> 'For this reason a man shall leave his father and mother and be joined to his wife, and the two shall become one flesh' (RSV).

The connective 'For this reason', although a part of the Genesis quotation and not Paul's own insertion, gives the impression in its new Ephesian context of logical dovetailing with Paul's contextual argument.[41] One could interpret the connection in either of two ways. First, 'For this reason' could join verses 25–30, or even the whole of 22–30, to the Genesis

[39] The only divergences from the Greek tradition are Paul's ἀντὶ τούτου for the LXX's ἕνεκεν τούτου and his omission of the pronominal αὐτοῦ after τὸν πατέρα and τὴν μητέρα. The definite article before πατέρα and μητέρα is also in question. None of these matters is material to the sense of the whole. *Cf.* BDF § 208 (1) on the force of ἀντί. Robinson (1904: 208) argues that Paul's use of ἀντί suggests not opposition but correspondence, offering as an analogy κακὸν ἀντὶ κακοῦ in Rom. 12:17.

[40] Gn. 2:24 is 'law' not only in that it is found in the Torah but, more particularly, in that it prescribes the norm for human marriage. See chapter 1. The future tenses of the Greek verse are probably imperatival in force. *Cf.* Turner (1963: 86), although he does not cite this verse. Curiously, the RSV and NRSV translate Gn. 2:24 with present tenses but Eph. 5:31 with future tenses – as if the force of the verbs in Genesis were customary but, when quoted as Greek in Ephesians, changed to the prescriptive sense.

[41] *Cf.* Paul's uses of the Old Testament in Eph. 4:25–26 and 6:2, where his quotation blends seamlessly into its new literary context without the sort of introductory formula that one observes in Eph. 4:8 and 5:14. It would seem odd if the Gn. 2:24 quotation were inserted as a whole block into the Ephesians passage, with its function there to be surmised from more subtle factors in the argument, while 'For this reason' stands there in the text pleading, as it were, for interpretative recognition.

quotation. If so, then the reason why a Christian husband and wife should aim at living out the Pauline vision of marriage (22–30) is that Genesis 2:24 honours such a relationship as truest to the 'one flesh' meaning of marriage (31).

If this is Paul's argument, then his thought flowing into verse 31 is concerned with a straightforward consideration of human marriage as such. The analogy of Christ and the church in verses 22–30 supplements Paul's pastoral admonition, but this Christological thread wound into his argument is incidental to the Genesis quotation. As a result, verse 30 lurches into verse 31 rather infelicitously. Moreover, this reading of the text renders the parallels with Christ and his church merely illustrative, sermonic figures for the dynamics of an exemplary Christian marriage. As a result, verse 32 cannot but blindside the interpreter as unnecessarily compounding the complexity of the argument, for the powerful directness of its proclamation concerning Christ does not comport well with the passage's earlier Christology functioning only as supplementary clarification.

This line of interpretation prompts one to wonder whether Paul's purpose even requires the Christ/church parallels with Christian marriage for his argument to succeed. Why drag in a supra-mundane spiritual vision, with its hermeneutical subtlety, if all that one intends is to encourage Christians in their marriages? The very features of the text which attract the reader's keenest interest become, by this line of reasoning, insipid distractions from the real thrust of the passage.

Alternatively, then, the logic signalled by 'For this reason' could be connected more particularly with verse 30, even as Genesis 2:24 flows directly out of 2:23:

Genesis 2:23–24	*Ephesians 5:30–31*
'This at last is bone of my bones and flesh of my flesh . . .'	. . . we are members of his body.
Therefore a man shall leave . . . and they shall become one flesh.	'For this reason a man shall leave . . . and the two shall become one flesh.'[42]

---

[42] It is worth noting that, in contrast with 1 Cor. 6:16, Paul uses 'body' and 'flesh' in nearly equivalent senses here, because he is bringing together his

If Paul's argument is moving along this line, then his reasoning is profound. Believers are members of Christ's 'body' (30), which warrants the 'one flesh' union of human marriage (31), unveiling the great mystery of Christ and his church (32); this instructs a Christian man to love his wife and a Christian wife to respect her husband (33). Read this way, the parallels with Christ and his church united together as one body are seen to be central to the apostle's argument. The great incentive and guide for the Christian marriage couple is the vision of Christ and his church in love together.[43]

Genesis 2:24 is now cast in a new light. 'This at last is bone of my bones and flesh of my flesh' (Gn. 2:23) and 'we are members of his body' (Eph. 5:30) function as equivalent premises, leading to the same conclusion, *viz.* that the two shall become one flesh in marriage (Gn. 2:24/Eph. 5:31).[44] With the reasoning of the text set forth this way, the Pauline 'we are members of his body' (30) and the Pentateuchal 'the two shall become one flesh' (31)

'Body of Christ' image of the church with the language of Gn. 2:24. But the categories operative in the Corinthians passage are different, as the inner logic of that passage requires. There, Paul is counting on a distinction between 'body' and 'flesh' as material to his message. The two words are ciphers for fundamentally different relationships, *viz.* a casual sexual encounter ('one body') *versus* marriage ('one flesh'). There, 'body' is prompted by the merely physical nature of promiscuity; here, 'body' is prompted by Paul's image of the church.

[43] *Cf.* Miletic (1988: 22): '. . . the husband and wife become "one flesh" not as the first Adam and Eve *were "one flesh"* but as the New Adam and Eve *are "one flesh"*.' (Italics his.) This overstates the case, for it is a matter of both/and, not either/or; but even in going too far he does highlight properly the primacy of Christ and the church in Paul's reasoning.

[44] It is important to bear in mind that Paul's emphasis in the quotation falls upon 'and the two shall become one flesh'. Only that part of the equation is held in common with Adam and Eve, Christ and the church, and the Christian husband and wife. Attempts to identify Christ's 'leaving his father and his mother' involve one in whimsical fancies as odd as if one had to conjure up the equivalent persons for Adam. *E.g.* Lapide (1874: XVIII:665) cites the following: 'Primus vates Adam, inquit Hieronymus, de Christo hoc prophetavit, quod scilicet Christus reliquerit patrem suum Deum, et matrem suam coelestem Jerusalem, et venerit ad terras propter suum corpus (Ecclesiam), et de suo eam latere fabricatus sit, et propter illam Verbum caro factum sit.' [The first prophet, Adam, says Jerome, foretold this concerning Christ, namely that Christ would leave his father, God, and his mother, the heavenly Jerusalem, and come to earth because of his body (the Church), and from his side he would form her, and because of her the Word was made flesh.]

spring to life as a breathtaking juxtaposition. The first Adam's love for his wife as *one flesh* with himself and the last Adam's love for his own bride, *his body*, are not, however, set alongside one another as a hermeneutical stunt; the typology serves Paul's pastoral purpose of providing a model for Christian marriage which is grounded in primeval human origins and reflective of ultimate divine reality.

Paul's line of argument implies not only that his doctrine of marriage is grounded in Old Testament precedent but also that the 'one flesh' union of Adam and Eve does not lie beyond the reach of a Christian husband and wife. Our union with Christ as his body restores us to such graces as to make deep marital union applicable and attainable, if not easy, for a Christian couple. The church's marriage to Christ is both prefigured in Adam and Eve and provides a Christian couple with the personal wherewithal for achieving marital unity at a profound human level.[45]

By connecting the truth that the church is Christ's body (30) with a larger, typological understanding of marriage as illuminated by the Genesis quotation (31),[46] Paul paves the way for his summarizing affirmation in verse 32. This interpretation of Paul's argument also prompts one to appreciate more meaningfully the richly theological flavour of his practical admonitions throughout the passage. The Christ/church parallel is not merely illustrative but the generating theological centre of his entire presentation. This explains why verse 33 seems to yank the discussion abruptly back to husbands and wives in the here and now; the theological and ultimate were so much at the forefront of Paul's teaching that they stood in danger of eclipsing the practical and immediate.

We are now prepared to consider verse 32:

---

[45] According to Calvin (*Inst*: 2.11.4), 'Nothing solid underlies this [*i.e.* the outward symbolism of the old covenant], unless it is surpassed with something more.' Since the symbol of human marriage continues until the eschaton, one may apply analogous reasoning here. Nothing solid underlies human marriage, unless it is surpassed with something more. Without the truth and power of Christ, marriage is liable to as much abuse and weakness as social trends will allow. It cannot retain its beauty, justice and self-renewing vigour without Christ, for it exists primarily for him and according to him.

[46] Barth (1958: III.1: 313–329) develops the connections between Gn. 2 and the rest of Scripture with deep insight at a number of points.

This mystery is a profound one, and I am saying that it refers to Christ and to the church.

If our interpretation of Paul's argument has been valid thus far, we are positioned to see 'this mystery'[47] as referring back to Paul's line of thought running throughout the passage, *viz.* Christ and the church reflected in the dynamic interplay of a truly Christian marriage.[48] The interlacing of the two themes, human marriage and divine marriage, is now seen unambiguously to be meaningful and appropriate, not arbitrary or incidental. Human marriage, as envisaged in Paul's instructions and as defined by Genesis 2:24, is to reveal the mystery of Christ loving his responsive church. Such a marriage bears living witness to the meaning of 'two become one', rendering visibly literal something of the eternal romance between Christ and his body.[49] Paul calls such marriage a 'profound' mystery presum-

---

[47] The Pauline 'mystery' is centred in Christ himself, for all that he is and means (Col. 2:2–3), as declared in the gospel (Rom. 16:25–27) by the God 'who reveals mysteries' (Dn. 2:29).

[48] It seems unlikely that 'this mystery' should refer back to the quotation of Gn. 2:24. ('The mystery is not itself revelation; it is the object of revelation', according to Bornkamm, *TDNT* IV:820.) That would also overrule the plain sense of the Genesis text. Grotius, in *Critici Sacri*, illustrates this line of interpretation in commenting on 'This mystery is great': 'Id est, verba ista quae apud Mosem extant explicavi vobis non κατὰ πόδας (ad verbum) sed sensu μυστικωτέρῳ (abstrusiore), במדרש (expositione allegorica).' [That is, these words which appear in the writings of Moses I have set forth for you not 'close on the heels' (literally) but in a 'more mystical' sense (more hiddenly), with 'midrash' (allegorical exposition).] Bockmuehl (1990: 204) argues not, in principle, dissimilarly: '. . . we are dealing here with an *exegetical* mystery: a deeper (in this case either allegorical or prophetic) meaning of a Scriptural text which has been elicited by means of some form of inspired exegesis. In other words, the deeper meaning of Gen. 2:24 points typologically to Christ and the church.' (Italics his.) I would prefer to distinguish typological exegesis from typological theology.

[49] This is not to affirm the Roman view that marriage is a sacrament. Marriage is a mystery, but a mystery is not a sacrament. Jerome's *sacramentum hoc magnum est* has worked mischief in this regard. Köstenberger (1991: 79–94) lists three alternative views of the 'mystery' in this passage: (1) human marriage as a sacramental vehicle of grace; (2) human marriage as a type of the union between Christ and the church; and (3) the union of Christ and the church. The second and third views are not exclusive of one another, however, and the second is required to avoid an allegorization of the Gn. 2:24 quotation in the logic of Paul's argument. Moreover, the profound interweaving of human

ably because the commonness of the institution may dull his readers' eyes to its true significance. This adjective calls the reader to alertness, to sensitive, respectful perception.

Verse 32b goes on to explain that Paul's foremost interest does not lie in human marriage as such, for its own sake. He is not a family therapist; he is a steward of the mysteries of God (1 Cor. 4:1). Human marriage claims his personal attention primarily because it speaks of Christ and the church, and he longs for the married people reading his letter to honour Christ in their marriages. Christ did not send Paul to baptize, or to teach 'marriage skills', but to preach the gospel. This verse, then, does not interject a surprisingly new Christological element into the thought of the passage. It does not call for the Christological allegorizing of Genesis 2:24. It simply restates with sharpened focus what has been Paul's primary burden all along, viz. the gospel mystery of Christ and the church.[50] And his point here is to emphasize his own sense of prophetic burden in declaring the great mystery. He is asserting something about himself,[51] openly declaring his agenda; he is not saying anything new about Christ and the church, since that point has already been well established in the context.

The net message of the text, then, is that a Christian marriage faithful to its 'one flesh' meaning incarnates the ultimate reality of sacrificial divine love in Christ wedded to joyful human devotion in the church. Paul's theological vision of the overtures of divine love finding a response in human hearts instructs believers as to how the Christian home reproduces in miniature form the beauty shared between the Bridegroom and his Bride. A Christian husband loves his wife by offering a lifetime of daily sacrifices, so that she might become ever more radiant as a woman of God. She, for her part, affirms and responds to her husband's Christlike initiatives. Through it all, the mystery of the gospel is unveiled.[52]

---

marriage with the divine throughout the passage favours a more inclusive referent.

[50] Cf. Sampley 1971: 89.

[51] Cf. BDF § 277 (1), where ἐγώ is interpreted as emphatic and contrastive in function.

[52] Batey (1971: 30) interprets the apostle's logic as a movement from human marriage to Christ and his church: 'The author sees in the "one flesh" concept where husband and wife become one body a key for understanding the unity

This passage, although it does not concern itself with spiritual harlotry, demands nevertheless to be included in this study. Along with Genesis 2:24, it opens up the theological substructure underlying the entire biblical vision of marriage, human and divine. From the beginning, the institution of human marriage embodied a message of divine romance pursuing a human response.[53] As God called Hosea to the tragedy of a broken marriage to symbolize Yahweh's love for wayward Israel, so the gospel calls a Christian husband and wife to 'one flesh' authenticity to symbolize Christ's love for his devoted church. And Paul is showing that these correspondences are not coincidental or whimsical but intrinsic to reality. Human marriage has always been only penultimate. No marriage is or can be a final experience. And every human marriage is truest to itself when it points beyond itself, representing something of Christ and the church in their perfect union.

Revelation 14:4

The awesome powers of darkness – a great dragon (12:3) commanding an angelic army (12:7), a beast rising up from the sea (13:1), another rising from the earth (13:11) – appear on the human scene, deceiving, blaspheming, intimidating. What will be left of God's kingdom after hell's boldest attempt to claim the world for itself? Revelation 14 projects the reader's imagination out to the dénouement of the great conflict, proclaiming the ultimate triumph of the Lamb and his church.

Separated out from the generality of mankind bullied by the agents of perdition, the 144,000 faithful, the whole people of God in the safekeeping of the Lamb on heavenly Mount Zion, join in a flood of worship filling heaven. God's own enter into

---

maintained by Christ and his Body, the church.' But Paul's argument moves in the opposite direction. Christ and the church in dynamic covenant together provide the paradigm to guide the Christian husband and wife. *Cf. The Book of Common Prayer* (1789): '. . . holy Matrimony, which is an honourable estate, instituted of God, *signifying unto us the mystical union that is betwixt Christ and his Church* . . .' (Emphasis added.)

[53] Calvin (*Eph*: 678) describes it well: '. . . we hear our Lord Jesus Christ call us to himself and tell us that we are so joined to him that he does not have anything of his own which he does not share with us, and of which he will not have us to be partakers.'

celestial intimacies reserved for them alone, according to verses 1–3. Surely, this future experience is worth any endurance now, even unto death.

Verse 4 then explains further what it means that the people of God have been 'redeemed from the earth' (verse 3). In what ways are they distinguished from the rest of the fallen human race?

> It is these who have not defiled themselves with women, for they are virgins; it is these who follow the Lamb wherever he goes; it is these who have been redeemed from mankind as first fruits for God and the Lamb.

Three affirmations are made about the character and the destiny of the faithful. First, they are spiritually chaste.[54] They have refused the drunkenness of Babylon's impure passion,[55] confessing the sober and pure reality of the kingship of the Lamb. They have resisted the allurements of Jezebel's doctrinal and moral, and of Babylon's political and commercial, seductions.[56] The faithful have made their inner 'virginity' manifest through lives undefiled by worldliness. Secondly, they have demonstrated a heroic loyalty to the Lamb, obeying his commands at whatever the personal cost, even as he himself obeyed fully.[57] Their spiritual purity is authentic; it commands their whole beings, so that they withhold nothing from the

---

[54] Lapide (1877: XXI:274) takes a familiar view in characterizing the 144,000 as 'Religiosi, qui angelicam puritatem consectantur' [the Religious, who seek angelic purity]. This anachronistic interpretation is of a piece with Roman ascetic spirituality, which is itself theologically invalid to begin with. *Cf.* 1 Tim. 4:1–5. The author's description of the faithful as 'virgins' undefiled with women is to be interpreted, as 1:1 (ἐσήμανεν) warrants, as a symbol functioning within the larger framework of his theology. The 144,000 include both women and men, and their 'virginity' is spiritual faithfulness to their Lord, which John's second affirmation implies.

[55] *Cf.* Rev. 14:8; 17:2, 4; 18:3.

[56] *Cf.* Rev. 2:20–22; 18:9; 19:2.

[57] 'Following' Christ 'wherever he goes' entails the acceptance of anything, even death, as his lordship requires and as he himself gave. *Cf.* Jn. 12:26; 21:18–19. BDF § 339 (3) construes the present participle as functionally equivalent to the imperfect here, paraphrasing, 'who (always) followed'. Along with ὅπου ἄν, this asserts the unqualified fullness of their steadfast constancy.

Lamb. Thirdly, they owe their Lord everything, for they were bought out of fallen humanity by his sacrificial death (5:9). And their redemption translates into their offering of themselves as a sacrifice of first fruits to God and to the Lamb.[58]

The full company of the faithful have been redeemed from a life smothered by terrestrial imperatives only. That is to say, negatively, they have not been degraded with conformist, worldly, spiritual harlotry. Positively, they have set their course to follow the Lamb, disregarding all costs and accepting all consequences; and they have been redeemed out of the mass of humanity to rise to God and to the Lamb as a sacred offering. However savagely the bestial powers of hell may rage against the church, her purity, obedience and value will be preserved for God.

Revelation 19:6–9a

The 'great harlot', the embodiment of human society fully given over to the lust of the flesh and the lust of the eyes and the pride of life, for all that such values mean and effect – 'Babylon the great' having fallen (chapters 17 – 18), another human society endures never to fall (chapter 19). In verses 1–4, the heavenly court above rings with praises for the justice poured out upon 'the great harlot who corrupted the earth with her fornication'. John records, in verse 5, hearing a voice authorizing God's servants, both those of great gifts and graces and those less privileged, to complement the praises of heaven with their own. But in the cosmic antiphony, while heaven exults in divine justice, earth celebrates divine love, 'the more intimate and tender aspect of the βασιλεία' (Moffatt 1970: V:464):

---

[58] *Cf.* Ex. 23:19; 34:26; Lv. 23:10; Nu. 18:12; Dt. 18:4; Pr. 3:9; Je. 2:3; Ezk. 44:30. As over against the usage of 'first fruits' in Rom. 8:23, 1 Cor. 15:20, 23, which suggests the first part of a larger whole, this use indicates the whole of the church as a perfect sacrifice to God. They have broken with the world and are fully devoted to God and to the Lamb, 'consecrated to and accepted of God, as the first-fruits were, being the only part of the world that are not profane', to quote Poole (*Comm*: III:987). The syntax (nominative ἀπαρχή with no connective or comparative particle) suggests the necessary relation between their having been redeemed and their offering of themselves in sacrifice.

⁶Then I heard what seemed to be the voice of a great
multitude, like the sound of many waters and like the
sound of mighty thunderpeals, crying out,
> 'Hallelujah! For the Lord our God
>   the Almighty reigns.
> ⁷Let us rejoice and exult
>   and give him the glory,
> for the marriage of the Lamb has come,
>   and his Wife has made herself ready;
> ⁸to her it has been granted to be clothed
>   with fine linen, bright and pure' –
for the fine linen is the righteous deeds of the saints.
⁹And the angel said to me, 'Write this: Blessed are
those who are invited to the marriage supper of the
Lamb.'

John hears the church, in verse 6, responding to the summons
of verse 5 by lifting up the last great song of the Revelation. The
sound breaks upon him as an overwhelming, thunderous,
powerfully dramatic exclamation of rejoicing.[59] The content of
their praises is twofold: the kingdom of the Lord our God the
Almighty has come in its fullness,[60] and the bride of the Lamb is
finally prepared for the marriage celebration.[61] For her there is
no more waiting, no more 'How long, O Lord?', as faith turns to

---

[59] The united (singular φωνήν) outburst of praise by the church is
comparable to the voices of Christ (1:15), one of the four living creatures
(6:1), the 144,000 (14:2) and the court of heaven (19:1), except that, with the
possible exception of 14:2, this cry of the faithful seems to exceed the others in
magnitude and intensity.

[60] The grammatical force of ἐβασίλευσεν in this context is either gnomic
(present tense in English, as in the RSV and NRSV) or ingressive ('has entered
on his reign', as in the REB). While one could insist upon observing a fine
grammatical distinction, it is somewhat relativized theologically. God reigns
eternally; but here his reign is made fully manifest, sweeping all opposition
aside and bringing to consummation his redemptive purposes. *Cf.* Rev. 11:15,
17. He had deigned to rule, in part, through his enemies; but now he rules
without them, so immediately that the yearnings of his people are satisfied.

[61] 'Hallelujah!' (the fourth and climactic last in the series of the chapter) is
paralleled and enlarged with 'Let us rejoice and exult and give him the glory.'
Each call to praise is followed by the incentive (ὅτι) for praise – the reign of God,
and the marriage of the Lamb. The second of these factors is elaborated upon
with the very features which the biblical-theological story up to this point most
urgently requires, *viz.* the full preparation of the bride with perfect integrity.

sight, hope to possession, mundane loss to heavenly gain and momentary sorrow to eternal pleasure.

The church rejoices, more specifically, because the marriage of the Lamb has come[62] and because his Wife[63] has prepared herself, according to verse 7. Unlike the failed marriage of Yahweh with harlotrous Israel, unlike the delicate betrothal of the fickle Corinthians, this perfect union brings together a triumphant Lamb and a pure Bride beyond the reach of hell and sin. She has prepared herself through faith, repentance and steadfast endurance, 'as becomes the bride who with joy awaits the coming of her bridegroom' (Düsterdieck 1887: 453). The hard path the church has taken to arrive at this moment has proved meaningful and fruitful, as she has been purified of all adulterous inclinations and is finally ready to give herself fully to her one Husband, and to no other, for ever.

The gracious character of her final preparation is made explicit in verse 8, where the church confesses that her lovely wedding dress of 'fine linen, bright and pure' – the righteous deeds[64] adorning her for her righteous Bridegroom – has been granted to her as a gift in the first instance.[65] Her Lover has indeed sanctified her, cleansed her and presented her to

---

[62] The aorist tense does not require that this moment be located chronologically prior to the last battle and final judgment (chapters 19 – 20). John is recording symbols of the ultimate without necessary regard to strict sequence. The wedding of the Lamb comes into view at this moment in the book, indicating that the End is fast approaching. The obstacles standing in the way of the consummation are falling rapidly, and the Bride is herself at last prepared. When this moment appears in fact, however, is a separate question.

[63] The RSV and NRSV render ἡ γυνὴ αὐτοῦ as 'his Bride' and 'his bride', respectively. It does not violate the imagery or theology of the passage, however, to translate the noun in its plain sense. Jeremias (*TDNT* IV:1099f.) explains (in connection with Rev. 21:9) that 'the designation of the bride as γυνή is in keeping with current Palestinian usage. According to later Jewish law the betrothal effects the "acquisition" (קנין) of the bride by the bridegroom and is thus a valid marriage. Though the bride still stands under the *patria potestas* until the marriage, she is legally a married woman from the time of the betrothal. She is called אשה (γυνή) and can become a widow, receive a bill of divorcement, or be punished for infidelity, etc.'

[64] The plurality of the noun makes it probable that concrete acts, not the church's state of grace in justification, are intended. This is congenial with the emphasis upon the church's 'works' in Rev. 2:2, 5, 19, 23, 26; 3:1, 2, 8, 15.

[65] The simple dignity of the Bride's wedding gown is to be contrasted with the meretricious finery of the great harlot, in Rev. 17:4 and 18:16. Grotius, in *Critici Sacri*, comments, 'Vides hic cultum gravem, ut matronae; non pompaticum,

himself in splendour, holy and without blemish (Eph. 5:26–27). Her faithlessness, persistent since remote times, is finally dissolved for ever in the chemistry of grace.

And who would not long to be there? Therefore, according to verse 9a, the angel addressing John (17:1) commands him to declare to the present generation suffering human tyranny the infinitely enviable status of those who are invited to the great nuptial feast of the Lamb.[66] The wedding is not to be perceived as an eschatological event in a remote and abstract sense but as a vividly personal experience awaiting and, as it were, beckoning those who have been invited. As they pay a price now for their allegiance to the Lamb, the elect may savour this hope 'when the trials of the former days are forgotten in laughter and happiness around the table of the Lord' (Beasley-Murray 1974: 274).

Revelation 21:1–3, 9–10

When the final spasms of defiant rage against the rule of God have been for ever quelled by 'the fury of the wrath of God the Almighty', and the devil and the beast and the false prophet, Death and Hades, and all whose names were not found written in the book of life, have been banished to eternal fire, history ends. Eternity descends.[67] A vision of the final moment, which is also the ever new beginning, opens up before the watching apostle:[68]

---

qualis meretricis ante descriptus.' [You see here the venerable appearance, as of a matron, not showy, as that previously described of the harlot.]

[66] *Cf.* Morris (1987: 221): 'In the troubled days of persecution it did indeed need emphasis that it was the persecuted saints who were blessed, not their persecutors.'

[67] Matthew Henry heads his comments on chapter 21 as follows: 'Hitherto the prophecy of this book has presented to us a very remarkable mixture of light and shade, prosperity and adversity, mercy and judgment, in the conduct of divine Providence towards the church in the world; now, at the close of it all, the day breaks, and the shadows flee away; a new world now appears, the former having passed away.'

[68] Caird (1966: *ad loc.*) puts it well: 'The clouds of glory have hung low over the camp of the true Israel in their wilderness wanderings. Now at last John stands on Pisgah and surveys the promised land. In some ways this is the most important part of his book, as it is certainly the most familiar and beloved. "If only we knew", the martyrs have cried, "where it is all going to end!"; and much of John's vision, and much of the human story it depicts and interprets,

[1]And I saw a new heaven and a new earth; for the first heaven and the first earth had passed away, and the sea was no more. [2]And I saw the holy city, new Jerusalem, coming down out of heaven from God, prepared as a bride adorned for her husband. [3]And I heard a loud voice from heaven saying, 'Behold, the dwelling of God is with men. He will dwell with them, and they shall be his peoples, and God himself will be with them.'

John's vision reveals more than the overthrow of Babylon. Far, far more, the very cosmos, tainted with the long and weary history of sin, is cast off like a worn-out garment and a bright new one appears to replace it, according to verse 1. The old has played its role in the drama and now must yield place to the new, which will last for ever as the eternal home of the people of God.[69] The most striking feature of this new order is the absence of the sea. John thereby proclaims the complete perfection of the new heavens and earth, for 'the sea', registering various associations with chaos and evil, finds no

becomes intelligible, credible, tolerable, when we know the answer. Here is the real source of John's prophetic certainty, for only in comparison with the new Jerusalem can the queenly splendours of Babylon be recognized as the seductive gauds of an old and raddled whore.'

[69] One is struck by the breathtaking claim of the biblical gospel. *Cf.* Rom. 8:18–25. Other gospels fiddle with the dilemmas of this life; the Christian gospel promises a new order altogether. The significance of John's vision becomes the more clearly evident when seen in connection with, *e.g.*, Rich (1977: 75f.), quoting Woody Allen: 'I always see the death's head lurking. I could be sitting at Madison Square Garden at the most exciting basketball game, and they're cheering and everything is thrilling, and one of the players is doing something very beautiful – and my thought will be, "*He's only twenty-eight years old and I only wish he could savor this moment in some way, because, you know, this is as good as it's going to get for him*" . . . The fundamental thing behind *all* motivation and *all* activity is the constant struggle against annihilation and against death. It's absolutely stupefying in its terror, and it renders anyone's accomplishments meaningless. As Camus wrote, it's not only that *he* dies or that *man* dies, but that you struggle to do a work of art that will last and then realize that *the universe itself* is not going to exist after a period of time. Until those issues are resolved within each person – religiously or psychologically or existentially – the social and political issues will never be resolved, except in a slapdash way. They'll never be resolved as long as people wake up each day and worry that they're finite, that they don't know why they're here or where they're going or when they're going to die.' (Emphases his.)

place there.[70] The settled order of righteousness now reigns in the renewed creation.

What draws John's attention primarily, however, is the holy city, a new Jerusalem, coming down out of heaven from the condescending, decisive grace of God, in verse 2, as a symbol of the new existence to be conferred upon the suffering, sinning people of God.[71] The new Jerusalem does not rise from the sea. It is not seated upon many waters. It does not even emerge Phoenix-like from the ashes of the old Jerusalem. It descends from heaven as the antitypical reality which the earthly Jerusalem had only dimly adumbrated. The city which had 'become a harlot', filled with violence (Is. 1:21), is replaced with the perfect dwelling of God with his people in holy communion[72] – the ultimate human experience and the end toward which salvation history has been pressing for so long.[73]

This inner meaning of the city of God is made explicit in verse 3, bringing to realization the promise implicit in the Old Testament tabernacle. Verse 2b conveys much the same idea

[70] The sea symbolizes the restless mass of godless humanity in Is. 57:20, and the first beast rises from the sea in Rev. 13:1. *Cf.* Rev. 17:15. Augustine (*City of God*, XX:16) comments not incorrectly but too generally, 'For at that moment this troubled and stormy era of mortal life, which he has portrayed with the word "sea", will be no more.' More particularly, Grotius, in *Critici Sacri*, interprets the sea as 'ingens illa idololatrarum multitudo' [that vast multitude of idolaters].

[71] *Cf.* Gal. 4:26; Heb. 11:10; 12:22; 13:14. Gladstone (1868: 197f.) renders the concept vivid: 'No man saw the building of the New Jerusalem, the workmen crowded together, the unfinished walls and unpaved streets; no man heard the clink of trowel and pickaxe; it descended *out of heaven from God.*' (Italics his.) And Lapide (1877: XXI:367) quotes Augustine's insight into the inner nature of this city as opposed to its degraded alternative: 'Duas, ait, in toto mundo civitates faciunt duo amores; Jerusalem facit amor Dei, Babyloniam facit amor saeculi.' [Two loves, it says, make two cities in the whole world; the love of God makes Jerusalem, the love of this age makes Babylon.] One discerns some fluidity in the concept of the holy city. In Rev. 3:12 it is distinct from the faithful believer and is promised as his eternal reward. Here in chapter 21 it merges into the people of God, the bride. This is consistent with the natural ambiguity which inheres in any city with its inhabitants.

[72] It is the *holy* city. There is neither secularism nor secularization there. All is sacred.

[73] *Cf.* Lv. 26:11–12; Je. 31:33; Ezk. 37:23, 26–28; Jn. 1:1, 14. The dwelling of God with man *in the form of a city* may also suggest the perfect social union of the redeemed with one another as God's final and eternal answer to the successive societal failures littering the course of human history.

but with the image of the bride, implying the uninhibited joy and tender intimacy of the divine-human communion. The fact that the city-bride comes from heaven guarantees her purity, which the word 'prepared' itself suggests. The new existence granted to the people of God adorns them in their finest raiment for their husband on the wedding day. The bride has never looked better. And as the people of God are united with their groom, there is at last no incongruity to spoil the moment:

> . . . as the bridegroom rejoices over the bride,
> so shall your God rejoice over you (Is. 62:5b, RSV/NRSV).

Three further points are made about the bride in verses 9–10, where John is granted a larger, fuller perspective on the things revealed earlier in the chapter:

> [9]Then came one of the seven angels who had the seven bowls full of the seven last plagues, and spoke to me, saying, 'Come, I will show you the Bride, the wife of the Lamb.' [10]And in the Spirit he carried me away to a great, high mountain, and showed me the holy city Jerusalem coming down out of heaven from God (RSV).

First, the very close resemblance of the wording of verse 9 to 17:1, where the judgment of the great harlot is announced, renders obvious the parallel intended between that ugly symbol and this glorious one.[74] The great harlot of Babylon is destroyed; the Bride, the wife of the Lamb, is exalted.[75] Wrath and love collaborate, in the ways of God.

Secondly, the identification of the bride with the new

---

[74] The words underlying 'full of the seven last plagues' are not matched in 17:1. The genitival τῶν γεμόντων is construed as a solecism typical of the Revelation in BDF § 136 (2). *Cf.* Turner (1963: 314). Interpreting this genitive as descriptive of τῶν ἑπτὰ ἀγγέλων rather than τὰς ἑπτὰ φιάλας forces a most improbable sense, which nevertheless is attempted in Alford (1958: IV:739).

[75] *Cf.* Beasley-Murray (1974: 315): 'The Revelation as a whole may be characterized as *A Tale of Two Cities*, with the sub-title, *The Harlot and the Bride* . . . The harlot-city reposes on the beast from hell – she partakes of the character of the devil, and the bride-city descends from heaven – she is the creation of God. But one thing they have in common. They stand alike on the earth, and invite humanity to come to them.'

Jerusalem is made explicit. In verse 2, the new Jerusalem is displayed '*as* a bride adorned for her husband'. The rhetorical device employed is simile, merely describing the city as a bride. In verses 9–10, the Bride appears *per se* and is equated with and identified as the new Jerusalem. This is presumably why the RSV translates 'bride' in verse 2 and 'Bride' in verse 9.[76] Verse 2 purposes to say something about the new Jerusalem, *viz.* it is like a bride dressed on her wedding day for her husband; verses 9–10 purpose to say something about the Bride, *viz.* she *is* the new Jerusalem. John mixes his metaphors, providing a richer understanding of the church triumphant as both the dwelling place of God and the beloved of the Lamb. The lines of expectation created by the fullness of Old Testament theology crowd into John's brief description of their final resolution.

Thirdly, verse 9 identifies the husband of the Bride as the Lamb. 'Her husband' is not further clarified in verse 2, because the function of 'bride' there is comparative in relation to the city. Now, the Bride is the central referent, which calls for the identification of her husband as the Lamb. And John's point in bringing the two together here is to hint at the final union of the church with her triumphant Lord and loving Husband. The perfect has come, the drama concludes, the marriage is consummated.[77]

John's pastoral purpose in setting forth this great vision of the end is focused into one sharply defined point in 22:17, where he calls the church to the single, essential response appropriate to all that has been shown:

> The Spirit and the Bride say, 'Come.' And let him who hears say, 'Come' (RSV).

The suffering church militant of this present evil age is to cultivate one great impulse throbbing in her soul, *viz.* an aching longing for the Bridegroom to come to her, to take her in his arms, with nothing within herself to wrest her away, and to be held there for ever. Until such time as he is pleased to come, she is to centre her life around 'the love of Jesus Christ, the King,

---

[76] Inexplicably, the NRSV renders both in lower case.

[77] The remainder of the section (21:9 – 22:5) teases out more fully various aspects of the glory of eternity.

Bridegroom, and Husband of his church, to her his Queen, Bride, and Spouse, and of hers to him, with

> 'those spiritually glorious interviews, holy courtings, most superlative, but most sincere, commendings and cordial entertainings of each other, those mutual praisings and valuings of fellowship, those missings, lamentings and bemoanings of the want thereof, those holy impatiencies to be without it, swelling to positive and peremptory determinations not to be satisfied nor comforted in anything else, those diligent, painful and restless seekings after it, till it be found and enjoyed, on the one hand; and those sweet and easy yieldings to importunity, and gracious grantings of it, on the other; with those high delightings, solacings, complacencies and acquiescings in, and heartsome embracings of, one another's fellowship . . . these vehement joint-longings to have the marriage consummated and the fellowship immediate, full and never any more to be interrupted.'[78]

[78] Margaret Durham, in J. Durham (1840: 13ff.).

Chapter Seven

Concluding reflections

Our conclusion will be limited to brief reflections on the hermeneutical, the theological and the pastoral. Hermeneutically, when we stand back and survey the whole biblical story, something striking appears. The primeval history opens with transcendent breadth, 'When', to quote Dryden, 'this universal frame began,

> 'When nature underneath a heap
>   Of jarring atoms lay,
> And could not heave her head,
> The tuneful Voice was heard from high,
>   "Arise, ye more than dead."
> Then cold and hot and moist and dry
> In order to their stations leap,
>   And Music's pow'r obey.'

As this glorious vision of biblical protology unfolds, creating expectations of ever greater sequels, a curious thing occurs. The attention of the text shifts from the heavens and the earth coming together in cosmic order (Gn. 1) to a man and a woman coming together in earthly marriage (Gn. 2). Even allowing that marriage is the most profound of human relationships ('one flesh'), one is still struck by the apparently incongruous movement from the universal to the particular, from impenetrable mysteries to familiar commonplaces. But there it is, this peculiar thing we call marriage, tenderly portrayed in its humble reality and delicate innocence against the enormous backdrop of the creation. Why? What does Scripture accomplish by this remarkable juxtaposition? The answer is not yet provided, but the question lingers as the story proceeds.

In the Pentateuchal and historical books, the larger significance of marital union continues quietly to call for recognition,

171

as the language of sexual misconduct ('to commit harlotry') provides a metaphor useful for describing Israel's defection from Yahweh. The literature tacitly assumes that Israel's bond with Yahweh entails marital exclusivity, so that sin is branded as a despicable 'sexual' offence.

Hosea and Isaiah, continuing and enlarging the accusation of spiritual harlotry along with Micah, exploit human marriage overtly as a symbol of Yahweh's covenant with his people. Later, Jeremiah and Ezekiel follow the same vector even more boldly and imaginatively, teasing out the entailments of the violated marital covenant.

In the New Testament, Jesus endorses the prophetic vision, identifying himself as the Bridegroom inviting the reluctant bride into the marriage feast. James, Paul and especially John move the theological drama toward its conclusion, opening up the prospect of the Bride's eternal purity and joy with the Bridegroom in a better world yet to be created.

So then, the biblical story opens up with human marriage as such, embedded in a context which creates the presumption of something more than immediately meets the eye. Then the histories intimate and the prophets declare that the covenant is a marriage between Yahweh and Israel. Finally, Jesus and the New Testament writers place the theme within a Christocentric frame of reference. But Paul is the one who lifts the hermeneutical capstone into place by revealing openly what our intuitions may have suspected all along, *viz.* that marriage from the beginning was meant to be a tiny social platform on which the love of Christ for his church and the church's responsiveness to him could be put on visible display. Human marriage is finally divulged to be emblematic of Christ and the church in covenant, destined to live together not as 'one flesh' for a lifetime in this world but as 'one spirit' for eternity in a new heavens and a new earth.

Therefore, marriage was not intruding itself into the story at a level out of its own depth back in Genesis 2. It had to be there, and it deserved to be there, for the typology to achieve its proper symmetry. The eschatology illuminates the true significance of the protology.

Theologically, the biblical story explains why Christian doctrine calls for marriage to be 'held in honour among all', and the marriage bed to be 'undefiled' (Heb. 13:4). Among all, men and women, married and single, the institution of marriage is to be honoured and its sexual parameters carefully observed. Why? Because marriage bespeaks a higher reality – the love of Christ for his church, and her joyful deference to him – and is itself enriched by what it bespeaks. Marriage is not just another mutation of human social evolution, like democracy. It is a divine creation, intended to reveal the ultimate romance guiding all of time and eternity. This is the real reason why premarital sex is wrong; it toys with the biblical mystery. The moral imperative is concerned with more than the folly of risking a sexually transmitted disease. God offers a theological rationale in Christ. This is why extramarital sex is wrong; it violates the mystery. This is why same-sex marriages are wrong; they pervert the mystery. And this is why every faithful and loving marriage is precious to God; it shines with the light of Christ's love for his people, and of their devotion to him, in the darkness of this present evil age.[1]

Pastorally, the biblical story lifts up before us a vision of God as our Lover. The gospel is not an imperialistic human philosophy making overrated universal claims; the gospel sounds the voice of our Husband who has proven his love for us and who calls for our undivided love in return. The gospel reveals that, as we look out into the universe, ultimate reality is not cold, dark, blank space; ultimate reality is romance. There is a God above with love in his eyes for us and infinite joy to offer us, and he has set himself upon winning our hearts for himself alone. The gospel tells the story of God's pursuing, faithful, wounded, angry, overruling, transforming, triumphant *love*. And it calls us to answer him with a love which cleanses our lives of all spiritual whoredom.[2]

[1] Human analogies are imperfect, and marriage is no exception. For example, it is possible for a woman to be widowed and then to remarry another man. This does not match the higher reality but is still legitimate. *Cf.* Rom. 7:2. The wide variation in human experience limits its capacity to serve as a model for that which is ultimate; but as long as any given marriage mirrors faithfully, even if imperfectly, the divine reality, it is fulfilling its holy calling.

[2] *Cf.* Johannes Oecolampadius (1525: 105), commenting on Isaiah 13: 'Et per eum quotidie in nobis expugnamus Babylonem. Plenum autem et verum mundi excidium sub finem erit huius mundio seculorum.' [And through him (*i.e.* Christ) daily we conquer the Babylon within ourselves. A full and true destruction of the world, however, will be at the end of the age of this world.] I thank Dr Vern Poythress for drawing my attention to Oecolampadius at this

If our covenant with God is a marriage, then its claims are to be strictly observed. This answers a popular objection to the gospel. Why does the gospel press its authority upon the whole of our lives? Would it not be more reasonable, and certainly more convenient, if the gospel were to content itself with serving us as religious ornamentation in our lives rather than rule as the governing centre of the whole of life? 'After all,' we complain, 'it's only religion!' But true religion is marital in nature. What sort of husband would look at his wayward wife and dismiss her adulteries by mumbling, 'As long as she and her lovers don't shake the bed and make too much noise, as long as I can get my sleep, what's the big deal? It's only marriage!'? No-one but a knave would own such a sentiment. So how can we trivialize our covenant with God? The covenant is a marriage. It is *the* marriage.

Questions of prophetic pointedness, therefore, are not non-questions. They are valid and urgently important to God. For example, what is the church's proper relationship with worldly political powers, of whatever philosophy? If the church seeks security and safety through the Assyrias, Egypts and Babylons of the modern world, insulting the power and protection of her Husband's loving all-sufficiency, then the church deserves to be confronted. And she would do well to listen, lest she risk being punished. Or, what is the church's proper relationship with popular consumer culture? At heart, are those who claim the betrothal gratefully contented with the providences of their Husband, or are they nervously addicted to the material goods of this world, as are those who have no higher love claiming and filling their souls? If the church seeks pleasure and luxury through the Baals and Asherahs of the modern world, insulting the value and joy of her Husband's loving all-sufficiency, then the church deserves to be confronted. And she would do well to listen, lest she risk being punished.

Such questions as these could be multiplied widely, as far as the particularities of human temptation branch out.[3] The point

point. The reader is also directed to the famous sermon by Rev. Thomas Chalmers (1780–1847), entitled 'The Expulsive Power of a New Affection.'

[3] I cannot cite all the work which might prove helpful to the reader in exploring this area further, but one could fruitfully consult the following: Jeremiah Burroughs, *Gospel Worship* (1648, repr. Ligonier, PA, 1990); D. A. Carson, *The Gagging of God: Christianity Confronts Pluralism* (Leicester, 1996);

to be emphasized here is that the biblical drama surveyed in this book makes such questions fair and meaningful. Questions of faithfulness to our heavenly Husband are not neurotic; to him, their importance is simply infinite. We must place ourselves, therefore, under the judgment of the Word of God, the covenant document. If at any given point we refuse to do so, we run the risk of being stripped before our seducers by our angry Husband, just as Israel and Judah were.

Matters of faithfulness to Christ deserve a place at the centre of church discussion rather than at the periphery, easily dismissed with self-congratulatory, unselfcritical answers. Outward prosperity and success are not infallibly accurate indicators of God's favour. They may be. And if they are, that is the ideal scenario we all desire. But Israel of Hosea's time was prosperous, and there was no smile of divine favour resting upon them. The external prosperity of popular appeal and pragmatic effectiveness *may* be, as Israel's prosperity surely was, the autumnal glow of departing mercy before the winter blast of oncoming judgment. And if that is possible, then we must be sincerely open to a more searching analysis of ourselves. It must not be disregarded as theoretical or prudish, or we risk terrible consequences.

Faithfulness requires a careful monitoring of ourselves. After all, who but an adulteress would be reckless in her relationships? Given the seductive power of our sinfulness, fidelity to Christ calls for a proper sense of self-doubt, for God searches deeply into the inner quality of his church with probing, inconvenient, embarrassing questions. His bride must remain open-minded and responsive to him, repenting and turning when his Word touches on some manifestation, however slight in our own eyes,

---

Andrew D. Clarke and Bruce W. Winter, *One God, One Lord: Christianity in a World of Religious Pluralism* (Grand Rapids, 2nd edn 1993); Thomas Doolittle, *Love to Christ: Necessary to Escape the Curse at His Coming* (1830, repr. Ligonier, PA, 1994); Jacques Ellul, *The New Demons* (New York, 1975); Os Guinness and John Seel, *No God But God: Breaking with the Idols of Our Age* (Chicago, 1992); John Piper, *Desiring God: Meditations of a Christian Hedonist* (Leicester, 1986); Francis A. Schaeffer, 'Adultery and Apostasy: The Bride and Bridegroom Theme', in *The Church at the End of the 20th Century* (London, 1970); Herbert Schlossberg, *Idols for Destruction: Christian Faith and Its Confrontation with American Society* (Nashville, 1983); Paul C. Vitz, *Psychology as Religion: The Cult of Self-Worship* (Grand Rapids, 2nd edn 1994); John White, *Money Isn't God – So Why is the Church Worshipping It?* (Leicester, 1993).

of unfaithfulness in our lives, our message, our policies or our ministry strategies. If, however, spiritual whoredom is perceived as too remote a possibility for the church, conservative or liberal, to take seriously, then we are all the more liable to being deceived along with previous generations of the covenant community.

More than our popular churches and institutions and movements, God wants us ourselves. He wants our hearts, our loyalty, our love for himself alone. He wants to find in us the same sense of intimate belonging to him that is appropriate to sexual union on the human level. More than our showing the world how 'relevant' the church can be, God wants us to show him how much we treasure him above all else. He wants to find in us the same sense of identification with him that is appropriate to human marriage. And we show him our love through doctrinal faithfulness to his Word, by following him heroically wherever he goes (we would rather *die* than turn aside, even one step, from following him to following the world), by resisting the world's radical pluralism demanding unlimited tolerance levels for its ideas and values, by restricting our ministries only to those methods which are warranted by his Word and consistent with prayerful dependence upon the power of his Spirit, by nurturing our 'vague half-believers in our casual creeds' into earnest, informed, gladly devoted lovers of Christ alone, and in many other important ways. But above all, we show him our love by savouring the hope of eternal union with him in the new Jerusalem above as our only true fulfilment.

The biblical theme of spiritual harlotry is not the whole of theology. It is only one strand woven into the fabric of Scripture, along with others, all of which are needed for the whole tapestry to shine forth in its complexity and fullness. But this strand of God's marital love and of his people's presently harlotrous but ultimately faithful response is too much neglected. And it is the overlooked themes of Scripture to which any given age of the church must pay special attention, for it is precisely there that we most urgently need to hear the Word of God again.

Appendix

The harlot metaphor and feminist interpretation

It would be impossible in an appendix to do justice to the nuanced variations and the significant bibliography of feminist biblical interpretation today; at the same time, it would be discourteous not to acknowledge something of the work being done in this area. One may at least take a sounding of feminist interpretation relevant to our study. Striking a course, therefore, which will likely please no-one, I intend here to respond briefly to critique of the harlot metaphor in Hosea, Jeremiah and Ezekiel – the point at which modern sensitivities may well be keenest – recently proposed by Athalya Brenner and Fokkelien van Dijk-Hemmes (1993: 167–193).

While some feminist biblical interpreters see the Bible as authentically egalitarian but too long misunderstood by patriarchal scholarship, others have given up on the Bible as hopelessly misogynist, at least at certain points. To be redeemed, the biblical text must be deconstructed. The authors surveyed here sympathize with the second approach.

With regard to Hosea, van Dijk-Hemmes notes that numerous male interpreters have construed Hosea 1 – 3 as a parable of divine grace and forgiveness, reflecting well on God. According to van Dijk-Hemmes, however, the text reveals 'sexual violence'. The metaphorical wife is 'victimized' by her husband. Because the wife expresses 'her desire for her lover', she is 'transformed into a harlot who shamelessly goes after her lovers (in the plural!)'. The 'male, misogynist metaphorical language', in calling people to return to Yahweh, is 'also, and simultaneously, an example of propaganda, addressed to men, extolling an ideal patriarchal marriage'.

Turning to Ezekiel 23, van Dijk-Hemmes premises her remarks with the idea that metaphors require their readers to 'participate in the construction of the metaphorical meaning' of the text, allowing her to distinguish between a male 'readerly response' to Ezekiel 23 and a female one. The literary strategies deployed in the text 'organize or mobilize' each reader's perception. Taking verse 48 as addressed to literal women, van Dijk-Hemmes reads the chapter as a warning to them. What then is its message?

Van Dijk-Hemmes sets out to explore the question by accepting as her point of departure 'a significant congruence between biblical and especially prophetic texts on the one hand, and modern pornographic depictions of female sexuality on the other hand', in both of which female sexuality is featured as 'a symbol of evil'. The function of pornography is to preserve 'male domination through a denial, or misnaming, of female experience'.

Van Dijk-Hemmes notes that the target audience of the oracle is 'required to hear the text via Ezekiel's (fictive) ears', that is, through a filter of male perceptions and interests. But she sees underlying the passive verbs of verse 3b ('their breasts were caressed . . . their virgin bosoms were fondled') male sexual molestation of the girls in Egypt. Where Ezekiel and a male reader may see female sexual profligacy, a female reader sees male sexual abuse. Far from sinning in Egypt, Israel was oppressed; but within an androcentric frame of reference the victim is blamed for her own suffering. The reader of the biblical text, at verse 8 and elsewhere, is 'seduced' into perceiving the abuse of Oholah and Oholibah in Egypt as something which all their lives they perversely enjoyed.

While most interpreters have failed to save themselves from its degrading influence, so successful is the male text's strategy, a feminist participating in the construction of the metaphorical meanings renders the male reading unnecessary. Thanks to a feminist reading, it is now possible to discern a pornographic interest in keeping female sexuality 'an object of male possession and control'.

Van Dijk-Hemmes acknowledges that the whole people of Israel, male and female alike, are drawn into the metaphor of Oholah and Oholibah. The 'androcentric-pornographic character of this metaphorical language must indeed be experienced as extremely humiliating by an M [i.e., a male] audience forced to imagine itself as being exposed to violating enemies'. It is the nature of the metaphor, however, which gives male readers an escape through identifying with the wronged husband or with the 'righteous men' of verse 45. Female readers are provided with no such expedient for moderating the power of the text's accusations. For them, 'the metaphorization of woman in Ezekiel 23 performs first and foremost a violent speech act' worse than that in Hosea.

Brenner introduces her critique by proposing that readers 'avoid falling into that trap of complicity with the text' by making allowances for it as prophetic. It is thereby 'too easily privileged' as superior to ourselves. Brenner prefers to approach Jeremiah not as prophecy but as poetry, and 'poetic-textual authority is easier to undermine than so-called prophetic authority'.

Arguing briefly that the husband-wife metaphor is a device used for propagandistic purposes, Brenner then goes on to define pornography in such a way that Jeremiah's literature falls within that category, in agreement with van Dijk-Hemmes. Brenner states, 'If contemporary pornographic literature is found to contain anti-female bias, the same should apply to pornographic biblical literature.'

To defend her charge of biblical pornography, Brenner finds in Jeremiah 2 – 5 the perception of female sexuality as 'irregular, abnormal', 'animalistic', and associated with bestiality. Male sexuality, by contrast, 'represented by God's behaviour, is praiseworthy both socially and morally'. She finds as the most striking and original feature of Jeremiah 2 'the animalization of the metaphorized woman-in-the-text', which amounts to 'dehumanization' and 'misogyny'.

The function of Jeremiah's text is to call the community to 'accept the validity of the poet's (male) perspective for his God and for yourselves'. The biblical text, defined as pornography, deals with 'the objectification and degrading of "woman" in a manner that makes the abuse of females acceptable or even commendable', it 'restricts female sexual choice to an actual state of slavery', and it 'stresses the nature and meaning of male power'. The cause of it all is 'male insecurity and need to affirm and reaffirm gender control in the face of change'. 'This [*i.e.*, Jeremiah, Hosea and Ezekiel] is M literature, not just androcentric but truly phallocentric and woman-suspicious.'

Brenner compares P. Reage's *Story of O* (1972), 'a modern piece of literary pornography', with 'Jeremian pornography'. She summarizes the plot and message of the *Story of O* as follows:

O, the focal figure of the narrative, is a young woman in love. She remains anonymous throughout the book: all the other characters apart from her, females and males alike, do have names. The story charts her journey from being a loving person to becoming a naked, abused sex object whose spiritual or physical death is imminent by choice. And yet, the literary O – and its authorial parent? – celebrates her situation. At the end of her story O is a non-person, a womb controlled by her lovers and open to all, an Orifice – and by her own testimony she views her condition as the uttermost condition she can achieve this side of death. No matter whether her death is symbolical, or will be realized shortly. Through an intense didactic effort on the part of her male mentors, through physical punishment ranging from beating to group rape to other sadistic forms of physical and mental violation, she becomes reeducated. Now naked, with a chain through her genitals for all to see, publicly displayed as a (positive!) lesson for other nubile females, she has fulfilled her destiny. She has come to realize that the punishment is no punishment, that the physical marks on her body are no mere torment marks. They are her masters' stamp, she finally belongs. Through whoredom she has achieved chastity, through sadomasochism an understanding and fulfilment of her latent female nature. She is ready. She is to be reborn as a male-acceptable, submissive female who is devoted to the idea/praxis of her gender – the predetermined bondage of love. In short, she has attained selfhood.[1]

Brenner affirms that in Jeremiah, Hosea and Ezekiel 'this fantasy', such as is illustrated in the *Story of O*, 'reaches its ultimate'. 'The (male) fantasy of (male) domination is acted out as total through the equation of male power with divine power.' Further, 'The (male) fantasy of (female) submission becomes total and totalitarian through the required recognition of male/

[1] I apologize to the reader for the heart-breaking and offensive content of this quotation, but it is material to the presentation being reviewed here.

THE HARLOT METAPHOR AND FEMINIST INTERPRETATION

divine authority.' 'The choice of metaphor is deeply rooted in (male) infantile fantasy.' In both the *Story of O* and the biblical text, 'verbal violence parading as rational wisdom, social and personal, is discernible'.

Brenner, in personal response, sees two alternatives before her: 'to identify with the male/poet/God's viewpoint; or to object to the kind of pornographic/religious pseudotranscend-ence prescribed by the metaphor, thoughtlessly if not necessarily unconsciously, for persons of my gender'. She concludes that she

> . . . can resist this fantasy by criticism and reflection. But I do so against odds, for I myself was raised and educated to comply with that fantasy and adopt it as my very own. Like other F [*i.e.*, female] readers, I deconstruct myself by having to fight a wish to reciprocate or even appropriate M fantasy.

How may one respond to this way of construing the prophetic metaphor? First, this proposal should be seen in connection with a larger move toward the deconstruction of biblical texts which contemporary concerns find unco-operative or offensive. This trend in biblical studies is itself part of a still larger drift toward nihilistic hermeneutics in the academic world at large. As the once-great edifice of modern certainties crumbles into the bits and pieces of postmodern radical subjectivism, knowl-edge implodes into the self, defined within some demographic or partisan collectivity. The truism that perspective influences perception, too grudgingly acknowledged by modernism, becomes the major premise of postmodernism. But the new outlook contains nothing within itself to moderate its own radical tendency to accelerate toward extremist denials of modest, but valid, objective understanding. One's views are confined to one's self, however the self is configured – sexually, politically, ethnically, religiously or historically. As a result, fair-minded exchange between widely differing but mutually sympathetic minds breaks down, with raw political power replacing reasonableness.

Secondly, a misogynist reading of the biblical text takes offence where none is given. This is not a matter of personal hypersensitivity, however; it is a function of interpretative theory, once it is allowed that a text may be confronted with a hermeneutic of suspicion. But this hermeneutic is simply unfair. The text itself gives no indication of the prophets' inner motives and attitudes. Were Hosea, Jeremiah and Ezekiel misogynist? They had no personal interest in advancing a system of male domination. They were unpopular with their contemporaries, among whom doubtless were men of an oppressive nature, for such men (and women) appear in every age due to human sinfulness. The prophets were challenging that sinfulness, not reinforcing it. That is why they suffered. To brand them as misogynist by reading one's own concerns in their texts is to assume the very point which has yet to be proved – and that is unfair-minded, trigger-happy judgmentalism.

Moreover, a metaphorical image is a carefully nuanced and delicately effective contrivance for conveying a certain, limited message, while also withholding all the conceivable implications. One hastens to concede that human language labours with ambiguities, and figurative language takes even greater risks by reaching for higher beauty, more compelling power or an ironic twist. In the book of Hosea, God is likened to a moth and dry rot (5:12). In Jeremiah, he is compared with a confused man (14:9) and a dangerous lion (25:38; 49:19). But is not the scope of each figure's intended message discernible in its context? Let there be no misunderstanding. The abuse of women is real, and I stand with van Dijk-Hemmes and Brenner in condemning it.[2] But it is not true that the metaphor of the harlot is 'verbal violence' toward women any more than the metaphor of dry rot is an attack on God. There is only partial conceptual overlap between metaphor and reality, as much or as little as an author wishes to use for accomplishing his purpose. And he expects the reader to be fair-minded in making all due allowances in such imaginative discourse, lest unintended entailments, violating the author's convictions, be mistakenly dragged in through inter-pretation. If the reader suspects that the figure deserves to be condemned as immoral, that judgment can only be due to the reader's assessment of the author's own personal moral character, not of the image itself.

Thirdly, the harlot metaphor is an apt figure for the sin it

[2] This appropriate concern is well expressed in Brenner & van Dijk-Hemmes (1993: 192f. n. 13).

points to. I affirm this, because I believe that in actual reality God *is* a perfect 'husband' to his people,[3] our sins really are a betrayal of him, and thus a moral category exists for which the image of a harlot is a reasonable fit. It is not the only metaphor useful for directing our thoughts toward this moral category; but when God's *love* is primarily in view, our 'harlotry' is a meaningful description of our rejection of his love for the love of others.

Last, the (appropriately) personal nature of Brenner's conclusion allows me to respond personally as well. Our human existence is like a Rorschach test. Its meaning is not self-evident. It allows for various interpretations, and competing proposals have stimulated dialogue for ages. This dialogue began in the garden of Eden. According to God, Adam and Eve, living within the circle of their God-ordained existence, were enjoying the richness and fullness of life; outside that circle lay the regions of death. According to the serpent, Adam and Eve, living within the circle of their God-ordained existence, were at risk of death; outside that circle lay the opportunities worthy to be called life. Two opposed readings of reality claimed the allegiance of Adam and Eve. They had to choose. Is our perception of our existence, as defined by the word of God, true to reality and the key to life? Or, is our perception of our existence, as defined by some other word, truer to reality and the real key to life? Each of us must choose as well.

I am persuaded that the biblical interpretation of reality is not a metanarrative giving privileged status to male domination or any other human ideology; it is the only explanation of the human plight which is *not* tilted toward the advantage of some special interest, except God's. And we are most dignified when he is most glorified. But if I subject Scripture to 'gender nuanced' deconstruction, I risk imposing my own cultural imperialism upon the biblical text. And why should anyone accept *that* metanarrative? Deconstruction subverts all persuasion, including its own. Rejecting all self-defeating hermeneutics, one must dare to make meaningful, sharable contact with

---

[3] We recall Paul's point in Eph. 5:31–32 that the profile of ultimate reality is a marriage in which Christ is honoured and we are loved with a love that satisfies our own aspirations for nobility. This passage is the hermeneutical intersection through which all theological questions related to marriage, manhood and womanhood and human sexuality must pass.

external reality as it is, even if one's perception of it is incomplete and imperfect. And I believe that such knowledge is both possible and obligatory, because God is there to illuminate the human mind.

That is why I remain optimistic. Where reasoned argument fails, regeneration succeeds. Jesus said, 'You must be born again' (Jn. 3:3). Deconstructing feminists, and all others, this author included, must be born again, or we will not see the kingdom of God. It is there. It is real. But we can fail to see it. Each of us needs illumination through personal renewal by the Holy Spirit, and it makes a hermeneutical difference.

> The one without the Spirit does not receive the gifts of the Spirit of God, for they are folly to him, and he is not able to understand them because they are spiritually discerned. The spiritual person judges all things, but is himself to be judged by no one. 'For who has known the mind of the Lord so as to instruct him?' But we have the mind of Christ (1 Cor. 2:14–16).

Personal illumination from the Holy Spirit of God establishes a commitment to objective truth. It places one within an interpretative framework where God's eternal, unchanging Word speaks judgment and salvation to the human soul with such power and clarity that the message is not deflected as sexist conquest or any other human game but is gladly welcomed as divine liberation from the prison of self.

Without the rebirth Jesus offers, one runs the risk of curing to an even harder temper the concrete of self-trust encasing the natural human soul. In a sense, one may trade one casing for another. One may be 'reborn' from traditional female subservience to feminist female defiance. One may be 'reborn' from cocksure male domination to timid male grovelling. One can modify one's self as times change and fashion dictates. But one can never break out of the failed cycle of merely human solutions contrived to solve our real human problems.

If we perceive the Rorschach pattern of life as a lonely fight for survival without the consolations of divine succour, so that we barricade ourselves within the apparent safety of the self, we discover too late that the lock on the door operates only from the outside. All we have left is an endless reconfiguring of the autonomous self, and we are incapable of release into the light and freedom of God's larger conceptual world. But, in the mercy of God, the biblical gospel intrudes its way into our prison as a blessed subversive agent, alerting us that that larger world really is out there and that God is able to break the lock of our self-imposed confinement, if only we will trust him enough to rise and follow.

> When anyone turns to the Lord, the veil is removed
> (2 Cor. 3:16).

Bibliography

Aalders, G. Ch. (1981), *Genesis,* Grand Rapids.

Ainsworth, H. (*Ann*), *Annotations on the Pentateuch* (1612, repr. 1991), Ligonier, PA.

Alford, H. (1958), *The Greek Testament* (1849–61), repr. Chicago.

Alter, R. (1981), *The Art of Biblical Narrative,* New York.

Andersen, F. I., & D. N. Freedman (1980), *Hosea,* New York.

Bailey, K. E., & W. L. Holladay (1968), 'The "Young Camel" and "Wild Ass" in Jer. II 23–25', *VT* 18:256–260.

Barth, K. (1958), *Church Dogmatics* III.1, Edinburgh.

Batey, R. A. (1971), *New Testament Nuptial Imagery,* Leiden.

Beasley-Murray, G. R. (1974), *The Book of Revelation,* London.

Bertman, S. (1961), 'Tasseled Garments in the Ancient East Mediterranean', *BA* 24/4:119–128.

Bird, P. (1989), ' "To Play the Harlot": An Inquiry into an Old Testament Metaphor', in *Gender and Difference in Ancient Israel* (P. L. Day, ed.), Minneapolis.

Bockmuehl, M. A. N. (1990), *Revelation and Mystery in Ancient Judaism and Pauline Christianity,* Tübingen.

Brenner, A., & F. van Dijk-Hemmes (1993), *On Gendering Texts: Female and Male Voices in the Hebrew Bible,* Leiden.

Budd, P. J. (1984), *Numbers,* Waco.

Burroughs, J. (*Hos*), *An Exposition of the Prophecy of Hosea* (1643–51, repr. 1863), Edinburgh.

Caird, G. B. (1966), *A Commentary on the Revelation of St. John the Divine,* New York.

Calvin, J. (*Jer–Lam*), *Commentaries on the Book of the Prophet Jeremiah and the Lamentations* (1565, repr. 1850–51), Edinburgh.

————(*Ezek*), *Commentaries on the First Twenty Chapters of the Book of the Prophet Ezekiel* (1565, repr. 1850), Edinburgh.

————(*Hos*), *Hosea* (1567, repr. 1986), Edinburgh.

————(*1 Cor*), *The First Epistle of Paul the Apostle to the Corinthians* (1546, repr. 1960), Grand Rapids.

————(*2 Cor*), *The Second Epistle of Paul the Apostle to the Corinthians and the Epistles to Timothy, Titus and Philemon* (1547, repr. 1964), Grand Rapids.

——————(*Eph*), *Sermons on the Epistle to the Ephesians* (1562, repr. 1973), Edinburgh.

——————(*Inst*), *Institutes of the Christian Religion* (1559, repr. 1960), Philadelphia.

Carroll, R. P. (1986), *Jeremiah: A Commentary*, Philadelphia.

Carson, D. A., D. J. Moo & L. Morris (1992), *An Introduction to the New Testament*, Leicester.

Cassuto, U. (1967), *A Commentary on the Book of Exodus*, Jerusalem.

Chavasse, C. (1939), *The Bride of Christ*, London.

Childs, B. S. (1976), *The Book of Exodus: A Critical, Theological Commentary*, Philadelphia.

Chomsky, W. (1952), *David Kimchi's Hebrew Grammar* (*Mikhlol*), New York.

Chrysostom, John (*1 Cor*), *The Homilies of S. John Chrysostom, Archbishop of Constantinople, on the First Epistle of St. Paul the Apostle to the Corinthians* (1854), Oxford.

——————(*2 Cor*), *Homilies on Second Corinthians*, in *A Select Library of Nicene and Post-Nicene Fathers* (P. Schaff, ed.), XII (1889).

Collins, O. E. (1977), 'The Stem *ZNH* and Prostitution in the Hebrew Bible', PhD thesis, Brandeis University.

Cooke, G. A. (1936), *A Critical and Exegetical Commentary on the Book of Ezekiel*, Edinburgh.

Davids, P. H. (1982), *The Epistle of James: A Commentary on the Greek Text*, Grand Rapids.

Davidson, A. B. (1904), *The Theology of the Old Testament*, Edinburgh.

Davies, G. I. (1993), *Hosea*, Sheffield.

Delitzsch, F. (1899), *A New Commentary on Genesis*, Edinburgh.

Dibelius, M. (1976), *James*, Philadelphia.

Driver, S. R. (1895), *A Critical and Exegetical Commentary on Deuteronomy*, Edinburgh.

Du Ry, C. J. (1969), *Art of the Ancient Near and Middle East*, New York.

Duhm, B. (1968), *Das Buch Jesaia*, 5th edn, Göttingen.

Durham, J. (1840), *Clavis Cantici* (1669), repr. Aberdeen.

Düsterdieck, F. (1887), *Critical and Exegetical Handbook to the Revelation of John*, New York.

Eichrodt, W. (1961), *Theology of the Old Testament*, Philadelphia.

——————(1970), *Ezekiel: A Commentary*, Philadelphia.

Fairbairn, P. (1960), *An Exposition of Ezekiel* (1851), repr. Grand Rapids.

Fishbane, M. (1985), *Biblical Interpretation in Ancient Israel,* Oxford.

Gibson, J. C. L. (1978), *Canaanite Myths and Legends,* 2nd edn, Edinburgh.

Gill, J. (*ExpOT*), *An Exposition of the Old Testament* (1748–63, repr. 1852–54), London.

Ginsburg, C. D. (1966), *Introduction to the Massoretico-Critical Edition of the Hebrew Bible* (1897), repr. New York.

Gladstone, W. E. (1868), *Ecce Homo,* London.

Godet, F. (1893), *Commentary on St Paul's First Epistle to the Corinthians,* Edinburgh.

Goppelt, L. (1982), *Typos: The Typological Interpretation of the Old Testament in the New,* Grand Rapids.

Gordon, C. H. (1962), *Before the Bible,* New York.

Guthrie, D. (1990), *New Testament Introduction,* 4th edn, Leicester.

Habel, N. C. (1964), *Yahweh versus Baal: A Conflict of Religious Cultures,* New York.

Hamilton, V. P. (1990), *The Book of Genesis: Chapters 1 – 17,* Grand Rapids.

Harrison , R. K. (1980), *Leviticus: An Introduction and Commentary,* Leicester.

————(1990), *Numbers,* Chicago.

Henry, M. (*Exp*), *Exposition of the Old and New Testaments* (1708–10, various reprs.).

Héring, J. (1967), *The Second Epistle of Saint Paul to the Corinthians,* London.

Hodge, C. (1973), *An Exposition of the Second Epistle to the Corinthians,* repr. Grand Rapids.

Holladay, W. L. (1986), *Jeremiah 1,* Philadelphia.

Hooker, R. (*Laws*), *Of the Laws of Ecclesiastical Polity* V (1597, various reprs.).

Hugenberger, G. P. (1994), *Marriage as a Covenant: A Study of Biblical Law and Ethics Governing Marriage Developed from the Perspective of Malachi,* Leiden.

Jacob, B. (1974), *Genesis,* New York.

————(1992), *The Second Book of the Bible: Exodus,* Hoboken.

Keil, C. F., & F. Delitzsch (1972), *Commentary on the Old Testament* (1861–75), repr. Grand Rapids.

Kidner, D. (1972), *Genesis: An Introduction and Commentary*, Leicester.

Kline, M. G. (1975), *The Structure of Biblical Authority*, Grand Rapids.

Köstenberger, A. J. (1991), 'The Mystery of Christ and the Church', *TrinJ* 12NS:79–94.

Lapide, C. à (1876), *Commentaria in Scripturam Sacram* XVIII, Paris.

————(1877), *ibid.*, XXI, Paris.

McComiskey, T. E. (1992), *The Minor Prophets*, Grand Rapids.

————(1993), 'Prophetic Irony in Hosea 1.4: A Study of the Collocation פקד על and its Implications for the Fall of Jehu's Dynasty', *JSOT* 58:93–101.

McKane, W. (1972), 'Jeremiah II 23–25: Observations on the Versions and History of Exegesis', *OTS* 17:73–88.

————(1986), *A Critical and Exegetical Commentary on Jeremiah*, Edinburgh.

MacLaurin, E. C. B. (1964), *The Figure of Religious Adultery in the Old Testament*, Leeds University Oriental Society, Monograph Series 6, Leeds.

Manton, T. (*James*), *A Commentary on James* (1693, repr. 1962), Edinburgh.

Mays, J. L. (1976), *Micah: A Commentary*, Philadelphia.

Metzger, B. M. (1971), *A Textual Commentary on the Greek New Testament*, London.

Miletic, S. F. (1988), *'One Flesh': Eph. 5.22–24, 5.31: Marriage and the New Creation*, Rome.

Milgrom, J. (1983), 'Of Hems and Tassels', *BAR* 9/3:61–65.

Moffatt, J. (1970), in *The Expositor's Greek Testament* (1910), repr. Grand Rapids.

Moo, D. J. (1986), 'The Problem of *Sensus Plenior*', in *Hermeneutics, Authority and Canon* (D. A. Carson & J. Woodbridge, eds.), Leicester.

Morris, L. (1987), *The Book of Revelation: An Introduction and Commentary*, Leicester.

Motyer, J. A. (1993), *The Prophecy of Isaiah*, Leicester.

Muggeridge, M. (1972), *Chronicles of Wasted Time: The Green Stick*, New York.

Muirhead, I. A. (1952), 'The Bride of Christ', *SJT* 5:175–187.

Mußner, F. (1975), *Der Jakobusbrief*, Freiburg.

Oecolampadius, J. (1525), *In Iesaiam Prophetam HYPO-*

MNEMATΩN, Basel.

Plummer, A. (1915), *A Critical and Exegetical Commentary on the Second Epistle of St. Paul to the Corinthians*, New York.

Poole, M. (*Comm*), *Commentary on the Whole Bible* (1685, repr. 1975), Edinburgh.

Rad, G. von (1962), *Old Testament Theology*, New York.

————(1972), *Genesis: A Commentary*, Philadelphia.

Rich, F. (1977), 'Woody Allen Wipes the Smile off his Face', *Esquire*, May.

Ringgren, H. (1987), 'The Marriage Motif in Israelite Religion', in *Ancient Israelite Religion* (P. D. Miller Jr, P. D. Hanson & S. D. McBride, eds.), Philadelphia.

Robertson, A., & A. Plummer (1914), *A Critical and Exegetical Commentary on the First Epistle of St. Paul to the Corinthians*, Edinburgh.

Robinson, J. A. (1904), *St. Paul's Epistle to the Ephesians*, London.

Ropes, J. H. (1916), *A Critical and Exegetical Commentary on the Epistle of St. James*, Edinburgh.

Rowley, H. H. (1956–57), 'The Marriage of Hosea', *BJRL* 39:200–223.

Rudolph, W. (1947), *Jeremia*, Tübingen.

Sampley, J. P. (1971), *'And the Two shall Become One Flesh': A Study of Traditions in Ephesians 5:21–23*, Cambridge.

Sayers, D. L. (1995), *Creed or Chaos?*, Manchester.

Segal, M. H. (1958), *A Grammar of Mishnaic Hebrew*, Oxford.

Skinner, J. (1930), *A Critical and Exegetical Commentary on Genesis*, Edinburgh.

Snaith, N. H. (1950), 'Wrath', in *Theological Word Book of the Bible* (A. Richardson, ed.), London.

————(1967), *Leviticus and Numbers*, London.

————(1975), 'The Meaning of שעירים', *VT* 25:115–118.

Stienstra, N. (1993), *YHWH is the Husband of his People*, Kampen.

Turner, N. (1963), *Syntax*, vol. III of J. H. Moulton, *A Grammar of New Testament Greek*, Edinburgh.

Vitringa, C. (1732), *Commentarius in Librum Prophetarium Jesaiae*, Basil.

Volz, P. (1928), *Der Prophet Jeremia Übersetzt und Erklärt*, Leipzig.

Weiser, A. (1969), *Das Buch Jeremia Übersetzt und Erklärt*, 6th edn, Göttingen.

Wells, D. F. (1994), *God in the Wasteland*, Grand Rapids & Leicester.

Wenham, G. J. (1979), *The Book of Leviticus*, Grand Rapids.

Westermann, C. (1969), *Isaiah 40 – 66: A Commentary*, Philadelphia.

——————(1984), *Genesis 1 – 11: A Commentary*, Minneapolis.

Whybray, R. N. (1995), *Introduction to the Pentateuch*, Grand Rapids.

Wolff, H. W. (1974a), *Anthropology of the Old Testament*, London.

——————(1974b), *Hosea*, Philadelphia.

Zimmerli, W. (1979), *Ezekiel 1*, Philadelphia.

Index of Scripture references

Index of authors